M Y C H A L   W Y N N

Increasing Student Achievement

VOLUME I: VISION

MYCHAL WYNN

Increasing Student Achievement

VOLUME I: VISION

RISING SUN PUBLISHING

For keynote addresses, administrator training, staff development, or school improvement training on the topics outlined in this book contact:

Rising Sun Publishing/Training and Staff Development
(800) 524-2813
E-mail: speaking@rspublishing.com

Increasing Student Achievement: *Volume I: Vision*

First Edition

ISBN 1-880463-10-5

Credits:
Pictured in cover photo: Mychal-David Wynn, Ashley Polyne, and Ghislaine Salhuana. Cover photo taken by Mychal Wynn. Cover design by Jennifer Gibbs.

Reference source for style and usage: *The New York Public Library Writer's Guide to Style and Usage*. Copyright 1994 by The New York Public Library and the Stonesong Press, Inc.

P.O. Box 70906
Marietta, GA 30007-0906
800.524.2813
FAX 770.587.0862
E-mail: info@rspublishing.com
web site: http://www.rspublishing.com

Printed in the United States of America.

Acknowledgements

I am deeply indebted to all of the teachers, administrators, superintendents, school support personnel, parents, business partners, and mentors who have contributed to the school improvement and strategic planning efforts in those schools that I have had the opportunity to work in and collaborate with over the past twenty years. Your thoughts, ideas, and work within the trenches have shaped the ideas, provided the synergy, and provided the proving ground for the operational strategies outlined within this, and the other volumes of the Increasing Student Achievement series.

I would like to thank my wife, Nina,
who works each day on behalf of thousands of children
whom she has never met with the same passion as she does
for our own two sons to ensure that schools
become places that are nurturing to their social,
emotional, and intellectual development.
I would like to thank my editor, Denise Mitchell Smith,
my proofreader, Laurie Lowe Sorrells,
and my graphic artist, Jennifer Gibbs.

Dedication

This book is dedicated to my wife, Nina, my sons, Mychal-David and Jalani, and to the teachers, who enter into our schools, frequently underpaid, often under-appreciated, and yet in spite of it all work tirelessly on behalf of children and their families.

Table of Contents

About the author

Mychal Wynn is the Chief Financial Officer of Rising Sun Publishing, Inc., an educational consultant, and the author of fifteen books that outline a plethora of holistic and systemic school improvement strategies. His personal experiences span nearly two decades of teacher/parent training, student presentations, research and collaboration with educators in primary, secondary, and post-secondary education throughout the United States, Canada, Africa, Bermuda, and in the Caribbean. His insight and perceptions regarding the processes required to pave the way to increasing student achievement and to closing the respective achievement gaps have been shaped through research and hands-on experiences over the course of thirteen years in the private sector, twenty years as an educational consultant, and thirteen years of parenting.

> *For over two decades, I have been working with schools. I have worked with parents, teachers, principals, superintendents, and students in every school setting (i.e., pre-school, elementary, middle, high, alternative schools, and community colleges) and I have personally witnessed what rings clear in the Texas Successful School-wide Research Study, 'There is no magic cure for increasing student achievement.' However, the research is clear and the anecdotal evidence is overwhelming: 'If you can successfully cultivate a socially supportive, emotionally nurturing, and intellectually stimulating school climate and culture, you can engage children in rigorous academic instruction and practical learning outcomes that will transform a school community into a place of passion and purpose.' As a parent, I want all schools to work for all children as passionately as I want my children's schools to work for them.*

Mychal Wynn, his wife, Nina, and their two children, Mychal-David and Jalani, live in Marietta, Georgia.

From the author

My life was forever changed in 1985, when, I volunteered to work with students at several junior high schools; most notably, Forshay Junior High School in Los Angeles, California, through the Proficiency in English Program (PEP) in the Los Angeles Unified School District. These young men and women were stereotypically representative of the children in our schools who dwell at the bottom of the achievement gap, African-American or Hispanic, and poor. I recall the day that we met. As they entered the media center they exhibited all of the stereotypical behaviors: pants sagging, unenthusiastic, non-standard English, and negative attitudes. Over the course of several weeks, we discussed their dreams and aspirations as we recited poetry to improve their diction and oral presentation skills. The culminating activity was a series of poetry readings in a school-wide assembly. Reciting poetry in an auditorium of junior high school students in South Central Los Angeles can be a nerve-racking experience, even for the most seasoned speaker. However, these young men and women, focused on their long-term dreams and aspirations, transformed in their current attitudes and behaviors, stepped confidently onto the stage and articulately presented individual and choral presentations that brought the house down. Witnessing the passion within those children, whom others had declared incapable of learning, inspired a passion within me that has consumed my life for the past fifteen years.

While it was those children who helped me to focus my writing on parenting, education, and school reform, I am deeply indebted to all of the conference organizers, school board members, superintendents, curriculum directors, principals, classroom teachers, counselors, parents, researchers, and countless others who have embraced my work, challenged my thoughts, and openly shared their insight, experiences, research, and best practices. And, I am eternally grateful to all of those individuals, too numerous to thank individually, whom I have seen model the types of practices outlined in this, and each of the other volumes in the Increasing Student Achievement series, and who have turned their schools and/or classrooms into nurturing, spirit-filled environments for learning.

Foreword

I have struggled to write this book. How do I begin to share the experiences that I have gained over the past two decades, working with teachers and children in schools in virtually every part of America? How do I help others to understand that the high standardized test scores and high academic achievement of my two sons (African-American males), students who most frequently dwell at the bottom of the achievement gap, can become commonplace, rather than an aberration, within our schools? My perspective has been further shaped by having attended the Chicago Public Schools, which (at the time) was noted as one of the worst school districts in America. Little has changed in the ensuing 30 years. The schools that I attended, Edmund Burke Elementary and Du Sable High School, were high poverty schools with over 98% of the students on free or reduced lunch. Nowhere in America is the achievement gap wider than between the African-American children in the largely segregated Chicago Public Schools and their white counterparts in the largely segregated suburban public schools. While I had a temporary reprieve from the fights and out-of-control classrooms when my parents enrolled me in Corpus Christi Middle School (a Catholic School), I know first-hand the boredom and terror that our children endure each day for what often amounts to an inferior education.

After doing my best to condense the issues, strategies, and instructional approaches to 800 pages in the initial draft, I realized from my experiences working with teachers and administrators, that few would read it all. And, yet, I believe that every page needs to be read if we are to truly transform schools into places of passion and purpose so that our children begin soaring beyond proficiency to realizing potential. In Ron Edmonds' groundbreaking research that provided the foundation and inspiration of the effective schools movement he stated:

(1) we can, whenever and wherever we choose, successfully teach all children whose schooling is of interest to us; (2) we already know more than we need to do that; (3) whether or not we do it must finally depend on how we feel about the fact that we haven't so far.

The challenge that we face is not to *discover* what is needed to cultivate the environment, put into place the practices, and initiate the collaborative strategies that will lead our children into higher levels of learning; we need to successfully put into *practice* what we already know. If we truly care about children we must stop doing what we've always done. We must not only do it differently, but we must continually re-evaluate what we are doing and ask the question, "Are we doing it right? Is what we're doing in the best interest of children?" In essence, "Step outside of the box." Inside the box, we can readily identify the problems, i.e., students don't complete their classwork, don't do their homework, are below grade level in reading, math, and much of the core curriculum, perform poorly on standardized tests, behave disrespectfully in classrooms, are frequently off task, lack proper nutrition, are frequently apathetic toward the whole business of schooling, and rarely perceive school and schoolwork as important to their long-term success. However, the solutions to these and the countless other issues impacting student and teacher success within our schools are found outside of the box, i.e., doing things differently, implementing innovative intervention strategies, creating holistic programs to cultivate parental involvement, using mentors and business partners to develop relationships with a caring adult for those students who don't have one at home, replacing ditto sheets with thematic and interdisciplinary units, providing brain-compatible instruction, and developing effective action-oriented problem-solving teams.

To facilitate this journey outside of the box into those strategies and innovative practices which can close the respective achievement gaps and lead all children to higher levels of learning, I have resolved to break the initial text into more palatable volumes:

- *Volume I: Vision*

- *Volume II: Climate & Culture*

- *Volume III: Curriculum & Content*

- *Volume IV: Instruction*

- *Volume V: Assessment*

Each volume provides specific insight and direction for anyone involved in a school or school district's reform efforts (e.g., state department of education, school boards, superintendents, administrators, teachers, parents, mentors, etc.). Those working on student achievement task forces or school improvement planning teams, educational consultants, or the many aspiring teachers in our colleges of education and teacher certification programs throughout the country will find these volumes helpful in understanding each of the components for which we must strive to develop operational strategies.

While anyone *can* become a catalyst for the needed changes to ensure that schools become more academically rigorous and socially and emotionally nurturing places for children, I believe that teachers *must* become the catalyst for such changes. If there is to be real meaningful and lasting reform within our schools, teachers must model instructional excellence within their classrooms, establish socially and emotionally nurturing classroom climates, and cultivate effective home-school communication and develop meaningful productive partnerships with parents and families.

Since 1982, I have worked with hundreds of schools in their school improvement efforts through staff training, parent/student presentations, writing curricula, and publishing supplemental materials. While the term *"School Reform"* has become popularized, I believe that the term *"School Transformation"* is more appropriate. Every school community exists somewhere along the transformation cycle or continuum of change, from those with the highest levels of academic achievement and standardized test scores to those with high numbers of low-achieving students, high truancy, and a high percentage of office referrals and suspensions. There is clearly a nationwide focus on raising test scores. However, such efforts must be guided by an understanding of the transformation continuum. Our efforts to increase test scores must take into account the subtle and not so subtle influences on student achievement e.g., the high number of suicides in seemingly high achieving schools; substance abuse; teenage pregnancies; gangs; drop out rates in high poverty schools; teacher turnover; decaying facilities; ineffective utilization of technology; office referrals and suspensions; the high numbers of children of color in general, and boys in particular, referred to special education; lack of parental involvement; teacher attitudes toward families and children living in poverty; and the multitude of other issues impacting school communities and, ultimately, the intellectual and mental health of students.

Despite claims to the contrary, e.g., *Eliminate the arts and focus on teaching the basics. Implement a stricter discipline policy. Require students to wear uniforms. Create single-gender classrooms,* there is no research that identifies any such one-dimensional strategy as providing a sustainable systemic solution to the complex problems which hinder our efforts to increase student achievement and close the varied achievement gaps. To the contrary, fostering a successful school community is an extremely complex process comprised of many large and many minute variables. Some are easily discernable; others are barely noticeable. Successful solutions are multi-faceted as noted in the *Successful Texas School-wide Programs Research Study* (University of Texas at

Notes:

Austin):

Before describing what we found, it is probably important to describe what was not found. First, if there is a magic formula, a simple prescription or a miracle program that makes all the difference, we did not find it. We found more differences than similarities in the instructional programs and approaches used in the 26 schools.

Some schools devote all of their attention and resources to instruction and discipline without understanding the holistic nature of teaching and learning. Subsequently, they focus on "new" programs without devoting the necessary time, energy, and resources toward cultivating the school-wide environment where excellence can occur. This is likened to purchasing the best lawn seed without devoting any time to surveying the land, ensuring that the grass is appropriate for the climate and environment (i.e., sun, shade, heat, soil type, etc.), rototilling and fertilizing the soil, ensuring adequate irrigation, germinating the seed at the appropriate time of the year, watering the seed once it germinates, spreading the proper weed killer, and cutting the grass to the appropriate height. We cannot just go out and purchase a bunch of grass seed (curriculum and staff development) without a clear vision of the type of lawn that we *want* to grow, and given our environment, that we *can* grow!

Effective school transformation is predicated upon conceptualizing and implementing holistic and multi-faceted solutions if schools are to fulfill their promise of effectively educating children.

Strategies regarding staff development, parent seminars, intervention programs, extra-curricular activities, school-wide processes and procedures, school-community partnerships, and data gathering and analysis must be identified, developed, and implemented within the school transformation framework i.e., developing a clearly-defined and commonly-shared vision; developing a school climate and culture conducive to learning; developing curricula that is meaningfully relevant and actively engaging; developing methods of instructional delivery that lead students into the ranks of disciplinary experts; and developing effective assessment tools.

Developing the school's vision, establishing effective stakeholder teams, implementing effective classroom management strategies and procedures, developing engaging thematic and interdisciplinary units, delivering brain-compatible instruction, developing effective intervention strategies for students identified as at-risk, helping teachers to overcome cross-cultural, cross-gender, cross-generational, and cross-socioeconomic communication gaps, making parents partners in their children's learning, and inspiring students to learn are only some of the pieces of the complex puzzle of increasing student achievement and achieving the Federal, State and local districts' learning goals.

Whether you are a government official, school board member, superintendent of schools, director of curriculum and instruction, principal, teacher, college student, support personnel or parent, what follows will help you to understand each of the critical components from which we are able to mold schools into rigorous academic and emotionally nurturing places for teaching and learning.

MYCHAL WYNN

Increasing Student Achievement

VOLUME I: VISION

Chapter 1

We have a total program that teaches all children that they are unique, special, and that they are too bright to ever be less than all that they can be. The 'I will not let you fail' statement is one that they seldom hear elsewhere.

As I listened today to three- and four-year-olds reading about Daedalus and Icarus, one four-year-old declared: 'Mrs. Collins, if we do not learn and work hard, we will take an Icarian Flight to nowhere.' I somehow wished that the whole world could see and understand that all children are born achievers and all they need is someone to help them become all that they have the potential to become.

— Marva Collins [Ordinary Children, Extraordinary Teachers]

Overview

Schools are complex organisms comprised of dynamic components subjected to literally thousands of daily influences, all changing each school year. Each year, the success of a school community is impacted by any number of variables, such as the experiences and creative capacity of stakeholders (i.e., administrators, teachers, support staff, parents, and students); teacher/student ability levels; teaching/learning styles; staff morale; teacher/staff turnover; administrative leadership; community perceptions; socio, gender, economic, and cultural diversity; available resources; school-community partnerships; along with a myriad of state and local mandates and accountability standards. Added to this mixture are the home, community, and societal forces that affect the attitudes and behaviors of teachers and students alike.

Despite these and thousands of other variables outside of the direct control of teachers, administrators, and the support staff, the doors open and children enter into our schools. Over the ensuing nine months (180 school days), school communities have the extraordinary opportunity to engage children in exploration and discovery, to cultivate their social, physical, artistic and intellectual development, to expose them to character values and life skills, to build relationships today and explore the promise and potential of tomorrow, to develop school spirit and national pride, to develop rituals and traditions, and to build communities and families.

From the opening to the closing bell, what occurs in our schools will have far-reaching ramifications for children, families, communities, and our nation.

For nearly two decades, I have observed six major components common to all school communities that represent the *Educational Continuum:*

- *Mission;*

- *Vision;*

- *Climate and Culture;*

- *Curriculum and Content;*

- *Instruction; and*

- *Assessment.*

The first of the six, Mission, represents the global purpose of the school and school district, i.e., "Educate children." The other five components, Vision; Climate and Culture; Curriculum and Content; Instruction; and Assessment formulate the framework for how the mission is fulfilled. Contained within each of these major components are the many issues (e.g., classroom instruction, standards-based performance, assessment methods, school safety, parental involvement, teacher retention, educational equity, character values, guiding principles, classroom management, inviting learning environment, cooperative grouping, brain-compatible instruction, teacher teaming, curricula and supplemental materials, utilization of resources, discipline policies, etc.) which create the mosaic of a school community. How successful we are at conceptualizing strategies and implementing action plans determines student success, how wide the various achievement gaps are, and whether or not a classroom or an entire school ascends to the ranks of excellence.

"Effective schools" research indicates that successful schools accept the challenge to conceptualize strategies and implement solutions to the issues unique to their school community. Developing a clear vision, cultivating a positive school climate and culture, engaging students in curriculum and content, delivering effective classroom instruction, and engaging in an annual assessment and effective pre-planning, are all components of a successful school. It is these efforts, rather than a student's background, that represent the greatest contributing factors to student achievement:

> *Effective schools research grew out of a challenge to the research of Coleman, et. al. (1966) which found a significant relationship between family background and how well children achieve. The research concluded that a school's resources have little impact on student achievement. While most evidence based on test results seemed to support Coleman's findings—children from middle- and upper middle-class families generally do demonstrate achievement levels above children from poor families—some educators disagreed with the conclusion that schools must have little impact. Effective school researchers acknowledged that family background contributes to student achievement levels. However, they disagreed with the conclusions of Coleman, et. al., that family background determines a child's educational attainment. Effective schools researchers found that if school resources are used effectively, schools can be successful in teaching all children the essential skills. Brookover, Levine, Stark, Edmonds, Lezotte, Rutter, and many others have identified schools that are successful at teaching all students, disadvantaged and nondisadvantaged, the skills needed to succeed at the next grade level.*

[National Center for Effective Schools]

The *Educational Continuum* (Illustration I-A) illustrates how each school's mission is the driving force into and through the other five components of the continuum. The school's mission, which must be aligned with the overall mission of the school district, provides the foundation from which each school community engages in the process of developing a vision; cultivating the needed school-wide climate and culture; engaging students in the school's (or school board's) curriculum and content; effectively delivering

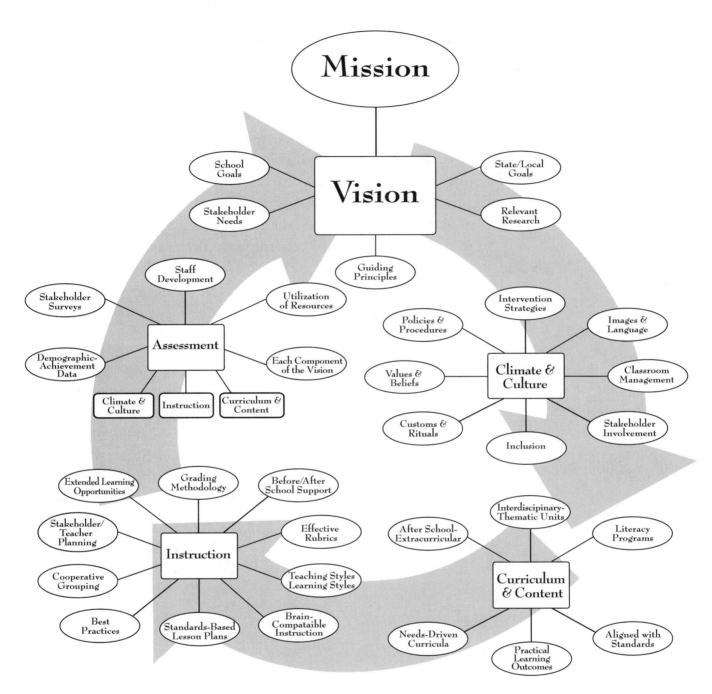

Mission

Vision

- School Goals
- Stakeholder Needs
- State/Local Goals
- Relevant Research
- Guiding Principles

Assessment

- Staff Development
- Stakeholder Surveys
- Utilization of Resources
- Demographic-Achievement Data
- Each Component of the Vision
- Climate & Culture
- Instruction
- Curriculum & Content

Climate & Culture

- Intervention Strategies
- Policies & Procedures
- Images & Language
- Values & Beliefs
- Classroom Management
- Customs & Rituals
- Inclusion
- Stakeholder Involvement

Instruction

- Extended Learning Opportunities
- Grading Methodology
- Before/After School Support
- Stakeholder/ Teacher Planning
- Effective Rubrics
- Cooperative Grouping
- Teaching Styles Learning Styles
- Best Practices
- Standards-Based Lesson Plans
- Brain-Compataible Instruction

Curriculum & Content

- Interdiscipinary-Thematic Units
- After School-Extracurricular
- Literacy Programs
- Needs-Driven Curricula
- Practical Learning Outcomes
- Aligned with Standards

Illustration I-A

Notes:

instruction; and assessing its success at fulfilling the school's (and ultimately the school district's) mission. Each school community—public or private, high- or low-achieving, urban or rural, affluent or with a high number of children on free or reduced lunch—will journey along this continuum every school year. The six components of the continuum are represented on the macro level of school-wide strategic-planning, which is where most school improvement and student achievement efforts *are* focused, and on the micro level of each classroom, subject area, grade level, intervention strategy, athletic program, extracurricular and co-curricular activity, and before/after school program, which is where more school improvement and student achievement efforts *need* to be focused.

Beginning the school year with a purposeful mission, creating a clearly-defined and commonly-shared vision (taking into account state/local learning goals, school goals, stakeholder needs, and driven by relevant research), and cultivating a positive, nurturing, and collaborative school/classroom climate and culture lays the foundation for engaging students within the school's curriculum and content areas. While the curriculum and content may be established by the state or local school board, the strategies, techniques, thematic and interdisciplinary units, alignment with state and local standards, methods for engaging all learners, etc., must be conceptualized and implemented by the classroom teacher and guided by curriculum development teams at the school site. The multitude of instructional strategies, including grading methodology, rubrics, standards-based lesson plans, hands-on activities, utilization of disciplinary experts, cooperative grouping, brain-compatible instruction, etc., must be consistent with the school's (and classroom's) vision and designed to measurably impact student achievement. All of the component strategies and related outcomes must be effectively assessed if we are to measure our progress toward achieving the school's vision and fulfilling its mission.

The school's mission provides the direction with the vision providing the compass that guides the way along the educational continuum and provides the barometer against which instructional practices, the utilization of resources, supplemental curriculum, extra- and co-curricular activities, and all school-wide and classroom programs must be measured.

Once clearly-defined Missions and Visions have been established, their value is only realized when they are used to drive all policies, programs, instruction, training, and school-wide activities:

1. The mission/vision must be clearly communicated and commonly-shared throughout the school community.

2. The vision must be used as the foundation for developing the school's core values, guiding principles, and ethical practices.

3. School-community partnerships and stakeholder teams must be developed for the purpose of conceptualizing and implementing the operational strategies needed to achieve the vision.

4. Experiential and researched-based strategies must be developed which meet the unique needs of the school-community and are driven by the school's vision.

5. Resources must be identified and utilized in a manner consistent with the school's vision.

6. Assessment mechanisms must be developed to measure the school's ongoing progress toward fulfilling the various components of the school's vision.

Notes:

7. Administrative leadership, instructional delivery, and home/school relationships must support student learning in ways that are consistent with the school's vision.

8. Staff development, supplemental curriculum, extracurricular activities, before/after school programs, and other enhanced learning opportunities must be consistent with the school's vision.

9. Staff hiring, volunteer support, consultants, guest speakers, and disciplinary experts (i.e., artists, authors, brick masons, hair stylists, research scientist, attorneys, chemists, etc.) must be driven by the school's vision.

10. The school's annual assessment, debriefing, and pre-planning efforts must be driven by the school's vision.

In essence, every decision that is made within a school community must be framed by two questions:

1. Is this consistent with our vision?

2. Is this in the best interest of our students?

At Marva Collin's Westside Preparatory School on Chicago's west side, they have embodied a vision that is clearly communicated and represents the driving force behind all school-wide efforts:

All students at Westside Preparatory School must also take an oral pledge before the entire group that they will never bring disgrace to the school and that they will, at all times, uphold the moral and academic standards of Westside Preparatory School and that any student who is guilty of omission in this area does not deserve the right to be called a Westside Prepian. The academic program at Westside Preparatory is nothing less than the basic three R's mixed with a total program that teaches every child that they are unique, special, and that they are too bright to ever be less than all that they can be. The 'I will not let you fail' statement is one that they seldom hear elsewhere. We also hold parent classes, and we teach the very same things to parents that we teach our students.

Restoring Public Confidence

The national focus on raising test scores, increasing reading proficiency, and expanding students' knowledge of the core curriculum has caused many school communities to become disconnected from children and their families. Increasing student achievement and strengthening relationships are not mutually exclusive but inextricably tied together. Public schools are part of the tapestry of communities.

1. They are often the most stable institutions within the community.

Notes:

2.   They represent the hope of families for the future of their children.

3.   They have extraordinary power to shape the future of entire communities and indeed of an entire nation.

While some principals, teachers, and support staff may view the dawning of the school year as just another day at the job, for children and their families each school year is fresh and new with potential and possibilities providing hope for the present and a promise for the future.

Walking through the corridors of a middle school in rural North Carolina I watched young boys and girls who, years ago, began school with divinely-given promise and potential. In most instances, they began kindergarten with high energy and inquisitive minds. Yet, now in the sixth, seventh, and eighth grades, they shuffled through the corridors without any sense of purpose or direction. They sat in classrooms half asleep, half paying attention, largely apathetic and uninterested in doing classwork or participating in classroom discussions. In some classrooms, students had such little interest in what was being discussed that they had fallen asleep. Not just one or two students; in several classrooms half of the students were asleep. On the faces of those still awake, I could see a lack of enthusiasm and a tragic sense of hopelessness. Most of them lagged behind grade level in nearly every academic area. A number of children were repeating their respective grades; some for a second time. Their daily rituals of clowning around, disrupting classes, disrespecting teachers, and engaging in any number of activities other than learning created a revolving door between their classrooms, in-school detention, and out of school suspension. With a student population under 400 students, there had been over 500 office referrals, and nearly half the school year remained.

I had been invited to the school to conduct a staff development on a curriculum entitled, *The Eagle Team: A Leadership Curriculum,* which contains a year-long series of units designed to cultivate leadership skills and to inspire self-directed behavior for high and low achieving students. However, the previous day, as I led teachers through a discussion of the *educational continuum* and some of the research studies which outlined components common to high achieving schools, I could see in their eyes and feel in their very spirits that attempting to implement the *Eagle Team Curriculum* would have been analogous to providing a pain-reliever to a patient suffering from appendicitis. While there might have been some temporary relief, without an operation the patient had little hope of surviving.

After meeting with the teachers and support staff I talked to parents regarding the at-home strategies outlined in my book, *Ten Steps to Helping Your Child Succeed in School.* I outlined strategies that they could use to support the school improvement efforts of teachers to ensure greater academic success for their children. I also shared examples of how my wife and I have developed effective communication strategies and forged teacher/parent partnerships with our sons' teachers, which has helped our children to become socially and academically successful. As we discussed issues of *Personality Types, Learning Styles, Multiple Intelligences,* developing effective at-home routines, and effective home-school communication mechanisms, it was glaringly evident that while most of the parents didn't know what to do, they were all anxious to learn and eager to become partners in their children's learning.

During my interaction with students, as the teachers had predicted, I was generally greeted with smart mouths and negative attitudes. However, since I had a clear vision of what I wanted to accomplish, and the experience of having encountered these type of behaviors hundreds of times in the past, I had a game plan (i.e., operational strategy):

1. Develop a relationship.

2. Demonstrate an interest in what "they" want to know.

3. Know more than they do.

4. Challenge them.

I had already taken steps to infiltrate their ranks. I had allies (relationships) in the persons of students whom I had interacted with the previous night at the parent meeting. For the students I was meeting for the first time, I knew how to get past their attitudes and how to make a connection. My battle wasn't with them. My enemy was the apathy and lack of enthusiasm toward learning that we have cultivated in our children and created in our schools. They weren't born like this. They hadn't entered into kindergarten like this. We, the parents, teachers, administrators, and those who profess to care about our children, have created boring, dreary, uninspiring schools. We have turned our children into worksheet junkies, filled their school days with boring, repetitive, and unchallenging tasks. We have told them to sit still and be quiet. And if they don't, we send them to the office, send them home, or send them to a doctor. Then we tell them to sit still, be quiet, and take a pill. My enemy wasn't the children. I understood why they were so unenthusiastic and what I needed to do—make a connection, build a relationship, inspire them, and convince them that I had something worth listening to.

There are many ways to develop relationships with children. In my book, *Building Dreams: Helping Students Discover Their Potential, Parent, Teacher, Mentor Workbook,* I illustrate the power of storytelling as a means of connecting with students:

> *I have discovered that a well-timed and well-told story or parable can be literally a life-saver when dealing with young people. It quickly grabs their attention in situations where all else seems to fail. It provides a means for the mentor [parent, teacher] to share a lot of personal information and experiences within a relatively short time span and provides a bridge of communication for the mentor to crossover and effectively open dialogue... Many people don't view themselves as storytellers. Either they simply don't believe that they possess storytelling skills or they don't believe that they have any stories to tell. However, when I work with parents and teachers, they*

frequently surprise themselves at not only their storytelling ability, but how many stories they have to tell.

I frequently tell the story outlined in my book, *The Eagles who Thought They were Chickens,* to capture their attention. Other times I will begin with observations that I have made at their school or at other schools. At times I may draw upon personal stories about my family, our hopes, and our dreams to make the connection. I use whatever stories or anecdotes that I believe can provide a lead-in to discussing their hopes, their dreams, their aspirations, and their attitudes toward school. As I listen to their hopes and dreams, I draw upon my beliefs and experiences to share my insight into ways of achieving what I've heard them articulate as being important to them:

> *As early as the second grade I had a passion for writing poetry. 'Roses are red, violets are blue, your dog is ugly, and you are too!' My early passion for writing poetry eventually evolved into my dreams of becoming a writer, which eventually evolved into my dreams of starting my own publishing company, which eventually evolved into my dreams of transforming schools into places of passion and purpose where students like you discover and pursue their own dreams.*

> *I don't know what your dreams are, but I do know that most of you have already wasted half of this school year. The human brain is the most powerful muscle in your body and most of you have exercised your brains as little as possible this school year. The human brain is composed of billions of neurons which send billions of billions of synaptic signals controlling conscious and unconscious thoughts throughout your lifetime.*

> *Just think, if you'd sat in your chair all school year by now your leg muscles would be so weak that you couldn't stand. The same is true of your brains, you've been sitting on them all year!*

Now that I had their attention, I began asking individual students what their dreams and aspirations were. I took the dreams of each student and created a dream map on the board so that they could "see" that their dreams weren't impossible, but with their behaviors and their attitudes toward learning, they were certainly improbable:

Of all of the areas that relate to your dreams, what have you learned this school year to take you closer to turning your dreams into reality? What have you read about, what have you studied, what have you researched, what have you done to acquire the education that you need to achieve your dreams?

The more I talked the more their body language changed as they began listening and thinking. Now I could challenge them:

You say that your dream is to play professional football. Okay, list three things that you have researched about muscular development and nutrition. What about the difference between animal and plant proteins on muscular development? Why is it important to load up on carbohydrates before practice? Who can tell me the three major muscle groups utilized by offensive linemen as oppose to the three major muscle groups utilized by a running back?

Oh, by the way, how many teams are there in the NFL, how many players are on each team, and what is the average career of a professional football player?

The bad attitudes and smart mouths quickly changed into insightful questions and positive comments. The teacher joined into the discussion, "Mr. Wynn, our community has such few resources, how does a student like Juan follow his dream of becoming a professional boxer when our community doesn't even have a gym?" My response was to illustrate the Multiple Intelligences identified by Dr. Howard Gardner in his book, *Frames of Mind: The Theory of Multiple Intelligences,* and how Juan could better utilize his experiences in school to expand his intellectual strengths, knowledge base, and subsequently, his opportunities to pursue his dreams and aspirations:

Let's look at the variety of aspects of Juan's dream of becoming a professional boxer and the impact that not having a professional training facility has on his dream.

Juan, since I am not an expert at becoming a professional boxer I can't speak specifically to what you need to do. However, if you and your classmates will help me we can look at some of the ways that you can become 'smart' enough to achieve your dreams. For example, we know that every person in this classroom can demonstrate intelligence, or be smart, in at least eight different ways. Let's look at some of these ways and how they might relate to a long-term dream of becoming a professional boxer.

Verbal/Linguistic Intelligence *involves being word smart. It deals with effectively talking, reading, and communicating orally and through written forms of communication. For example, how you would articulate yourself in an interview following a fight, your ability to read and understand a contract, and your ability to write and verbally communicate your thoughts.*

Logical/Mathematical Intelligence *involves solving problems. It involves your thinking skills in understanding complex problems and developing a sequence of steps like those typical in math and science. For example, your ability to analyze the fighting style of a boxer you're about to fight and developing an effective strategy. It may also involve rethinking and changing your strategy during the fight itself. It would also deal with developing investment strategies, managing your winnings, and negotiating a contract with a promoter.*

Bodily/Kinesthetic Intelligence *involves effectively using your body. It involves conditioning and training your body to perform well within the confines of a boxing match. This is where your lack of a professional training facility could be a problem. However, a training facility is only one component of enhancing this area of intelligence. It also involves guidance from someone knowledgeable in the sport, a professional trainer. It would also involve understanding muscular development, the difference in eating and training for quickness versus bulk, strength and endurance.*

I went on to discuss the other areas of *Visual/Spatial, Interpersonal, Intrapersonal, Musical/Rhythmic,* and the *Naturalist Intelligences* with Juan and the rest of the classroom. On the chalkboard, I illustrated the types of decisions, strategies, fight preparation, and career choices which would all be impacted by decisions made within each of the intellectual domains.

We were all in agreement that there were many things that Juan could do to pursue his dream in spite of the lack of a local training facility. Juan agreed that he was concentrating all of his efforts on developing Bodily/Kinesthetic intelligence and had paid little attention to developing any of the other intelligences, all of which he would come to rely upon, if he was to increase his chances of achieving his dream.

Juan then asked, "Mr. Wynn, if you're a writer, how do you know so much about achieving my dream of becoming a boxer?" To which I responded, "Juan, the cornerstones of how a person follows any dream are: reading, thinking, understanding, planning, and following your plan. All of these are taught or strengthened each day in school. However, you have acknowledged that you have not been applying yourself to developing the skills and acquiring the knowledge available to you each school day. If you are serious about achieving your dreams, then it's time that you seriously begin reading, thinking, understanding, and developing your plan. If you truly want to become a boxer, then you must become a thinker."

No more smart mouths. No more negative attitudes. No more disrespectful behaviors. This wasn't an aberration. Developing a relationship and using our beliefs and experiences as a foundation for making a connection between the sterile learning of school and the richness of the world of a child's dreams, hopes, and aspirations opens a doorway to learning that both student and teacher may enter together. Taking the time to paint the broad strokes of passion, purpose, and inspiration across the canvas of schooling evolves from internalizing Marva Collins' belief, *"All children are born achievers and all they need is someone to help them become all that they have the potential to become."*

By and large, children are inspired to learn. When the actions and behaviors of adults, within their school community, conveys a sense of confidence that the adults themselves know what they are doing, they provide children with a sense of clarity about what they must do to become successful. Being concerned with the interests, hopes, and aspirations of children is no small concern. We need to understand that children are not intellectually limited little creatures whom we are to toss bits and pieces of information toward until we decide to momentarily stop tossing them information and assess how much of the bits and pieces they have absorbed. We must nurture each child's greatest gift, "the passion for learning." Children enter into our schools excited about learning, with many areas of interests, unique gifts, and aspirations for their futures. Perhaps our greatest challenge will be to stop our busyness and to work harder toward building relationships with and "hearing" our children.

A boy of five, on the first day of kindergarten, asked his teacher, 'When am I going to learn to read?' She said, a bit absently (for there was a lot going on), 'Oh, that won't happen until next year, in first grade.' He didn't say anything, but an hour or so later, she noticed that he had slipped away when no one was looking. He walked out of the room and continued home (which fortunately was only a few blocks away). He went up to his startled mother and said, 'I'll go back next year...when they're ready to teach me to read.'

[Schools That Learn]

Many of the children in this middle school, like thousands of their counterparts throughout the country, entered school below grade level in various academic areas. Many of them also came from difficult home situations, particularly, families living in poverty. Such children and their families may have already internalized a sense of hopelessness as it relates to school and learning. It is important to recognize that for them, the first days of school must become spirit-filled days in which we build relationships in an inviting and reaffirming learning environment, tap into their interests and intrinsic desires to learn, and convince them of our belief that we are capable of teaching them and preparing them to pursue their dreams and aspirations. We must diligently work to restore the public trust and to inspire public confidence in our schools. For most of our children, the journey through our schools will take thirteen long years. However, the vast majority of them will spend just one year at each grade level. Although a classroom teacher may teach a particular subject, or at a particular grade level year after year, for most children we have the one year that they are with us to inspire them and to reassure them and their families of the hope and promise of the current school year.

What do YOU believe?

I spent the balance of my time at this middle school outlining the steps needed for the administrative team to put together a *Core Team* (Chapter 7), and how to cultivate effective, and much needed school, parent, and community partnerships. The principal asked each teacher, administrator, and support person to write a note indicating whether they were interested in becoming a part of the Core Team and/or willing to make a commitment to engaging in the processes needed to improve their school.

During my meeting with the principal, I asked, "Now that your staff has a sense of the amount of work involved and the commitment needed to pave the way to increasing student achievement, how many staff people do you believe are interested in becoming a part of your Core Team?"

Notes:

The principal was confident that the majority of the staff was committed to doing whatever was necessary to ensure the success of their students. While she didn't believe that all staff members would be willing to become a part of the Core Team, she was confident that *all* staff members would be in support of the school's efforts.

The first responses she received turned her optimism into astonishment. Once confronted with the reality that increasing student achievement does not occur by accident or because we "wish" it to occur, the principal received letter after letter indicating that few of her staff were willing to do what was needed to lay the foundation for creating a high achieving school.

Typical responses from teachers and support staff were:

- *"I am unwilling to participate in this process because students' lack of enthusiasm, low self-esteem, and low test scores are not our fault. All of the blame lies with their parents."*

- *"I'm looking for a job closer to home."*

- *"This sounds like a very good idea, but I am not willing to commit myself."*

- *"I don't want to commit to something because I'm not sure whether or not anything would work with these kids."*

- *"We already have enough responsibilities."*

Ultimately, it is the individuals within each school community who will pave the way to heightened student achievement and close any student achievement gaps. Their attitudes, beliefs, experiences, and willingness to identify and implement the needed solutions to the complex issues confronting the school will ultimately impact upon climate, culture, and student achievement levels.

Admittedly disheartened by the lack of support from those who had always *talked* about being committed to their students' academic success, the principal's hope for her students was brightened by the commitment and reassurances from other staff members:

- *"I want to make a difference. Show me my role. I would love to become a part of the Core Team."*

- *"I'm ready to see a change. I'm willing and ready to be dedicated and to help out in any way that I can."*

- *"I am willing to work with any program that can help our students."*

- *"I will support whatever it takes to make our school the best in the county."*

- *"I am truly committed. However, to be honest, I don't think that our entire staff would be dedicated to the challenge. Count me in!"*

The questions that must ultimately be raised within each school community are:

1.   What is our mission, i.e., "What is our purpose?"

2.   What is our vision, i.e., "What must we do to fulfill our mission?"

3.   What are the issues hindering our school from achieving our vision and fulfilling our mission?

4.   What are our goals and what strategies are needed to successfully achieve them?

5.   What work must be done to implement the strategies?

6.   Who will do the work?

1. What is our mission, i.e., "What is our purpose?"

2. What is our vision, i.e., "What must we do to fulfill our mission?"

3. What are the issues hindering our school from achieving our vision and fulfilling our mission?

4. What are our goals and what strategies are needed to successfully achieve them?

5. What work must be done to implement the strategies?

6. Who will do the work?

Excellence Does Not Occur by Accident

Cultivating schools of excellence, increasing student achievement, closing the various achievement gaps, and creating school-wide cultures that are socially and emotionally nurturing for children are not achieved by wishful thinking and do not occur by accident. Nor can they be mandated by the superintendent, legislated by the general assembly or written into teachers' contracts by the school board. Schools that best serve children evolve from the collaborative efforts of the stakeholders within the school community (i.e., central office personnel, administrators, teachers, support staff, parents, students, mentors, tutors, bus

Notes:

What is the school that you envision
and what efforts are needed to create it?

drivers, custodians, and business/community partners) who are driven by a clear vision of what they want to achieve. In essence, the school's vision provides a mental picture of the school community that they want to create.

Cultivating effective collaboration is no small task, which accounts for the fact that there are so few schools of *real* excellence. I say *real* excellence because excellence in academics or performance on standardized tests only represents academic or test performance excellence. Schools that demonstrate high academic achievement and yet have high numbers of

students committing suicide, suffering from depression or any number of anxiety disorders, disproportionately high numbers of students (typically boys) being prescribed Ritalin or labeled as ADD or ADHD, that have school-wide cultures that tolerate racial, social, economic, athletic, and academic cliques that emotionally abuse and verbally ridicule students, that have identifiable achievement gaps where ethnic or socioeconomic groups of students are relegated to lower level courses, have disproportionate drop-out rates, are disproportionately assigned to special education classes, and/or are disproportionately referred to the office, in-school detention or are suspended from school, should never be confused with excellence no matter how high the test scores.

Schools of excellence operate holistically. They cultivate high academic achievement, positive social interactions, and are emotionally and socially nurturing places for children and occur by design, not by accident. Academic achievement is driven by teams of individuals who commit to identifying the curriculum, instructional strategies, lesson plans, study groups, tutorial assistance, etc., which pave the way to high academic achievement. An emotionally- and socially-nurturing school climate and culture is cultivated by teams of individuals who commit to identifying the needed customs, rituals, instructional lessons, guest speakers, extracurricular activities, and intervention programs. This paves the way for nurturing the emotional health of the very children whom we are leading toward high academic achievement. True schools of excellence are comprised of many pockets of excellence, all holistically-integrated to cultivate high student achievement and which nurture the personal and emotional development of students.

Don't Play the "Blame Game"

In low-achieving schools, rather than focusing on proactive strategies to cultivate effective collaboration, the energies of both the school and community are frequently directed toward affixing blame. Blame is directed at teachers, parents, society, the media, and at the children themselves for the failings of schools and the underachievement pathology prevalent within so many schools and school districts throughout the country. Letting go of old paradigms and shedding preexisting stereotypical beliefs about what is wrong with children and their families is the first step toward change.

Notes:

A common thread woven through all of the educational research regarding successful schools is a belief by teachers and the support staff in *their* ability to help students achieve academic success. They believe that they can make a difference within the lives of their students. Becoming an integral part of the process of helping a school to navigate its way along the educational continuum into the ranks of a school of excellence requires a level of commitment from teachers beyond just showing up and delivering instruction within the classroom. While it probably means working harder, it definitely means working smarter. Many traditions, instructional strategies, and school-wide initiatives are driven by a lot of hard work. No matter how ineffective, many traditions refuse to die and teachers refuse to let go of them as they proudly proclaim, "We've always done it this way!"

The traditions of a school community are particularly mystifying when they relate to the area of parental involvement. Research study after research study identifies parent and community involvement as essential to school success. Yet, the tradition of parental involvement in many school communities is that parents are involved in elementary school, less involved in middle school, and tragically absent in high school. Teachers have accepted this tradition and are apt not to change it, despite the fact that everyone seems to know that as students grow older, are confronted with increasingly negative peer pressure, deal with issues of adolescence, emerging sexuality, and the complexity of relationships, they need MORE parental involvement, not LESS. While some traditions are healthy for school communities, many traditions should be discarded in favor of traditions more in line with the type of school that the school community envisions creating. We must create more traditions that celebrate teachers, children, parents, support staff, and the many partnerships that must be created to best serve the needs of students and their families.

We must create traditions that develop and celebrate relationships.

We Cannot Legislate Passion

North Carolina, as are many other states, is working hard to help its public schools better educate its children and has established state-wide learning goals and School Accountability Standards.

The General Assembly believes that all children can learn. With this as a guiding mission, the State Board of Education is charged with developing a school-based management and accountability program with improving student performance as the primary goal.

Despite such efforts, many of the students in this middle school, and thousands of their counterparts throughout the state, don't care about the standards and aren't reaching the levels outlined in the learning goals. They are not making a connection with their teachers and they remain unmotivated to engage in the rigors of higher-level learning. In essence, their schools have failed to cultivate the level of collaboration needed to transform the culture of the schools, and subsequently, the attitudes of the students.

In poor rural and urban communities students are entering each school year with a sense of hopelessness and disillusionment. They are not reading; they are not thinking; they are not writing; and they are not computing. In essence, they are just coming. They are turning off to education and tuning out their teachers. An equally tragic situation is that many teachers are turning off their students and tuning out the accountability standards. Fewer and fewer schools are places of passion and purpose and fewer and fewer schools believe that "academic excellence" is achievable.

At Bertie County High School in Windsor, North Carolina, I had the opportunity to speak to all of the students during two assemblies. During the first assembly of ninth and tenth graders, I talked about my dreams, my family, and the reality of education being the key to unlocking the doorway to opportunity. During the question and answer exchange with students, one young lady took issue with comments in which I stated, "I intend for my children to attend college as surely as I intended for them to attend elementary school."

Mr. Wynn, how can you say that your children are going to go to college? If they don't want to go to college you can't make them go to college!

Her question lead to an enthusiastic exchange with other students as I went on to outline the vision that my wife and I have for our sons. That vision guides the expectations that my wife and I have of our children, and the rules and restrictions that we enforce in our household (e.g., no TV during the week, and no TV on the weekends unless all schoolwork has been completed and turned in during the week, etc.). Our rules are consistent with achieving our long-term vision, "to raise spiritually-centered, socially conscious, intellectually and artistically successful children." I remained steadfast in my position, "It is our responsibility as their parents to ensure that our children have every opportunity to pursue their respective dreams and aspirations. Doing well enough in school to ensure that they can attend and graduate from a four-year college or university is one of the keys to furthering their opportunity." Following this statement, a young man stood and said:

> *Mr. Wynn, I can see that you care about your children and that you are determined that they become successful in school. But what about people like me, whose parents aren't involved like you, and whose teachers don't care? Many of the teachers here don't care whether we do the work or not.*

Without debating whether or not the young man's comments were accurate, the fact that this was his perception of the school community was important for us to hear as adults. Of all of the efforts that we are engaged in to increase student achievement, we are failing to listen to our children and involve them in the process of transforming our schools. Far too many children lack pride in their schools and confidence in their teachers.

During the remaining dialogue, I outlined why students had to take ownership of their own learning and why going to college should not be an option if they wanted to expand their opportunities for becoming successful. I told them that even if they currently aspired to pursue a trade or enter into the Armed Forces, college should be part of their life's plan. I admonished them, "You have to take responsibility for your own learning." However, we must not forget that they are children. We must accept that a part of our responsibility is not to simply educate them, but to inspire them to want to learn. We have to change the spirit within our schools from one in which many of our children "believe" that teachers and counselors don't care about their success to one in which our children begin to believe that we, in fact, "believe" in their success, and care about their dreams. After the two assemblies, I met with groups of students in the media center and showed them how to do internet research, gather information, and develop plans for pursuing their dreams and aspirations. The eagerness, enthusiasm, and self-directed behavior that I witnessed by those students is what I believe we want for all children within our schools. However, inspiring such behavior in all children requires that we first ask ourselves, "What do we want to inspire within *our* children?"

What Do You Want for YOUR Children?

I have two sons who currently attend public schools. I realize that no matter what my wife and I do as parents, they are going to spend nearly 14,000 hours and 13 years of their lives in schools (elementary through high school) where they will be influenced by teachers and have the values and beliefs of our household challenged or supported by their peers. While my wife and I can afford to send our children to private schools, we are committed to our public schools (a commitment that is challenged more and more each school year as we encounter middle and high school teachers and administrators who are less and less child-centered, who are uninterested in establishing effective lines of communication with families, and who view parental involvement as burdensome rather than as an essential element in a child's success in school). Like millions of today's children, my wife and I grew up poor and we had no choice but to attend the

Would you want your own children attending your school?

Notes:

public schools. My parents tried to exercise "choice" by enrolling me in Chicago's parochial schools. However, with the negative peer pressure from the children within my community, and the abusive attitudes toward poor children from those within the very schools where my parents sent me to be educated, I discovered that the choice that they were making was forcing choices upon me that I was neither intellectually or emotionally prepared to deal with. Why couldn't they make the schools in my neighborhood better? Where were the advocates for the public schools in my community?

I don't want my children to relive my experiences within the Chicago Public Schools or my experiences within Chicago's Catholic Schools. I don't want them to be intimidated by gangs. I don't want them to be bullied. I don't want them to be verbally abused by a popular peer culture of put-downs and ridicule. I don't want them attending school for 13 years without discovering the interests, dreams, and aspirations that might become their life's work so that they can process their many hours of classwork within a meaningful and relevant context. Thus, I am involved in the schools where my children attend. And, if they are in the public schools, then other children benefit from my advocacy. As a parent, I want the public schools to become places of passion and purpose because that's where my children attend school.

On a flight from Atlanta, Georgia, to Rochester, New York, I was sitting next to a business consultant. He was well dressed, articulate, and apparently was a highly-paid expert in the area of Human Resources. He noticed me working on a manuscript and asked what I did. When I told him that I was an educational consultant, he immediately began talking about all that is wrong with our schools. He articulated many of the stereotypical beliefs prevalent today regarding public education. "Teachers don't care; children don't want to learn; parents aren't involved, etc."

After patiently listening, I asked the following questions:

1. "Where do your children attend school?" (All of his children had attended private schools and had subsequently graduated from college.)

2. "When was the last time that you were in a public school?" (Not since he had graduated from high school in the 60s.)

I went on to state, "Years ago, when I was speaking at a conference, a reporter asked my opinion regarding the 'Ebonics Movement.' I told him that I wasn't aware that there *was* an Ebonics Movement, just some well-publicized newspaper stories regarding issues that were being discussed within one of the Northern California school districts. The reporter continued to press me for an opinion to which I responded, 'I don't know much more than what journalist have reported. Also, I do not have a linguistics background, so I am unqualified to comment on the linguistics or dialect issues being raised in the discussion. My position is, if I don't know what I'm talking about, we would both be better served if I didn't say anything!' "

From the look on his face, I don't believe that this fellow quite grasped from my illustration, that I was suggesting that he should shut up. If you don't have children attending public schools, and if you haven't been in a public school recently, then you don't know what is going on in our public schools. And, if the tragic state of public education that you have been reading or hearing about is true, the fact that you aren't actively involved in changing what is going on is even more tragic.

In many school districts, embodied within the mission of the district is such language as, "creating productive citizens." We have obviously missed fulfilling this mission when so many of the students who attend our public schools, like this fellow, grow up to become adults who have nothing to do with ensuring the success of our schools.

Notes:

I believe that children like those in the North Carolina middle school, despite their occasionally disrespectful and apathetic behaviors, are basically good people who largely lack focus on the future. They don't understand how the very education that we are holding them accountable for can help them to achieve their dreams and aspirations. Tragically, most of them have no dreams and aspirations. For many of them, school is simply a social experience that they are forced to endure until they reach legal age or until their parents allow them to stop going altogether.

I believe that teachers, despite their occasional frustration and cynicism regarding students (and their parents), are basically good people who want to be effective and who want to see children learn. I have found that cultivating the dynamics within a school community that builds a relationship between these two groups of people so that teachers teach with passion and students learn with purpose is the miracle that must be expected if we are to truly achieve the highest levels of student achievement. Such a miracle doesn't occur by berating schools and teachers; by condemning parents for their lack of knowledge; by condemning students for their lack of enthusiasm toward learning what "we" believe to be important; nor, does it occur by living in denial about the magnitude of the problems confronting us within each school community and the depths to which we must reach to identify solutions.

Courage: The Fundamental Core Value

Whether or not you would want your own children to attend the school where you work and to be taught by your colleagues is analogous to asking the question of a waitress, "Would you eat the food that you serve?" or a mechanic, "Would you want the people you work with servicing your car?" or better yet, a doctor, "If you were gravely ill would you want to be brought to the hospital where you work?" If the administrators, teachers, and support staff have confidence in their colleagues, in the instructional practices occurring within the classrooms, in the school-wide climate and culture, in the administrative leadership, in the curriculum, and in the extra- and co-curricular activities of the school in which they work and are willing to have their own children educated where they work, then it is probably a good school for all children. If not, then the most effective reform movement for such a school is for the teachers and support staff to commit their efforts toward implementing those strategies, identifying those resources, and creating the type of school community where they would want to bring their own children.

We tend to personalize the education of our own children. But what about the other children? One thing is for sure: If you have the courage to become an advocate for all children, it will almost ensure that you won't be popular [at least not until courage becomes one of the commonly-embraced core values of your school community]. Being an advocate for children requires that we continually question what we do and why we are doing it; it requires standing up for a child whom we believe is being overlooked, mistreated, undereducated, or in the worst case, miseducated. When teachers are not delivering effective instruction within their classrooms, we must have the *courage* to either help them or to inform parents that their children are not being effectively educated. When adults within a school community lack professionalism and integrity, we must have the *courage* to hold them to the same professional standards that we would if the children and families which they serve were our own. When cafeteria workers speak to children as undeserving of kindness, respect, and compassion; when custodians do not take pride in a clean school; and when teachers and the support staff dress in a way that communicates less than the highest standards, we must have the *courage* to ask, "Why do you believe that our students and our school are deserving of less than your best?"

When we begin to stand up and speak out on behalf of all children with the same passion as we would for our own children, we will begin to raise the standards throughout the school community. Thusly, we will begin to raise expectations which, ultimately, will convince children and their families that we care about them and their futures. This is not to deny that parents and students within many school communities behave disrespectfully toward teachers and school property. However, as we will examine later in great detail, school climate and culture is either defined within each school community by the adults or it defaults to the children! Children and their parents behave within each school community commensurate with the standard of behavior that is modeled by administrators, teachers, and the support staff.

What are YOU Willing to Do?

Nothing has more profound meaning within a school community than the statement, "Lead, follow, or get out of the way!" Staff responses to the principal at the North Carolina middle school represent important individual decisions that will directly determine the future of the school. Those teachers who enthusiastically responded that they were willing to accept leadership roles on the Core Team were stating, "I'm willing to lead." Those who indicated that they weren't sure of the role they needed to play, but were willing to do whatever was needed to help to improve the school were stating, "I'll follow." Those teachers unable to lead and unwilling follow must get out of the way.

Within each school community, school board members, superintendents, principals, classroom teachers, counselors, psychologist, custodians, cafeteria workers, social workers, support personnel, and parents must decide, "Will I lead?" "Will I follow?" or, "Will I get out of the way?" Even this decision requires courage. Schools that fail children are frequently dominated by adults who won't lead, won't follow,

and who won't get out of the way. The complexities of the problems within school communities can rarely be solved individually. Even in the most extreme cases where there is a visionary principal who brings order to chaos, there are always individuals who get behind the principal to follow his or her lead. Lorraine Monroe, principal of the Frederick Douglass Academy High School in New York, in her book, *Nothing's Impossible*, writes:

> *Seek, too, a leader who aspires to a noble ideal of education. Noble because this work of transforming children's lives is particularly ennobling. Noble because the work has merit only when done for no reason except to transform children's lives... And once you've identified the leader who will spearhead your new creation, surround him or her with a group of insanely dedicated followers, a few people who can infect the rest of the staff with the values and ideals that make education or any work exciting, fruitful, and worthwhile.*

Notes:

Lead

There will be times when each of us has the experience and knowledge required to resolve some of the complex issues confronting a school community. Systemic, sustained change can only occur when we are willing to step forward into a leadership role. Later, when we explore Howard Gardner's research in the area of Multiple Intelligences (M.I.) Theory, as outlined in his book, *Frames of Mind: The Theory of Multiple Intelligences,* we will examine in great detail how M.I. theory provides an effective framework for teaming individuals according to their highly-developed intellectual domains for problem-solving purposes. Within such a framework, individuals must assume leadership roles for applying their intellectual strengths for problem-solving and for leading the charge to implementing the operational strategies needed to achieve the school's vision.

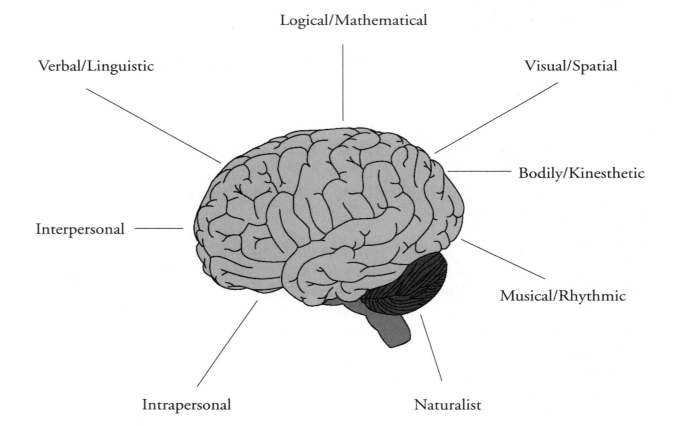

Follow

There will be times when we won't know what must be done and must accept a support role and allow others to lead the way. This is evident when evaluating the multi-faceted strategies that evolve out of M.I. grouping. Those who have a heightened understanding of how to build relationships (Interpersonal Intelligence) may conceptualize viable parent involvement strategies that those who have a heightened understanding of processes and procedures (Logical/ Mathematical Intelligence) don't fully grasp and would never have conceptualized themselves. In like fashion, those who have a heightened understanding, and unique talents and abilities, in the area of visual imagery (Visual/Spatial Intelligence) may conceptualize inspiring architectural designs, bulletin boards, murals, and other visual imagery, design, and utilization of space, which those who have a heightened understanding of language (Verbal/Linguistic Intelligence) would not have conceptualized and may even find superficial. Typically, in school communities, rather than valuing and validating the varied intelligences, individuals become roadblocks to the school improvement process by persistently questioning, "Why is that important? That doesn't make sense to me. Why don't we just...?" instead of accepting a support role, "How can I help?"

Get Out of the Way

Finally, there may be times when we lack the experience and knowledge and are so confused by the problems that we can't lead. We may not have enough confidence in others, or are simply unwilling to follow. Subsequently, we are relegated to the role of observer. As such, rather than hindering the efforts of others, the school is better served if we simply *get out of the way*. Perhaps we will stay and watch what happens, and at other times, the school community may be better served if we would just *go away*.

The Question that Must be Answered

Each of the 17,000+ public school districts throughout the United States, as well as each of the thousands of public and private schools internationally, despite the diverse student populations and communities they serve, is confronted with the singular question:

> **How do we help our children to learn more during the 13 years that they are in our schools—from kindergarten through the twelfth grade?**

Avoid the platitudes of those who would attribute all that is wrong in our schools to parental apathy, student apathy, or the lack of morality popularized within today's pop and hip-hop culture, and engage in a critical review of each school's demographic data.

- Does the data reveal an achievement gap between identifiable groups of students (i.e., migrant children, reservation children, mountain children, trailer park children, project children, children from the Barrio, black boys, eighth graders, etc.)?

- Does the data reveal a gender gap in areas of the core curriculum such as honors or Advanced Placement classes?

- Does the data reveal identifiable groups of students (i.e., socio- economic- or cultural) who are not demonstrating proficiency on the end-of-grade exams?

- Does the data reveal identifiable groups of students who are involved in a disproportionately high number of discipline-related incidents?

- Does the data reveal identifiable groups of students who are disproportionately referred to the office or suspended from school?

- Does the data reveal identifiable groups of students who are disproportionately placed into Special Education as opposed to the Talented and Gifted programs?

Each school community must engage in a critical review of its data to identify those groups of students who are not achieving.

Whether your school community is located in one of the United States urban or rural school districts; in Canada; in Bermuda; or on any one of the many Caribbean islands, you must engage in an honest and objective review of your school's data. Whatever disparities or unique challenges lead you to the micro view of your school communities' problems, the overriding question remains the same, *"How do we help our children to learn more during the 13 years that they are in our schools—from kindergarten through the twelfth grade?"*

Once the question is raised, each stakeholder within a school community from building custodian to district superintendent must answer the question, **"What will I do?"**

Dr. Ann Hart, the Superintendent of Schools in Hickory, North Carolina, invited me to speak on the opening day of school to all of the school district's employees. This was the first time that all of the district employees had been gathered together for one big meeting. As the new superintendent, Dr. Hart wanted to use this meeting to share her vision and to have an inspiring kick-off to the school year.

In one of our early conversations regarding the scope of my presentation, Dr. Hart shared with me, "Mychal, you may not remember me, but I've heard you speak on several occasions. When I was an assistant superintendent in the Chapel Hill Public Schools [North Carolina], my son was a student at Ephesus Elementary School. You spoke to the staff at Ephesus and got them so fired up about talking to children about their dreams and aspirations and how their education can empower them to achieve their respective dreams and aspirations. One day shortly after you spoke to the staff, my son came home from school excited that children had been talking about and researching their dreams. He asked me to come to school with him to see his star hanging on the wall that talked about his dreams. I've never forgotten how excited he was about school and how insistent he was that I come to the school to see how his school was helping him to pursue his dreams and aspirations. As a parent, I have always treasured that moment, and I want you to share that inspiration with our school district's employees so that they begin this school year with a focus to help our students discover their dreams and how what we're teaching can help them to achieve those dreams."

Whether you are a cafeteria worker or the school psychologist, it is important for everyone within a school district who is in contact with children to understand the many pieces that must be put into place if we are to help each child create his or her mosaic of learning. After exploring each of the steps outlined in developing your school's mission, vision, operational strategies, and implementation plans that follows, each of us must resolve to *lead, follow,* or *get out of the way.*

Discussion Questions

1. What is the Mission of your school district and where is it printed and/or posted?

2. What is the Mission of your school and where is it printed and/or posted?

3. What is the Mission for your grade level, department, athletic program, extracurricular activity, or after school program, and how is it communicated to students and families?

4. How does the fulfillment of your Mission (i.e., department, program) impact student achievement?

5. How do the student demographics of your school at-large compare to the demographics of students in your gifted, advanced, honors, or AP classes?

6. Is part of your Mission (i.e., personal or departmental) to ensure equity in student enrollment in advanced classes and/or increased achievement on standardized or EOG testing?

7. Write down the name(s) of at least one low achieving student whom you are willing to accept personal responsibility for his or her personal growth and academic success.

8. What steps can you take to build or strengthen your relationship with this student?

9. What passions, interests, dreams, or aspirations does this student have that you can use to build a bridge between learning and outcomes?

Chapter 2

*Can you go two weeks without milking the cow and then get out there and milk like crazy? Can you 'forget' to plant in the spring or goof off all summer and then hit the ground real hard in the fall to bring in the harvest? We might laugh at such ludicrous approaches in agriculture, but then in an academic environment we might cram to get the grades and degrees we need to get the jobs we want, even if we fail to get a good general education. The only thing that endures over time is **the law of the farm**: I must prepare the ground, put in the seed, cultivate it, weed it, water it, then gradually nurture growth and development to full maturity—there is no quick fix, where you can just move in and make everything right with a positive mental attitude and a bunch of success formulas. The law of the harvest governs.*

— Stephen R. Covey [Principle-Centered Leadership]

What is the Mission?

As Covey states in his book, *Principle-Centered Leadership*, "the law of the harvest governs." Before forging ahead to deal with the real or perceived problems within your school community, we must determine the mission. Is the obscure Mission Statement that is posted in the principal's office the true mission of your school? Is anyone aware of it, outside of the principal? An argument may be made that the mission of every public school is to educate its students. This education may be stated as, "creating lifelong learners, productive citizens" or "100% proficiency on the end-of-grade exams."

Whatever language your school community chooses to articulate its mission, the Mission Statement itself must be visually displayed and verbally articulated to every person within your school community to ensure that everyone knows what the ultimate goal of the school is. The mission should clearly state what your school community is attempting to achieve.

Mission: The Foundation of the School House

The process of constructing schools of excellence is analogous to building a home. The mission represents the overall concept of the house that we're attempting to construct (i.e., Victorian or Contemporary), with the vision representing the actual blueprint.

1. You begin with the concept, "Mission."

2. Your concept must be translated into an architectural design, "Vision."

3. That "Vision" guides the efforts of subcontractors, e.g., ordering materials, excavating the land, pouring the foundation, putting up the frame, etc.

4. You cultivate the necessary working conditions, "Climate and Culture," that allows people to work effectively to achieve the vision.

5. You identify all of the needed areas of expertise, "Curriculum and Content," i.e., interior, exterior, swimming pool, roofing, excavating, concrete, landscaping, permits, etc.

6. You identify, and/or train individuals who can put into practice, "Instruction," the required expertise, i.e., carpenters, brick masons, electricians, architects, plumbers, dry wallers, roofers, landscape experts, interior designers, etc.

The Animal School

Once upon a time, the animals decided they must do something heroic to meet the problems of a new world. So they organized a school. They adopted an activity curriculum consisting of running, climbing, swimming and flying. To make it easier to administer the curriculum, all of the animals took all the subjects.

The duck was excellent in swimming; in fact, better than his instructor. But he made only passing grades in flying and was very poor in running. Since he was slow in running, he had to stay after school and also drop swimming to practice running. This was kept up until his webbed feet were badly worn and he was only average in swimming. But average was acceptable in school, so nobody worried about that except the duck.

The rabbit started at the top of the class in running, but had a nervous breakdown because of so much make-up work in swimming.

The squirrel was excellent in climbing until he developed frustration in the flying class where his teacher made him start from the ground up instead of from the treetop down. He also developed a charlie horse from over-exertion and then got a *C* in climbing and a *D* in running.

The eagle was a problem child and was disciplined severely. In the climbing class, he beat all the others to the top of the tree, but insisted on using his own way to get there.

At the end of the year, an abnormal eel who could swim exceedingly well and also run, climb and fly a little, had the highest average and was valedictorian.

The prairie dogs stayed out of school and fought the tax levy because the administration would not add digging and burrowing to the curriculum. They apprenticed their children to a badger and later joined the groundhogs and gophers to start a successful private school.

— George H. Reavis
Former Assistant Superintendent of the Cincinnati Public Schools

The 4 Levels of Mission

The mission, as it relates to student achievement occurs on four distinctive levels within a school community:

1. The first level is the guiding mission of the school district.

2. The second level is the guiding mission of the school itself. Guided by the school district's mission, the mission of the school provides a global focus of what the school is attempting to achieve, e.g., productive citizens, students capable of entering into four-year colleges or universities, students well-rounded in the arts, technology, etc.

3. The third level is the guiding mission of departments or programs within the school, that, when fulfilled, allows the school to fulfill its mission. Such Mission Statements would reflect the unique focus of grade level, subject area, extracurricular activities, special focus areas, and support functions.

4. The fourth and final level is the guiding mission of those individuals responsible for performing the work that allows the school to fulfill its mission, i.e., the personal mission of administrators, classroom teachers, school support staff, volunteers, mentors, tutors, central office support, etc.

    While it is the job of those employed by the school to help the school to fulfill its mission, it is in the best interest of students and their families if they too, develop a personal mission of becoming partners in the success of the school.

To illustrate how the respective missions, once aligned, impact student achievement consider the following:

The school district's mission is, *"Engage students in the highest levels of learning."*

The high school's mission might be articulated as, *"Provide enhanced and extended learning opportunities for students through a broad range of curricular and co-curricular activities."*

The math department's mission might be articulated as, *"Inspire student enrollment in Advanced Placement and honors classes in applied mathematics."*

A math teacher's mission might be articulated as, *"Engage students in rigorous classroom instruction and provide before/after school strategies to cultivate the highest levels of student achievement."*

A school counselor's mission might be articulated as, *"Identify, inspire, encourage, support, and prepare targeted groups of students (e.g., children of color or children from households living in poverty) to enroll, and succeed, in Advanced Placement and honors mathematics classes."*

If the mission of the high school can be embraced by the middle school, strategies will be developed to identify, support, encourage, and prepare students to enroll, and succeed, in such classes.

The significance of administrators, counselors, grade level teams and individual teachers developing individual and departmental missions, which are aligned with the overall mission of the school, and their impact on overall student achievement is clearly outlined in the *Texas Successful School-wide Research Study* (University of Texas at Austin):

A focus on the academic success of every student was articulated through a fundamental belief that they (teachers) could succeed with every child. 'These schools did not simply have mission statements, their sense of mission was articulated in every aspect of their planning, organization, and use of resources.'

Heightened levels of student achievement and the narrowing of the various achievement gaps occurs within those schools that are guided by a clear mission that cultivates a school-wide focus on student achievement. The school's mission provides the impetus for the vision and operational strategies that follow.

In the book, *The Strategy-Focused Organization*, the authors note:

The mission and the core values that accompany it [the vision] remain fairly stable over time. The organization's vision paints a picture of the future that clarifies the direction of the organization and helps individuals to understand why and how they should support the organization. In addition, it launches the movement from the stability of the mission and core values to the dynamism of strategy, the next step in the continuum. Strategy is developed and evolves over time to meet the changing conditions posed by the real world.

The Mission of the School District

Each school district in America has formulated some type of Mission Statement as it relates to the education of its students. They embody such terminology as, "creating productive citizens, lifelong learners, implementing quality practices, creating safe schools, creating leaders, and preparing students to participate in a global economy."

Following are examples of the Mission Statements from school districts from three different states.

The Memphis City Schools (TN)

The mission of the Memphis City Schools is to prepare all children to be successful citizens and workers in the Twenty-first Century. This will include educating them to read with comprehension, write clearly, compute accurately, think, reason, and use information to solve problems.

The Greenville County Schools (SC)

The mission of the Greenville County Schools is to provide educational experiences, in cooperation with the home and community, that prepare students for lifelong learning and for ethical, productive participation in a democratic society and global community.

The Pinellas County Schools (FL)

The mission of the Pinellas County Schools is to create systems that align all resources to assure that each student achieves at his or her highest level.

Such statements are representative of the mission statements of school districts throughout the country. Despite such lofty statements, each of these school districts continue to experience huge achievement gaps between their highest performing and lowest performing schools. They aren't *preparing all children to be successful.* They aren't *preparing all students for productive participation in a democratic society and global community.* And, they aren't *aligning resources to ensure that each student achieves at his or her highest potential.*

Remember the four levels of mission. If individual schools don't align their mission and subsequent practices with the mission of the school district; if each grade level, subject area, and school-based program doesn't align their missions with the mission of the school; and, if the administrators, teachers, and support staff don't internalize a clear personal mission that will help the school to fulfill its mission, the school district's mission will represent little more than lofty words that hang in the central office.

When my oldest son was in the fifth grade at Perkins Elementary School of the Visual and Performing Arts (Pinellas County Schools, FL), I raised the question at a district-wide meeting of administrators, "Despite a 33% school-wide population of African-American students, my son is the only African-American child in the fifth grade Talented and Gifted program while his counterparts are overrepresented in special education classes. Is he the only African-American child who is Talented and Gifted or are we not inspiring or identifying other children who are intellectually capable?"

Nearly four years have passed since I made that statement, and despite a mission statement that says, *The Pinellas County Schools will create systems that align all resources to assure that each student achieves at his or her highest level* no systems have been created or resources aligned to change this dynamic and the district continues to experience a huge achievement gap between African-American and white students, and disproportionately high special education placements, office referrals, and suspensions of African-American children.

The Memphis City School District recently received national headlines as having deplorable student achievement and was identified among the lowest achieving districts within the state of Tennessee. Clearly, the district's mission has not led to systemic operational strategies within their schools. Therefore, their mission remains unfulfilled. Large numbers of their students are not "being prepared to become successful citizens, productive participants in a democratic society, or achieving at their highest level." The rhetoric of the school district's mission has not translated into a clear mission and effective operational strategies within their schools.

To ensure that the district's mission is achieved at the school level each school must develop a clear mission that will guide its programs, people, and instructional efforts:

Notes:

1. *What programs, processes, partnerships, curricular, and co-curricular activities must we put into place to ensure that our students are reading with comprehension, writing clearly, computing accurately, thinking, reasoning, and using information to solve problems?*

2. *How must we communicate our mission to our students and their families so that they understand what it means to read with comprehension, write clearly, compute accurately, think, reason, and use information to solve problems?*

3. *What must we tell our students and their families that we need for them to do to help us fulfill our mission?*

4. *What assessment methods must we utilize and how frequently and accurately must we assess student learning?*

5. *What methods must we use to review our instructional practices, curriculum, supplemental materials, and home/school communication to ensure that they are aligned with our mission?*

6. *What discipline policies, intervention programs, extended learning opportunities, and partnerships are needed to fulfill our mission?*

7. *What professional and staff development, consultants, stakeholder committees, and resources are needed to fulfill our mission?*

These are only some of the questions that must be answered if the individual schools within the district are to turn the rhetoric of the school district's mission into the operational strategies required to fulfill the mission within the schools themselves. However, whether or not such questions are even raised depends in large part on whether the district's mission can evolve into a clearly-defined mission/vision that is embodied by the school's stakeholders.

The realization of each school district's mission can only occur at the school site. The school board doesn't run the day-to-day operations within the school and the superintendent doesn't teach the classes.

The Mission of the School

As previously stated, the Mission Statement of each school district must be used as a framework for establishing the mission of each school within the district. For a mission statement to be meaningfully relevant to the education of students and to move plans into practice, it must be relied upon as the foundation from which operational strategies evolve. In essence, those who create the mission to begin with must be held accountable to make decisions and utilize resources in ways that are consistent with fulfilling the very mission which they have articulated.

The mission of a school is unlikely to be as simple as photocopying the school district's mission. The school district's mission represents the end result of an effective pre-K through 12 educational system. The following questions should guide the development of the school's mission:

Notes:

1. What is the national mission of public education?

2. What is our state's mission?

3. What is our local school district's mission?

4. What part of the pre-K-12 system does our school represent, i.e., pre-K, elementary, middle school, or high school?

The fulfillment of the pre-K mission provides a building block upon which the elementary school can fulfill its mission. The fulfillment of the elementary school's mission provides a building block upon which the middle school can fulfill its mission. The fulfillment of the middle school's mission provides a building block upon which the high school can fulfill its mission. The successful fulfillment of the high school's mission should result in the fulfillment of the pre-K through 12 mission of the school district.

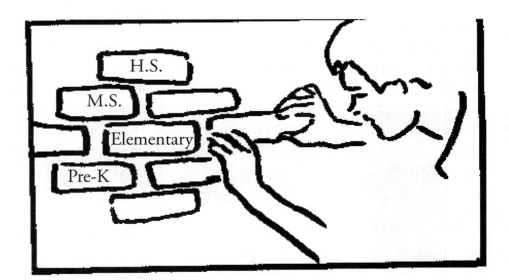

The mission of each school must be aligned to ensure that students achieve the overall mission of the school district.

Notes:

Lorraine Monroe, in her book, *Nothing's Impossible*, articulates her mission at the high school level:

Our goal [mission] at the Frederick Douglass Academy was to create a school concerned with excellence, quality, and equity, one that would train kids to be competitors at the highest level. I knew that the quality we sought would be based not on our location or on the ethnic and social makeup of the neighborhood, but on the high level of expectations and beliefs of the person in the front of each classroom, and on the vision, acts, energy, and courage of the person in the principal's chair...

I wanted to offer our students an academically rigorous college-preparation program to train them for competition beyond what they'd find in the local high schools. At the same time, I wanted to balance the academic rigor with lots of extracurricular club and team activities. When I interviewed potential staff members, I asked, 'What two other things can you offer kids other than your subject?'

Dr. Patricia Charthern, principal of the Harry Daniels Primary Center (Roosevelt, NY), has a student population of 300 students (90% African-American and 10% Latino) in Kindergarten through Third Grade. She and her staff have cultivated a school community that is driven by their clearly-stated primary school mission:

Harry Daniels Primary Center

The Mission of the Harry Daniels Primary Center is to provide children with a standards driven curriculum and literate environment that will foster mastery of academic skills, an appreciation of cultural heritage and mutual cooperation between school, home and community.

Notes:

Evolving from that mission is a vision and school philosophy that has shaped staff development efforts, curricular and co-curricular activities, and other school-wide program initiatives that have led to a 93% attendance rate. She and her staff have led 93% of their third grade students to minimum state levels in reading and 99% to minimum state levels in math proficiency.

Vision

The Vision of the Harry Daniels Primary Center is stated through our School Wide Goals:

- **To provide a literate learning environment which will be a cooperative effort among school, students, parents and community.**

- **To provide opportunities for students to develop skills necessary for Oral and Written communication; and to increase achievement in Math Problem Solving and Concepts.**

- **To provide a curriculum strong in Cultural Arts in order to maximize the multiple talents of each student.**

- **To provide opportunities for students to display their talents and be recognized for their academic, artistic, athletic, and personal achievements to the school and community.**

- **To provide activities for students to develop a positive self-concept and positive attitude toward learning and school.**

The Harry Daniels Primary Center has chosen for their Mascot the 'Eagle' because they are among the most majestic and powerful of all birds. The Eagle is an intelligent bird and they soar gracefully high in the sky. The students and staff at the Harry Daniels Center model after the characteristics of the Eagle. We are majestic, powerful and intelligent. We all strive to soar towards high standards.

The Daniels Primary Center, "Home of the Eagles" is a wonderful place where children learn with care, concern, competence and consciousness.

School Philosophy

We believe that all children can learn and are able to reach set academic standards. We believe that children achieve higher levels of academic success when expectations are high.

We believe that all children can develop positive cultural, social and emotional behaviors and attitudes.

The staff realizes that educating children is a moral obligation. Therefore, the staff accepts the responsibility of nurturing and motivating children thus creating a meaningful learning atmosphere to promote successful achievement.

Mrs. Lessie Hamilton-Rose, principal of Flower City School, #54 (Rochester, NY), has a student population that is over 90% African-American and Hispanic in grades 3 through 5. She and her staff also have a clear sense of their elementary school mission that has led to a clearly-defined vision and statement of beliefs:

This clear sense of mission has led Flower City School in developing the strategies that produced one of the largest gains in reading within the Rochester Public Schools, a 26% increase during the 1999/2000 school year. Evolving from that guiding school-wide mission, teachers developed personal missions of becoming recognized as "Best Practices" instructors within the various curriculum and instructional areas (i.e., Math, Social Studies, Standard English, Classroom Management, and Multiple Intelligences). Their school-wide mission was the driving force behind such initiatives as the vertical teaming of teachers, establishing learning communities, establishing a "Back Pack Book Club"

Notes:

to improve literacy, and establishing a 3rd through 5th grade college tour (and the establishment of a college scholarship fund for alumni who attend college). Local business and mentoring partnerships have also evolved from their mission.

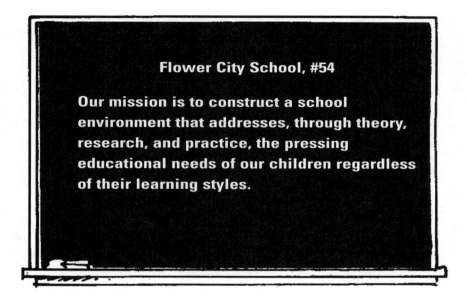

Barbara Hires, principal of Maximo Elementary Microsociety Center for Economic and Visual Arts (St. Petersburg, FL), and her teachers aligned their elementary school mission with their school district's mission:

> **The mission of Pinellas County Schools is to create systems that align all resources to assure that each student achieves at his or her highest level.**
>
> **The Pinellas County Schools' (Area III) mission is to provide leadership through integrated management systems that will create and support exemplary teaching and learning to ensure highest achievement for all students within our schools.**
>
> **The mission of Maximo Elementary School, in partnership with our families and our community, is to develop high achieving and responsible students by working cooperatively a safe, nurturing environment and applying continuous quality improvement processes.**

The Maximo Elementary School Principal's mission is to create a safe and supportive environment where children can learn and teachers can teach in order that all stakeholders will achieve at their highest level. I will accomplish this mission by modeling and implementing quality processes, and providing necessary training and resources.

Maximo Elementary School, despite having 55% of its student population on free and reduced lunch (the barometer most often used to "explain" underachievement) has been recognized as an "A" rated school within the state of Florida and is one of the highest achieving elementary schools in the Pinellas County Schools.

The parents, teachers, and administrators at the 1100-student Mt. Bethel Elementary School (Marietta, GA), revisit their mission and vision annually. Despite being ranked in the top five public elementary schools within the state of Georgia, Mt. Bethel Elementary applied for and was granted Charter School status. The parents, teachers, and administrators felt that while the student population clearly exceeded the state standards, they were not being challenged to stretch toward their potential.

Mt. Bethel Elementary School

We, the Mt. Bethel community of learners, will meet the needs of our unique population through the modification of content, process, and product expectations.

The vision of the Mt. Bethel staff, parents, and students is to create a strong foundation which will challenge our community to produce leaders and responsible decision-makers.

The Mt. Bethel Elementary School's mission and vision guides the school community through establishing stakeholder committees, expanding the curriculum, and exposing students to a wide range of opportunities beyond those available to students in other public schools within the county.

At the 1500-student John Hopkins Middle School (St. Petersburg, FL) the mission was succinctly stated as:

John Hopkins Middle School

The mission of John Hopkins Middle School is to create a supportive educational environment that develops school pride in highest student achievement.

Guided by that mission, I worked with a group of parents, teachers, central office representatives, business partners, and the administrative staff to develop a school-wide Vision, Statement of Beliefs, and Core Values. These guiding documents provided the impetus for operational strategies and a number of school-wide initiatives. The school, which had the dubious distinction of being recognized at one time among the lowest achieving middle schools within the state of Florida, became the most successful middle school within the county. John Hopkins was the only middle school in the Pinellas County Schools accredited by the Southern Association of Colleges and Schools and had the highest increase in Florida's FCAT scores of any middle school in the county during the 1999/2000 school year. The school received a $152,000 award from the State of Florida for recognition in increasing its state grade.

Each of these schools provide examples of how a school's mission provides the guiding force behind the instructional and operational strategies needed to ensure high student achievement levels and cultivate a nurturing school community. However, we can only ensure systemic and sustainable increases in student achievement when each pre-K program, elementary school, middle school, and high school develops missions that are aligned with the mission of the school district and are interconnected with each other.

Your Personal Mission

Schools and school districts are institutions and as such, their missions represent an institutional focus. Whether or not those missions are fulfilled occurs from the work within the trenches, the day-to-day leadership, classroom instruction, coaching, feeding, nurturing, and guidance of the children and families within our schools. Neither the Daniels Primary Center, Flower City School, Maximo Elementary School, or John Hopkins Middle School taught, nurtured or guided students. Schools don't develop strategies, implement action plans or cultivate student achievement, people do. It is the people within school communities who create the customs, rituals, and traditions that fulfill the school's mission. Dr. Patricia Charthern, Mrs. Lessie Hamilton-Rose, Mrs. Barbara Hires, and their teachers and support staff were guided by their own personal missions to teach, nurture, enable, and empower children. It was their personal missions that ultimately led to the levels of student achievement that allowed their respective schools to fulfill their missions.

Barbara Hires, principal of Maximo Elementary School, stated her personal mission as the principal:

The Maximo Elementary School Principal's mission is to create a safe and supportive environment where children can learn and teachers can teach in order that all stakeholders will achieve at their highest level. I will accomplish this mission by modeling and implementing quality processes, and providing necessary training and resources.

Her mission is used to frame discussions between parents, teachers, and students. Her personal day-to-day planning and school-wide operational strategies are guided by her mission as the school's principal. Her teachers have developed personal and grade-level mission statements that guide their planning efforts, intervention strategies, parent conferences, and instructional strategies. Subsequently, the school's "A" grade was not achieved by accident, but is the result of the clarity and focus of the principal, teachers, and support staff, which all began with their individual missions.

In staff training that I conduct, the question is often raised, "If we have a school mission, why must I develop a personal mission?" The answer is simply:

The school's mission provides focus while the personal mission of each individual within the school community directs their actions.

The personal mission of each parent, teacher, administrator, and support staff within a school community provides the keys to developing and carrying out the needed operational strategies to fulfill the school's mission. Remember: "Lead, follow, or get out of the way." What you decide will, in essence, become your personal mission. It will provide focus and clarity about what you, personally, are attempting to accomplish. You will likely revisit your personal mission many times over. As you gain experiences and expand your beliefs you should continually re-evaluate your mission relative to your school's needs and your abilities.

In the book, *The Path: Creating Your Mission Statement for Work and for Life,* Laurie Beth Jones states:

A mission statement is, in essence, a written-down reason for being—whether for a person, or for a company. It is the key to finding your path in life and identifying the mission you choose to follow. Having a clearly articulated mission statement gives one a template of purpose that can be used to initiate, evaluate, and refine all of one's activities.

She goes on to outline three simple elements to a good Mission Statement:

1. *A Mission Statement should be no more than a single sentence long.*

2. *It should be easily understood by a twelve-year-old.*

3. *It should be able to be recited by memory at gunpoint.*

Too often the busyness of life keeps us distracted from the business of life. We rush to work, rush to open the school year, rush to teach the curriculum, and rush to assess what we've done. Perhaps a moment to reflect on our professional and personal missions is in order.

What is my professional mission?

What is my personal mission?

Taking a break from the busyness of life to reflect on my personal and professional missions (i.e., husband, father, author, and consultant) has guided my way, focused my efforts, and brought about a spiritual calmness that has steadied my course through life's uncertain and often turbulent storms. Because of my missions to develop a successful marriage, be an effective parent, remain healthy enough to enjoy the fruits of my labor, and help schools to become places of passion and purpose, I have consciously sought the knowledge and applied my efforts in ways consistent with fulfilling each respective mission. This has translated into an eagerness to learn and a willingness to acknowledge what I do not know. Little of my formal schooling prepared me to develop a successful marriage, be an effective parent, live a healthy lifestyle or understand how to transform a school into a place of passion and purpose. However, my personal mission gave birth to a guiding vision of what a successful marriage, successful children, healthy life, and a successful school would look like.

My mission relative to my marriage:

To live my life in accordance with the vows that I made before God on our wedding day.

My mission relative to my role as a parent:

To nurture my children through developing the spiritual, moral, and intellectual foundation from which they may engage in the passionate pursuit of their dreams and aspirations.

My mission relative to my health:

To consciously nurture my spiritual, emotional, and physical health.

My mission relative to my children's schools:

To help my children's schools become the most academ-ically and socially nurturing school communities possible.

My mission relative to the process of school transformation, as outlined in my published works and public speaking engagements:

To guide parents and educators through the process of transforming schools into places of passion and purpose leading to the highest levels of student achievement.

Undoubtedly, you may experience turbulent times in the pursuit of your professional, or any of your personal missions. Due to circumstances beyond your control or as a result of poor decisions, you may struggle with fulfilling one or more of your missions. Nevertheless, a clearly-defined sense of mission provides an anchor to steady ourselves during the inevitable storms of life.

The Mission of the Principal

If there is one person within a school community who has the greatest level of responsibility for ensuring the best possible education for its students, it is the principal. While it is the classroom teacher who actually delivers instruction, it is the principal who has the overriding responsibility to ensure that:

- *the school has a clear Mission, Vision, and Statement of Beliefs.*

- *the school is engaged in an effective, ongoing analysis of its data to ensure that children are learning.*

- *the school community is safe.*

- *teachers adhere to professional standards and deliver effective instruction.*

Notes:

- *gender, ethnic or socioeconomic disparities in achievement, special ed. placement, or discipline enforcement is identified and that action plans are developed to ensure equity.*

- *students understand the school's fundamental values and principles.*

- *the best possible match exist between students and teachers.*

- *parents are invited to become partners in their child's learning.*

- *there is an active and effective outreach to cultivate business and community partnerships.*

- *there are effective teacher teams.*

- *the school's primary focus is on teaching and learning.*

- *resource allocation, program evaluations, and decisions made throughout the school community are in the best interest of children.*

While most school children have never met the members of their local school boards or the superintendent of schools, they must know who the principal is and what the principal believes about their school community. The principal is the person responsible for setting the tone for what happens each day within the school. As such, the principal must lead the school through

the transformation process so that teachers are effective within their classrooms and children are learning.

This can only occur when the principal has a clear sense of his or her personal mission. The principal should be able to answer the question, "What significant thing will occur within the lives of these children who have been entrusted into my care at this school?"

The Tennessee Value Added Assessment System (TVAAS) was a three-year, longitudinal study of third-, fourth-, and fifth-grade students in 54 Tennessee school districts. The TVAAS outlined the importance of the role of the principal within a school community:

- *Administrators must believe that each child will learn if given the appropriate instruction.*

- *Every effort must be made to secure qualified teachers who also believe that their students can learn.*

- *Given the national shortage of teachers and the large number of new teachers, each building administrator, as well as master teachers, must go beyond mentoring and actively coach novices to help them succeed and to retain them in the profession.*

- *Professional development must correlate with the building plan and the district goals; academic growth must be a part of every school improvement plan.*

- *Assessment data and information gleaned from teacher observations must be considered when student assignments are made. Perhaps because many administrators have been reluctant to assign or accept responsibility for poor student performance, some tend to abdicate their responsibility in the critical duty of assigning students to teachers and classes.*

Notes:

The role of the principal is so vitally important that sustained and systemic high student achievement levels are improbable unless the principal has a clear sense of mission and a commitment to implementing the needed processes and operational strategies.

The principal's mission might be articulated as:

To cultivate the most academically rigorous, socially, and emotionally nurturing environment possible for the highest levels of teaching and learning to take place.

The Mission of the Classroom Teacher

Classroom teachers may be certified to teach math, science, social studies, art, language arts, music, physical education, special education, etc., however, if the mission of the school is to educate its students, boundaries cannot be drawn that define science, social studies, language arts, math, or reading as representing the totality of a child's education. To do so suggests that character values, life skills, morality, compassion, citizenship, and community service are not worthy of teaching. In fact, character values and life skills are inescapable building blocks of a positive school climate and culture.

The African proverb, "It takes a village to raise a child," has been widely quoted. Yet, teachers who don't recognize their roles as members of a larger community may refer to the children within their classroom as "my children" while referring to other children within the school community as the "bus children" or the "special ed. children" or the "minority children" or "the trailer park children" or "the project children" or "the free lunch children" or "the neighborhood children."

I was working with children at an elementary school in Annapolis, Maryland, when one of the teachers approached me and asked if I would speak to Brittany. 'Mr. Wynn, will you talk to Brittany? Brittany is an evil child! She always talks about people and is always fighting and getting into trouble.'

I invited Brittany to join me for lunch. Brittany came into the cafeteria with five other little girls. Brittany and her little friends strutted into the cafeteria as though they were in charge and they were not to be messed with!

As the little girls approached me, Brittany said, 'Are you that man that we are supposed to talk to?' 'What man is that?', I said. Brittany placed her hand on her hip and snapped, 'You know that you are that man. They told you that we were bad, didn't they?' I smiled at this delightful child and said, 'Honey, my name is Mr. Wynn and I was so tired when I arrived at your school this morning. Last night I flew into Baltimore from Atlanta. That's where I live with my wife and children. I have been traveling so much this month that when I got to your school I just asked if they could send the six prettiest little girls to have lunch with me.'

Brittany, batted her eyes and said, 'For real?' To which I responded, 'Brittany you have the prettiest eye lashes.' Brittany, flashed her big beautiful smile and turned to her little friends and said, 'Come on y'all, we have to get our lunches so that we can have lunch with Mr. Wynn.'

As Brittany and the other little girls sat down at the table, I began talking about my family. I shared with them what our dreams were. I told them about my wife and my children. I went on to ask each of the girls what their dreams were. Without hesitation Brittany said, 'Mr. Wynn, I want to be a doctor.' I asked, 'What type of doctor would you like to become, Brittany?' Again, without hesitation, Brittany said, 'A pediatrician.' One of the other little girls at the table said, 'What type of doctor is that?' Brittany responded, 'A baby doctor, fool!'

This was my opportunity to 'connect' Brittany's long-term dreams with her current behavior. 'Brittany, is that the way you would speak to one of your patients if they had a question regarding your diagnosis?' Brittany thought for a moment and looked at the little girl, 'That's a baby doctor. Okay?'

After discussing the dreams and aspirations of each of the young girls I asked, 'How do you like your school?' As if on cue, in unison all of the little girls responded, 'We hate this school!' I then asked, 'What don't you like about the school?' Brittany responded, 'They call us the Bus Children. The children are always calling us names and the teachers don't like us.'

I went on to learn that Brittany and her little friends, who live in the public housing projects, ride the bus to the school. The school is located in an upscale community near the waterfront and the neighborhood children are predominately white and middle to upper class. Brittany, and all of the 'Bus Children' are black and poor.

After our delightful lunch, each of the little girls left affirming their dreams and aspirations. Brittany got up from the table, threw her trash away, waved good-bye, and walked away with her head held high. She walked away with the confidence that she could, in fact, become a doctor.

I went on to share my delightful lunch experience with the teacher who had asked that I speak to Brittany. 'Did you know that Brittany wants to become a doctor?' The teacher immediately responded, 'Well, Brittany is retarded, Mr. Wynn!'

Unless teachers internalize a personal mission to encourage, inspire, and teach *all* children within their school community it is impossible for the school to fulfill its mission. While Brittany may have been labeled mentally handicap, she and her friends were smart enough to know when they were unwelcome and when some of the teachers didn't have a personal mission to teach them.

For a school community to embody the proverb, "It takes a village to raise a child," teachers must accept as their mission to nurture, inspire, motivate, and encourage students. These must all be done within the context of a emphatic and uncompromising mission to teach.

The Tennessee Value Added Assessment System study determined that the effects of teachers on children are cumulative, *"race, socioeconomic level, class size, and classroom heterogeneity are poor predictors of academic growth. Rather, the effectiveness of the teacher is a major determinant of student academic progress."*

- *For grades three through eight, the cumulative gains for schools across an entire state have been found to be unrelated to racial composition of schools, the number of students on free and reduced lunch or the mean achievement level of the school.*

- *Students from the highest achievement groups show somewhat less academic growth unless they are assigned to teachers in the top twenty percent of effectiveness. It cannot be assumed that these students can make it on their own.*

- *The highest gains occurred in the lowest achieving groups of students.*

- *Ineffective teachers were ineffective with all groups of students regardless of the students' prior achievement level.*

Notes:

- *There are residual effects of poor teachers on students.*

- *Although African-American students and white students with the same level of prior achievement made the same progress when assigned to comparable teachers; the study found that more African-American students than expected are assigned to the least effective teachers.*

- *Three consecutive years of effective teachers in grades three through eight can virtually close the gap between African-American and white students.*

- *Students in high poverty schools are less likely to be taught by a teacher who majored in the subject he or she is teaching.*

The researchers concluded:

The most important factor affecting student learning is the teacher. In addition, the results show wide variation in effectiveness among teachers. The immediate and clear implication of this finding is that seemingly more can be done to improve education by improving the effectiveness of teachers than by any other single factor.

A school of excellence cannot occur without excellence within the classroom. Excellence within the classroom cannot occur without the classroom teacher understanding the tremendous power that he or she has to shape the lives of the children who pass through his or her doors.

The mission of the classroom teacher might be articulated as:

To provide the most academically rigorous, and socially and emotionally nurturing environment possible that will lead students to their highest level of academic and social skill development.

Such a mission does not deny that children may enter into the school with little at-home support; they may be below grade level in any number of subject areas; they may have been the victims of abuse; they may have been exposed to violence and profanity either at home, within their communities or through film and videos; or they may simply be uninterested, apathetic, and turned off to school. The classroom teacher cannot control what goes on within the lives of children outside of the school. However, if the mission of the classroom teacher is clear, proper preparation will follow.

Marva Collins, in her book, *The Marva Collins' Way*, articulates a clear personal mission as it pertained to her students:

Throughout the year, as in every year of my teaching, my main goal [mission] was to motivate the students to make something worthwhile of their lives. Everything we said or did in class was directed toward that aim. More than anything I wanted to supplant apathy and defeatism with positive expectations. I didn't want my children to feel stigmatized by where they lived. I didn't want them to succumb to a ghetto mentality. If I had my way, they would dream and hope and strive and <u>obtain</u> success.

Notes:

I have come to a frightening conclusion: I am the decisive element in the classroom. It is my personal approach that creates the climate. It is my daily mood that makes the weather.

As a teacher I possess tremendous power to make a child's life miserable or joyous. I can be a tool of torture or an instrument of inspiration. I can humiliate or humor, hurt or heal. In all situations, it is my response that dictates whether a crisis will be escalated or de-escalated and a child humanized or de-humanized.

— Dr. Hiam Ginott

The Mission of Parents

As I outlined in my book, *Ten Steps to Helping Your Child Succeed in School: Volume I,* whatever else parents do to ensure that their children have every opportunity to become successful in school, parents must develop a personal mission to become partners with their children's school(s). Regardless of whether a home/school partnership is encouraged or discouraged by the administrators, their children's teachers, or by their children themselves the personal mission of parents must be to become partners with their children's schools and stakeholders in their children's learning. The dynamics of meaningful parental involvement and effective parent/school partnerships affect everything from what goes on in the classroom to what goes on in the restroom. As previously stated, the mission embodied by my wife and me reflects such a parent-school partnership.

Our mission is:

To help our children's schools become the most academically and socially nurturing schools possible.

Notes:

It is this sense of mission that guides our efforts each school year. We volunteer to work on school-based committees and we work with the school's principal to ensure clarity of the school's mission/vision. We share books and materials with our children's administrators and teachers. We send in a packet of information to each of our sons' classroom teachers outlining their personality types, learning styles, and best and worst learning situations. We talk to their teachers to develop the best at-home strategies to support the instruction within the classroom. I have spoken in school-wide assemblies, volunteered in classrooms, and met with children in small groups to help cultivate a positive social experience for my children. My wife volunteers in the classroom, meets with other parents, and attends school activities to develop personal relationships with parents, teachers, and other students. Because each school year brings with it different teachers, different teaching styles, different personalities, and our children are entering into different developmental levels, our strategies may change; however, our mission remains the same.

The Mission of Students

The passion, enthusiasm, and excitement of elementary school students is all but lost by the time the final bell has rung in our high schools. While principals and teachers have defined their missions we have forgotten about the children. The principal's lead, the teachers' teach, but what about the children? What is their mission? Where do they want to go in life and how will what we are teaching help them to get there? The earlier we can help children identify their unique gifts, talents, interests, and abilities the sooner we can lead them into the earnest pursuit of their dreams and aspirations. Each school year we can assist children in developing personal missions within the larger context of developing life plans.

- Be aware of what students are interested in learning.

- Help students to develop personal goals across an array of interest areas and intelligences.

- Help students to make the connection between what is being taught and their long-term aspirations.

- Help students to develop long-term plans specific to their interests and aspirations.

- Help students to understand who they are (i.e., personality types) how they learn (i.e., learning styles) and how they're smart (i.e., Multiple Intelligences).

Helping children to develop goals, identify long-term dreams and aspirations, and better understand their unique talents and abilities can all help to shape a child's mission. For many children it is essential that we convince them of the potential, possibilities, and opportunities that will result from an education, and that our mission to teach and their mission to learn can become instrumental in emancipating them from poverty and catapult them toward the promise of the American dream.

Mrs. Lessie Hamilton-Rose, principal of the Flower City School, #54 (Rochester, NY), gives her students a college-bound vision. Each year her fourth and fifth graders visit a local college for a "Live Your Dreams Day." While on campus, they create dream collages, visit classrooms, the gymnasium, auditorium, library, and research facilities. They talk to students and professors. Throughout the school year students are introduced to programs, activities, field trips, and guest speakers. Many low-achieving students are inspired to develop personal missions to excel academically and individual visions of attending college. To keep her students focused on their respective missions, Mrs. Rose created a

Notes:

scholarship fund that Flower City alumni can apply for when they graduate from high school and are accepted into a college, university, or junior college. She hosts a gala scholarship banquet each year to recognize the scholarship recipients. Due in large part to the ongoing encouragement of the principal, teachers, and support staff many of her students leave Flower City and  enter into middle school with a college-bound vision driven by a personal mission of academic excellence.

Achieving the school's mission cannot be done in isolation from helping students to develop their own personal sense of mission. Students have to be personally driven toward high academic achievement and high standardized test scores in the same way that they are toward developing a cross-over dribble or scoring the next touchdown. The intrinsic motivation to excel should be self-imposed, but it can also be externally stimulated. As the sense of mission and standard of behavior of the professional staff within a school is positively or negatively influenced by the climate and culture of the school, so too, is the sense of mission and standard of behavior of students influenced by the climate and culture of the school, particularly amongst peers. Being a Trojan, Panther, Tiger, or Buccaneer (i.e., school mascot) must be significant within the minds and spirits of students. Customs and traditions should instill a sense of pride and inspire students to develop a personal mission to achieve excellence.

My mission is:

To actively engage in learning and to apply myself in a way that will allow me to achieve my God-given personal potential.

Without the guidance of parents and teachers, many children would be content to embody a sense of mission that minimizes the importance of academic achievement and maximizes the importance of socialization. While getting students to develop and internalize a mission that embraces academic achievement can be an arduous task, avoiding the effort is likely to result in students developing a sense of mission more akin to:

My mission is:

To disrupt my classes, annoy my teachers, and focus all of my energy on socializing.

The latter is more common within low-performing schools.

Notes:

The Mission of Everyone Else

If the principal and classroom teachers have a clear mission to lead and teach, respectively; if parents have a mission to support their efforts; if students have a mission to apply themselves academically, then each of us who affirms U.S. citizenship must accept some personal sense of mission as it pertains to American public education. Whether that sense of mission is to directly participate in the decision-making process at the federal, state or local level; contribute tax dollars to ensure that every American child has access to a quality education; volunteer to ensure that every school has community support and involvement; or to serve as a mentor to ensure that every child has a relationship with a caring adult to inspire and encourage them, we all must have a personal sense of mission as it relates to our public schools.

I frequently speak with politicians and business leaders who have strong opinions regarding what is wrong with our schools, however, by and large, they don't enroll their children in public schools. They don't work in public schools. They don't mentor children who attend public schools. And, it has been years since they have walked into a public school.

The future of American Public Education requires each of us to become a catalyst for the changes needed within our schools to ensure the highest level of education possible for America's children who cannot afford to attend private schools, cannot be home schooled, and will never be served by parochial or charter schools. Your personal mission must be to do more than condemn the schools or teachers. To become a catalyst for change, you might embrace the following mission:

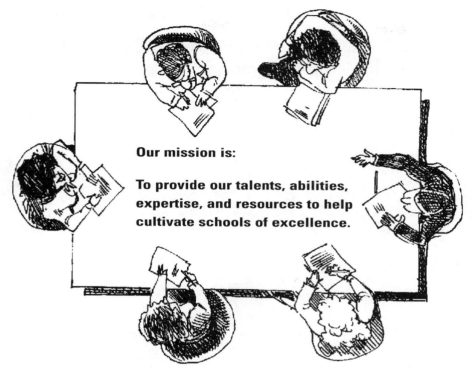

Each of us has the power to influence change within our schools. However, whether our influence and the subsequent changes are to the benefit or detriment of children will be guided by our personal mission.

Notes:

Your Mission Should Reflect Student Needs

Maslow's Hierarchy of Needs should be used to guide your efforts in establishing your mission:

There is little dispute that we must satisfy the physiological, esteem, social, and safety needs of children to cultivate the environment for teaching and learning to occur. Without ever stating it as our mission, we feed, clothe, bathe, medicate, and inoculate children in our schools. So, why stop there? Why not accept as our mission to satisfy whatever needs we are capable of satisfying, including "Self-actualization?" Satisfying a child's physiological, esteem, social, and safety needs without inspiring hope and providing frequent opportunities for them to apply what they know will fail them and will ultimately fail us as a society.

We must overcome our maternal instinct to feel sorry for poor children and teach them. Not only so that they might know, but so that they might do. So that they might become. Our mission must be to provide students with self-actualizing experiences where they actualize interests, abilities, and learning outcomes. Once we have fed, bathed, clothed, medicated, and inoculated them our school community should be filled with such actualizing experiences as entrepreneurship, banking, writing and delivering mail, creating audio/video recordings, delivering motivational/informational speeches, cooking/baking, discovering/experimenting, creating published works/musical compositions, choreography/performing, carpentry, running for/serving in political office, building/repairing computers, teaching, creating/selling products, creating/reciting poetry/stories, creating/showing/packaging and producing works of art, photography, graphic designs, library management, radio/television hosting, managing stock portfolios, veterinary medicine, accounting, computer programming, personal training, creating nutritional menus, landscaping, automotive repair/restoration, and brick masonry.

Our mission would embody the belief to "teach so that they might do." Rather than *receivers*, students would become *seekers* of knowledge—intrinsically desiring to learn so that they might do. My thirteen-year-old son has been pursuing his dreams of becoming an artist since his first grade stick people inspired within him a passion for illustration. Now, an eighth grader, he has published a line of note cards that carry his illustrations dating back to his second grade art projects. His series of note cards have inspired him to pursue other publishing projects such as illustrating a coloring book and other note cards. As he stood in the printing plant watching his original artwork being turned into film for a four-color printing press, the entire curriculum came to life: science, art, grammar, word processing, and graphic design. As he discussed and debated pricing and packaging, he was able to apply mathematics and critical thinking to solving real-world problems. He was catapulted from the ranks of receiver to seeker of knowledge, from abstract to real-world application.

Notes:

Levels of learning are deepened whenever students have the opportunity of applying what they've learned within a meaningfully relevant context.

More than any federal, state, or local mandate, it is our mission that has the power to guide us toward consciously cultivating a school community that inspires within its students and teachers a personal quest to achieve the level of self-actualization where the highest levels of learning and application of knowledge take place. Children discover how the curriculum is meaningful and relevant to their lives through self-actualizing events. Abraham Maslow, in the book, *Maslow on Management,* comments:

> *A musician must make music, an artist must paint, a poet must write, if he is to be ultimately at peace with himself. What a man can be, he must be. This need we may call self-actualization... It refers to man's desire for self-fulfillment, namely to the tendency for him to become actually engaged in what he is potentially to become everything that one is capable of becoming.*

Carter G. Woodson, in his 1933 book, *The Miseducation of the Negro,* comments:

> *Unless [African-Americans] receive an education befitting to their peculiar situation, they would never enter fully into the economic, political and social institutions in the United States of America. The mere imparting of information is not education, above all, the effort must make a man think and do for himself. The program for the uplift of the [African-American] in this country must be based upon a scientific study of the [African-American] from within to develop in him the power to do for himself. To educate the [African-American] we must find out exactly what his background is, how to begin with him as he is and make him a better individual of the kind that he is.*

Nearly seventy years ago, Dr. Carter G. Woodson was an advocate for teaching so that we might do, identifying what children and whole communities needed, so that they might become.

Notes:

When children enter into our schools with a passion for sports we must engage them in the totality of learning through the very window of opportunity which they have eagerly opened for us. Instruction in nutrition; physical fitness and muscular development; bone structure and density; joints, cartilage, and flexibility; how the organs work and how diet, nutrition, cardiovascular activity, and age impacts upon their development; mathematical calculations in terms of weights and measures; how the heart functions and the impact of anaerobic versus aerobic activity on heart rate and size; how muscles stretch and tear; and how bones dislocate and break. Not only would many of our now, professional athletes, better understand the wear, tear, and pain to be anticipated on the human physiology from their sport of choice, but having been engaged in discussions and hands-on application in such areas as entrepreneurship, investing, negotiating, rates of return, and financial management when they first began shouting from the rooftops, "I want to play ball!" they would have more highly-developed critical-thinking skills in regards to investing their money and managing their lives.

Instead of questioning, "How do we convince our children that their aspirations of becoming a professional athlete are unrealistic?" our focus should be to teach so that they might do. Deepening a child's depths of learning in their interests and aspirations will heighten their critical-thinking skills thereby allowing them to make more informed choices and decisions. Their expanded knowledge will broaden their understanding and often lead them into new directions and career aspirations, with their choice, rather than our lecture, becoming the motivating factor.

Students enter into our schools with a passion for developing their physique, wearing/designing clothes, and adorning the most fashionable hair styles. They are interested in learning about the chemical reactions of products which they put into their hair and ingest into their bodies. They want to know how their metabolic rates are influenced by diet and lifestyles and how to focus diet and exercise on reducing or enlarging certain body parts. Their interests can be woven through the curriculum, i.e., social studies, science, mathematics, history, language arts, physical education, character values and social skills.

Through their interests we can lead them into reading, writing, computing, and thinking, i.e., written and oral presentations, engaging in speech and debate, developing models and displays, dialoguing with guest speakers, producing documentaries and publishing books/articles.

Our schools are continually-evolving dynamic organisms whose teachers have the intellectual and creative capacities to shape our curriculum with meaningful, relevant lessons that captivate the interest and engage the intellectual capacities of children. Dittos, worksheets, and a rigid focus on drilling and testing students do little to tap the intellectual and creative capacities of educators let alone students. Thematic and interdisciplinary

Notes:

units that tap into the diverse interests, aspirations, learning styles, and cultures of students pave the way to more engaging classroom instruction, deepened learning, and in the final analysis, higher test scores.

For nearly twenty years, I have advocated that the dreams and aspirations of children become a part of the educational equation. Their passions and interests should be identified as a means of hooking them on learning and a conduit to lead them through the core and elective curricula. For twenty years I have met with resistance from educators who proclaim, "We don't talk about their dreams because many of these children have no dreams." What is being said, is that many of today's children *come* to school uninspired with a sense of hopelessness and we allow them to *leave* our schools uninspired with a sense of hopelessness. When children enter into our schools not reading, our mission is to teach reading. When children enter into our schools with poorly-developed mathematical abilities, our mission is to teach mathematics. However, children today can still enroll into our schools in kindergarten, and graduate 13 years later from our high schools without ever having been meaningfully engaged in the research, analysis, discussion, debate or pursuit of their dreams and aspirations. Quite simply, this has not become part of our mission.

The research is clear on why students' interests must become a part of our mission. Alfie Kohn, in his book, *Punished by Rewards,* writes:

> *...just as adults who love their work will invariably do a better job than those goaded with artificial incentives, so children are more likely to be optimal learners if they are <u>interested</u> in what they are learning. Several studies have found a positive correlation between intrinsic motivation and academic achievement for children of different ages. Most of this work has been correlational, which means that we can't necessarily assume the child's motivation causes achievement to go up or down; indeed, there is reason to think that achievement may*

affect motivation, too. Still, at least one researcher has concluded there is a causal relationship: 'reduced intrinsic motivation produces achievement deficits.'

William Glasser, in his book, *The Quality School Teacher*, notes:

If, in the frequent teacher-student discussions that are held in a quality school, the students express a desire to learn some particular information, teachers would do their best to teach it or to help students find where to look it up.

Eventually, as part of teaching students to speak competently, you would discuss with them what they want to read, but, in the beginning, you should provide them with useful material to read and, in the primary grades, teach them to read it. To get them interested in learning how and then continuing to read, research shows that there is no better way than reading to them. To emphasize the importance of books, teachers in a quality elementary school might, with the help of the students, build libraries in their classrooms.

Consider what our schools might become if children entered each day in the diligent exploration and pursuit of their dreams and aspirations led by teachers who inspired their dreams, encouraged their passions, helped them to hone their unique gifts and abilities, and convinced children of the power of education to overcome their circumstances. Rather than attempting to pre-determine a child's potential based on learning assessments and socioeconomic status, teachers would encourage children to spread their wings and soar. Through the ongoing discussions, debates, research, and analysis children would learn to use the skills and apply the knowledge acquired each school year to closely examine what they think their dreams are in the course of discovering what their dreams might become.

The kindergartner who dreams of becoming a pediatrician, after learning what a pediatrician does, might expand his dream to becoming a child advocate through

Notes:

articles and lectures. The fourth-grader who dreams of becoming a professional football player, after learning about the injuries and assorted surgeries that professional athletes undergo, might instead dream of a career where he can work with his hands, albeit an artist or a carpenter. The seventh-grader who develops a passion for learning a second and third language might dream of a career where she can utilize her linguistic abilities, albeit a teacher of foreign languages or an interpreter for migrant workers. Giving children a purpose for their education paves the way to cultivating passionate, inspiring learning environments, and creating

schools and classrooms that provide hope for families and communities. The relationships forged between children and their families would reduce teacher turnover, increase staff morale, and provide teachers with the opportunity to see the fruits of their labors as generations of dreamers pass through their classrooms and return to their schools with testimonials

of the power of education and the significance of their teachers. While a child's dreams might change many times over the course of their school-aged years, what motivation toward learning does the child have who has no dreams?

Whether you agree or disagree with my views on schooling and my philosophical position that "inspiring" learning is important to student achievement keep in mind that it is our beliefs and our experiences that frame what we do. As my beliefs (i.e., that children should be engaged in the early exploration of their dreams and aspirations) and experiences (i.e., that inspired children are more engaged learners) shape my mission, so, too, will your beliefs and experiences provide the framework for your personal mission.

Write Your Mission

As you write your personal mission, ask yourself the question, "What significant thing will happen within the life of a child as a result of their coming into contact with me?"

If you are a classroom teacher, principal, counselor, school bus driver, cafeteria worker, custodian, office staff, paraprofessional, superintendent, school board member, volunteer, media specialist, coach, mentor, business partner, pastor, central office staff, psychologist, reading specialist or any of the countless numbers of adults who have the awesome power to touch the life of a child, you have a duty to answer this question.

There, undeniably, will be a multitude of things outside of your direct control, e.g., class size, school supplies, class schedules, parental support, budgets, the district mandated curriculum, maintenance of the school buses, availability of coal for the furnace, etc. However, the moment that you find yourself within the presence of a child, despite all that you cannot control, you can decide what you will do.

- If you are a school bus driver, you decide how you greet children each day as they board your bus and what you say to children each day as they depart your bus.

Notes:

- If you are a classroom teacher, you decide how you greet children each morning as they enter into your classroom and how you send children out of your classroom at the end of the day.

- If you are a mentor, volunteer or business partner, you decide whether or not you will ask such questions as, "What are your dreams? What types of things would you like to achieve in life?", when you meet children within our schools.

- If you are the school's principal, you decide whether or not you will assign wall space within your school to themes that provide visual representations of children's dreams and aspirations.

- If you are the school's custodian, you decide whether to put forth the effort needed to create an aesthetic environment of excellence that communicates the highest regard toward the school's staff and students.

- If you are the school's counselor, you decide whether or not you will encourage children to pursue life's extraordinary possibilities or whether you will discourage their dreams and predict their futures based upon their socio-economic status, family background, or previous failures in school.

Like it or not, the actions and/or inactions of each adult within a school community impacts upon the attitudes, perceptions, consciousness, dreams, and aspirations of students. For better or worst, how we discipline, how we inspire, how we greet, how we teach, and how we guide children will impact their lives for years to come.

In my book, *Follow Your Dreams: Lessons That I Learned in School,* I recounted the impact that my high school guidance counselor had on my life long after I had graduated high school.

> *I approached Mr. Jones with my dreams of becoming a writer, 'Mr. Jones, I want to become a writer. What do I need to do to become a writer?' Mr. Jones' response to me after reviewing my school records was, 'Mychal, there ain't no jobs for no Negro writers. You have high scores in math and science you should become an engineer.' From that single conversation in Mr. Jones' office, my life was directed toward attending college to study engineering. I enrolled into the Northeastern University's College of Engineering and majored in electrical engineering. Prior to coming full circle to pursue my dreams, the next decade of my life was committed to a course in life as the result of that conversation with Mr. Jones. This is the power that teachers, counselors, principals, and others within our schools have over the lives of children.*

The mission of my high school guidance counselor was not to help students discover and pursue their respective dreams and aspirations. His mission was to direct students toward what he perceived to be good jobs. His personal mission may not have been posted on the door. It may not have been formally written as a mission statement. However, that unspoken, unpublished mission guided his efforts in reviewing academic, discipline, and student demographic data (i.e., socio, economic, ethnic, and gender) and the guidance that he subsequently provided students. So too, will your mission guide your efforts.

Answer the following questions and write your personal mission.

1. List three things that you believe are essential to a child's success within your school community for each of the categories indicated within "Maslow's Hierarchy of Needs."

Notes:

Following are examples of needs that might be perceived to be important to a child's success in school:

Physiological:

- *I believe that children must have the proper daily nutrition to optimize learning;*

- *I believe that the school must have an appropriate physical environment; and*

- *I believe that children, themselves, must have the appropriate personal hygiene.*

Safety:

- *I believe that the school community must be free from bullying and verbal put-downs;*

- *I believe that the school must take reasonable steps to limit access to school grounds by those who do not have business within the school; and*

- *I believe that the school must have appropriate logistics for ensuring the safe and orderly movement of students throughout the school.*

Social:

- *I believe that children must have positive and rewarding social experiences within the school community;*

- *I believe that children must develop the social skills to become successful in their future jobs and careers; and*

- *I believe that adults must model appropriate social behaviors.*

Esteem:

- *I believe that children must be encouraged and supported in taking risks within the classroom;*

- *I believe that each child must be consciously and publicly validated, encouraged, and uplifted; and*

- *I believe that if taught appropriate social behaviors that children will feel more comfortable in new and diverse social situations.*

Self-Actualization:

- *I believe that children must have frequent opportunities to apply what they learn in practical and real-world applications;*

- *I believe that children must learn how their talents, interests, and unique abilities can have value within the larger society; and*

- *I believe that children should learn "how" their education can help them to actualize their interests, dreams, and aspirations.*

2. Use the issues that you identified as essential to a child's success as the framework for developing your personal mission statement.

    For example,

    > *My mission as a Seventh Grade Science Teacher is to provide a safe, nurturing, and collaborative environment within which children can explore the many and diverse facets of science and scientific thinking.*

    > *My mission as a Fourth Grade Teacher is to provide a safe, nurturing, and collaborative environment within which children can develop the social and academic skills that will provide them with the*

foundation to discover and pursue their life's dreams and aspirations.

The general statement of your mission is an inextricable building block to developing a more comprehensive vision. The resulting vision will provide the framework for conceptualizing action plans, establishing goals, and implementing the operational strategies needed to fulfill your mission. For example, the phrase *"safe, nurturing, and collaborative environment,"* within your mission statement must result in a vision of what a "safe, nurturing, and collaborative environment," might look and feel like. Perhaps it's a classroom where students do not engage in verbal put-downs, bullying, or sarcasm. One in which students work in collaborative groups on projects that recognize and value a wide range of talents and abilities. One in which differing ideas and opinions are encouraged. Where ideas are rigorously debated without personal attacks on the individuals who argue them. Despite a mission that desires such a classroom environment, or a vision that creates a mental image of such a classroom, the challenge remains, "How do we develop the strategies and techniques that will, in fact, cultivate such a classroom?"

Dee Blassie, a former second grade teacher who co-authored the book, *Building Dreams: K-8 Teacher's Guide*, clearly articulated her personal mission:

Mrs. Blassie's mission is to help each student to become successful academically and socially as a stepping stone to their discovering and pursuing their dreams and aspirations.

From that personal mission, Dee developed a vision of what an academically and socially successful classroom that nurtured a child's dreams and aspirations would look and feel like. To achieve that vision she developed a classroom motto, "Welcome to Success," which she used to frame every question with students, "Honey, how can Mrs. Blassie help you to become more successful?"

Each year in her classroom she engaged students in such activities as:

- *A put-down-free classroom where students received a "Thumbs Up" for incorrect answers and applause for correct answers.*

- *A "Star of the Week" corner where every student was recognized and celebrated.*

- *Daily readings of inspirational poetry and quotations.*

- *A "Welcome to Success" pledge that students recited each morning.*

Notes:

- *A "Popsicle Sticks" activity where a popsicle stick, representing a student, was selected randomly at the beginning of each day. She observed the student, without the student's knowledge, throughout the day and sent a note or made a phone call to the student's parent to share some pleasant attributes about the student.*

- *A Multiple Intelligences bulletin board where the unique intelligences of each student were identified and celebrated.*

- *Encouraging students to set daily, weekly, yearly, and life goals.*

- *Filling shortened days with dream exploration activities such as creating collages, performing research, and playing games that related to student interests.*

- *Hosting an annual "Dream Day" where guest speakers, e.g., Fire Fighters, veterinarians, politicians, college professors, artists, insurance agents, psychologists, stock brokers, electricians, brick masons, airline pilots, professional athletes, pastors, entrepreneurs, and others who represented professions relating directly and indirectly to the dreams and aspirations of students talked about their jobs and provided "How To" guidance.*

- *Creating Dream Trees, Dream Portfolios, Guest Speaker Wall of Fame, and other visual imagery designed to encourage and inspire student aspirations.*

- *Creating classroom clubs such as "Models Alert," "Aspiring Artists," "Aspiring Writers," and "Future Teachers of America" to provide extended learning opportunities for students to explore and further develop their interests.*

- *Developing a yearlong series of study trips to expose students to a broad range of careers and future opportunities.*

Guided by a clear mission that gave birth to an all encompassing vision of how children should be nurtured and encouraged, Dee created a classroom environment and a yearlong schedule of planned experiences for her students that had parents lining up to have their children placed into her classroom. That guiding mission helped Dee to cultivate a fight-free, put-down-free, zero referrals classroom. In her classroom, students developed social skills and internalized character values as part of learning to become the persons of their dreams.

Once you have completed a preliminary draft of your mission, measure your first draft against the following:

1.   Has it been stated in one sentence?

2.   Can it be recited from memory?

3.   Does it provide a quest that is not likely to change?

Prominently display your mission in your office, classroom, school bus or in a visible location where you can see it each day.

Begin each day by questioning, "What must I do today to fulfill my mission?" Perform your job or volunteer your time in a manner in which your actions, attitudes, and behaviors are consistent with achieving your mission.

Stay focused on your mission, keeping in mind that it is not fixed and should be expanded or more narrowly defined as you expand your knowledge, beliefs, and experiences.

Notes:

What Will You Accept As Your Assignment?

Now that you have stated your personal mission, what is your assignment? What role will you accept to ensure that your school community achieves its mission and that you fulfill your personal mission? If you are employed within a school, your assignment will usually be much broader than the scope of your job description.

For example:

The job description of a math teacher outlines preparing lesson plans, developing assessment tools, and engaging in instructional delivery of the district's curriculum. However, a math teacher must recognize that his or her job description doesn't fully define his or her assignment. An undeniable part of any teacher's assignment is to cultivate a positive and nurturing atmosphere within the classroom that paves the way to effective instruction.

The math teacher who doesn't view *effective* instruction as part of his or her assignment will likely attribute student failure to the students themselves (e.g., "They are unmotivated. I told them to read the chapter. Their parents don't care. They should have been paying attention. They're so unorganized. They don't care about school.").

The math teacher who accepts effective instruction as part of his or her assignment has a more personal investment in student learning and in his or her role in cultivating it. This personal investment leads to a more proactive and creative approach leading to such initiatives and operational strategies as:

1.   Maintaining open communication with students and families to ensure that instructional methods and problem-solving methodology are understood.

2. Outlining strategies for parents and students to deepen learning through rituals, routines, extended learning opportunities, supplemental materials, or via step-by-step approaches to problem solving.

3. Talking with colleagues, reading professional literature, attending conferences, and participating in professional development to continually reassess and enhance instructional strategies.

4. Developing a rigorous and engaging classroom environment where students work effectively, are encouraged to ask questions, and are provided with clear and effective problem-solving strategies.

5. Compensating for student organizational weaknesses by visually sequencing and flow charting classroom and homework routines.

6. Developing an open classroom where administrators, parents, and other teachers are invited to observe instructional lessons.

7. Collaborating with colleagues to plan interdisciplinary, thematic, or expanded instructional units.

8. Developing support mechanisms (i.e., study groups, before/after school tutoring, student tutors, monthly calendar of tests, quizzes, and lectures, etc.) designed to inspire students, deepen learning, and enhance instruction.

9. Writing curriculum units that tap into students' preexisting knowledge, interests, and real-world application of classroom instruction.

Notes:

10.   Developing math decathlons, academic challenges, quiz bowls, inter/intra-school competitions, before/after school programs, mentors, study trips, and other extra- or co-curricular activities that provide competition and hands-on application of mathematical concepts.

The job description of the school bus driver may be to safely, and in a timely manner, transport children to and from school.

However, school bus drivers must recognize that their assignment extends to eliminating negative language, verbal abuse, physical altercations, and other inappropriate behaviors during the morning/afternoon bus rides. Student behaviors on the school bus have a direct impact upon school climate and culture after the children depart the school bus and, thusly, on the school's success in achieving its mission.

Identifying and accepting your assignment provides clarity of focus and establishes your role in helping the school to fulfill its mission:

• *What is my assignment and how will it allow me to carry out my mission?*

• *What role will I play within my school community (as parent or teacher) to ensure that children are being prepared to become successful?*

• *If I successfully fulfill my assignment who will be served?*

There was an engineer who inherited 3,000 acres of land. The land had been in his family for generations and was given to him upon the death of his grandfather. The engineer and his family lived in an urban area near his place of employment. The local schools were overcrowded and the city was experiencing a crime wave. He was largely dissatisfied with his job and was eager to retire and move his family to the country. The engineer didn't know a lot about farming but he was able to plant crops on a couple of acres of land and grow enough fruits and vegetables to feed his family. He used a few more acres of land for livestock. However, in the town, just a stone's throw away from the land that he had inherited, was a mill that had long since been abandoned. Many of the people had moved away and many of the small farmers who stayed lost their land. Only those people who were too poor, too old, lacked formal education or were simply unable to move remained in the town.

The engineer continued to farm his two acres of land, raise a few cows and chickens, and was able to feed his family. However, his children had no one to play with because the town's children eventually grew too sickly to play. The engineer's wife had no one to converse with because eventually the town's women grew bitter and resentful of the engineer and his family.

Eventually, the schools in the town became run down and were unable to effectively educate the town's children as the teachers moved away to other towns. Finally, after much contemplation, the engineer put a "For Sale" sign up on his land and moved his family back to the city where he began working as an engineer again.

The engineer had 3,000 acres of land, but he didn't have the knowledge or ability to farm all of it. The town had many people who needed food and some of the town's people were farmers, but the engineer never recognized that he and his family were part of a community. He only thought in terms of taking care of those within his household. The engineer had the resources, but lacked the vision to utilize them. His mission was too narrowly defined, "I need to grow enough to feed my family."

Notes:

If your mission is not to cultivate a school community that meets the needs of all children and if your personal assignment is not integral to the success and survival of the community, you may awaken one day to discover that the rest of the community has died, dropped out, or moved away.

Which Assignments Will You Accept?

There are many assignments within a school community, each providing a building block toward cultivating school-wide excellence. The greater the number of individuals willing to accept areas of responsibility, the greater the potential for the school community to achieve excellence. Following are some of the assignments which exist within each of the primary components of the educational continuum (i.e., vision, climate & culture, curriculum & content, instruction, and assessment).

Vision

As will be outlined in great detail later, the school's vision is the compass that guides your way through the process of conceptualizing and implementing the needed strategies to ensure an academically-engaging and socially- and emotionally-nurturing school community.

What assignment will you accept in helping your school community to clarify its destination or to succeed in its journey?

Some of the components that directly relate to the school's vision are:

Vision Development: responsible for writing, publishing, evaluating, assessing, and if needed, rewriting the school's vision.

Cross Collaboration: responsible for identifying, establishing, and cultivating the collaborative efforts required to effectively pursue the school's mission/vision. Typical areas of cross collaboration:

- *High school teachers/counselors with local college and trade schools*

- *Ninth grade high school teachers with middle school teachers*

- *Sixth grade middle school teachers with elementary school teachers*

- *School-wide collaboration with such organizations and agencies as mentoring programs, community agencies, internship programs, job placement programs, law enforcement agencies, foundations, scholarship programs, before/after school programs, summer camps, special interest programs, local/state/national competitions, etc.*

Student Recognition: identifying and recognizing student achievement. Establishing customs, rituals, symbols, and ceremonies that celebrate student achievement in all areas pertinent to student esteem, school success, and the pursuit of the school's vision, i.e., athletic, academic, artistic, community service, modeling the school's core values, etc.

Guiding Principles: engaging in the ongoing assessment of whether the school's core values and guiding principles are being effectively communicated throughout the school community, i.e., through the core curriculum, extracurricular activities, visually, verbally, systemically, through the school's discipline policies, and through the school's established customs and rituals.

Notes:

School Goals: engaging in the ongoing assessment, analysis, and reporting of school-wide goals and their correlation to the school's stated mission/vision.

Creating a Safe School: proactively cultivating relationships between stakeholders throughout the school and surrounding community. Identifying appropriate instructional programs, community partners, logistics, strategies, and techniques to help cultivate a safe school community. Continually evaluating systems, technology, and student attitudes.

Office Referrals and Suspensions: engaging in experimentation, data gathering, analysis, and developing in-school experiential and research-based strategies designed to eliminate office referrals and suspensions thereby enhancing classroom instruction, student learning, and building positive relationships throughout the school community.

Relevant Research: identifying pertinent research, practices, and data that will help to achieve the school's goals. Identifying and reviewing local and national models as the foundation for engaging in experimentation, data gathering, analysis, and developing in-school research-based models.

Understanding Stakeholder Needs: gathering data, surveying families, and communicating with community organizations and agencies to identify and understand stakeholder needs. Identifying pertinent research, practices, and resource materials that provide greater insight into, and understanding of, those needs (i.e., children living in poverty, cultural dynamics and icons, community history, etc.). Developing a community-resource database.

School Goals, Resources, and Programs: developing a central information source (i.e., brochure, press kit, binder, computer database) of school-wide programs, school-based initiatives, extra and co-curricular activities, program goals, academic and performance-based achievements, customs, and rituals.

State and Local goals: developing a central information source of all state and local learning goals and creating a matrix showing how the school's curriculum, study trips, guest speakers, and extended learning opportunities correlate with those learning goals.

Grant Writing: identifying and writing grants to further the school's efforts toward fulfilling its mission and achieving its vision.

Developing a Foundation: identifying the necessary professional resources (i.e., attorney, board of trustees, etc.) to establish a non-profit foundation for engaging in fundraising efforts to provide funding for teacher, student, and school-wide initiatives.

Climate & Culture

The climate and culture of each school community is either defined, taught, and reinforced by the adults of the school community or by default, it is defined by the children. Cultivating the climate and culture needed to establish high academic, social, and moral standards within a school community, as in the case of developing the school's vision, is arduous and painstaking work. Let's face it, children are children. Many of today's parents are only slightly older than the children they send to school. Popular culture, promoted through film, television programming, music videos and music, encourages children to be smart-mouthed, disrespectful of authority, and promiscuous. Children are further encouraged to use violence as a primary means of problem-solving and sarcasm as their primary communication mechanism. If we are to turn our schools into places of passion and purpose; if we are to help children to understand and embody our core values and guiding principles, we must prepare ourselves to define what they are. Teach children our values and beliefs. And continually model and reinforce our expectations.

Why freak dancing freaks out schools

All this bumping and grinding — in the most intimate of ways — is a dance-floor craze that some say these suggest more than freedom of ex...

By Forrest MacCormack for USA TODAY

Everybody dance now: At the Planet Club in Chantilly Va., kids

By Olivia Barker
USA TODAY

At the Bar Code club in Cranston, R.I., a handful of kids meld into a kind of Conga line that redefines the term "joined at the hip," as their pelvises into girls' behinds to their pelvises into girls' behinds to hip-hop anthem Big

▶ Upper Darby phia instituted things

The sexual revolution hits junior high

...oing more than baring bellies: They're ...s with their anything-goes behavior

USA TODAY ph

Caught in the catty corner

Experts call it 'relational aggression,' but adolescent girls say peers are just mean

By Nanci Hellmich
USA TODAY

Katy Montague's seventh-grade year was a girl's worst nightmare.

She was excluded from parties, lunch table groups, conversations and cliques. She was teased and taunted about her looks and her glasses. She was treated this way by "the meanest people I ever met, and they were all girls," says Montague, of St. Louis.

"There was a lot of plotting and scheming behind people's backs. It was horrible. I don't remember anything I learned that year."

But there was a silver lining: She met her best friend during that trying time. "We do almost everything together. She's always there for me," says Montague, now 17.

Montague's experience mirrors that of millions of girls across the country as they make their way through the often painful passage of adolescence. Out of this pain often comes strength of character and genuine friendships, but while it's happening, a girl's life can be total misery. Now, some behavior experts are doing research to try to understand this phenomenon. And while they realize they may not be able to — and perhaps shouldn't — totally change it, there may be ways to help girls get through it with fewer scars.

Experts use the term "relational aggression" to describe the cattiness, meanness and nastiness that happens between some people

Cover story

but especially among girls.

Girls may gossip, spread malicious rumors, write nasty e-mails, give the silent treatment, exclude people from social events, betray secrets or snicker about people's clothes and mannerisms behind their backs. They may tell a girl that they're not going to be friends with her unless she does what they want.

"We all get angry. We all have the need to control others and our environment, and boys and girls have tendencies to do those things in different ways," says Nicki Crick, a professor of child development at the University of Minnesota-Minneapolis. She has studied relational aggression in thousands of people, from preschoolers to adults.

Boys and girls are equally capable of being kind or unkind, she says. "But where boys might use physical intimidation, girls will say, 'I won't be your friend anymore,' or "I'm not going to talk to you.' "

Several researchers, including Crick, are trying to figure out why this happens so frequently, especially among girls from third grade to seniors in high school, when they really value close friendships.

This spring, several books are coming out to help parents understand the phenomenon, including *The Secret Lives of Girls; The Friendship Factor; Trust me, mom — everyone else is going!; Queen Bees & Wannabes; Odd Girl Out.*

Psychologists believe there are several explanations for some of this behavior. One may be that girls are under enormous pressure to be nice and sweet. Unlike boys, girls have few opportunities to openly express their aggression or anger, so they strike out

e-schoolers. Perhaps you imagine s trying out eye shadow, boys azines.
of increasingly concerned edu-

recently started a program to anned to offer it to seventh-s to target fifth-graders — be-y were having sex.
f, Iowa, middle school, says from boys and girls in her dress code, girls come to . "They'll leave the house y start disrobing."
her in Omaha, recently el most comfortable" as ut themselves. A group ut receiving oral sex.
to do without dress ntories of forbidden . Schools that used sis now must have

ORY next page ▶

Sex by age 14
Kids (15 and older) who say they had had intercourse by age 14:

Girls — 11% (1988), 19% (1995)
Boys — 21% (1988), 21% (1995)

Source: Child Trends, a Washington research group

By Julie Snider, USA TODAY

Cover story

In addition to defining your school's core values and guiding principles, cultivating the climate and culture needed to pave the way to high academic achievement and cultivating an emotionally- and socially-nurturing environment for children requires creating a web of relationships that nurture, encourage, teach, and support children.

Alumni/Booster Club: identifying and recognizing alumni or developing a booster club of school supporters. Creating an alumni wall of fame, listing of guest speakers, business/community partners, mentors, and recognition events.

Business-Community Partnerships: cultivating business and community partnerships as a means of building relationships, providing a broader base of experiences and expertise, expanding volunteer efforts, identifying mentors, identifying community-relevant service projects, expanding resources, and supporting school-based initiatives.

Classroom Management Practices: developing expertise in classroom management practices for the purpose of modeling or coaching other teachers, with the goal of cultivating positive student-student interactions and increasing instructional effectiveness within the classroom.

Parental Support: developing innovative programs that are designed to cultivate parental support of, and involvement in, school programs. Identifying and recognizing parent/family needs and developing effective parent communication mechanisms, and family support programs (e.g., parent communication/newsletter, interest-specific volunteer opportunities, town hall styled meetings, parenting seminars, book clubs, breakfast club, parenting tips, parent recognition programs, birth announcements, etc.).

PTA/PTSA: developing a clearly-focused PTA/PTSA which may involve coordinating school opening activities, teacher/student recognition programs, creating effective fundraising initiatives, collaborating with other school-based groups (i.e., booster club, alumni association, etc.), sponsoring study trips, guest speakers, parenting seminars/workshops, etc.

School-wide Policies and Procedures: engaging in an ongoing audit of school-wide policies and procedures to ensure consistency in the school's mission/vision. Reviewing such processes as student movement, class schedules, classroom procedures, parent conferences, home-school communication, etc., within the context of age-appropriate student behaviors to ensure that school-based strategies and procedures are effective in cultivating the school-wide climate and culture envisioned.

Values and Beliefs: engaging in the ongoing analysis of the school's core values and guiding beliefs to ensure that they represent the driving force behind school-wide policies and practices as they impact upon school climate and culture, that beliefs are clearly stated, and that they are recognizable parts of customs and rituals (i.e., opening sporting events, assemblies, etc.).

Teacher/Staff Morale: developing school/community teacher recognition programs, identifying local/state/ national teacher recognition programs, recognizing and celebrating instructional excellence and community/family service, planning staff events, welcoming new staff, conceptualizing special interest activities, developing teacher/staff support programs, and developing customs, rituals, and traditions that value and validate professional and support staff.

Student Performances: creating customs and rituals that foster school and community pride in student performances (e.g., plays, oratorical programs, speech and debate, talent shows, art exhibitions, field days, entrepreneur fairs, etc.).

School Closing/Opening: planning the school closing/ opening in a way that best meets the needs of the school community, cultivates a positive school climate and culture, and fosters school spirit and pride. Planning the end of year debriefing, staff retreat, and pre-planning efforts.

Customs & Rituals: ensuring that appropriate customs and rituals become ingrained into school culture for the recognition and celebration of each area identified as a component part of the school's mission/vision.

School Image: coordinating and developing banners, posters, flyers, buttons, bumper stickers, t-shirts, mugs, pennant flags, and other paraphernalia to foster a heightened sense of school spirit and pride.

Intervention Strategies: identifying intervention strategies and research-based models that deal with the unique needs of the student population. Developing initiatives directed at identifiable student needs such as:

- *homelessness and students living in poverty,*

- *children of working parents,*

- *children of divorced parents,*

- *children living in extended families,*

- *children living in foster care,*

- *children experiencing cultural isolation,*

- *culturally or gender-specific underrepresentation in science and math,*

- *culturally or gender-specific underrepresentation in gifted, higher level, honors, and AP classes,*

- *culturally or gender-specific overrepresentation in alternative or special education,*

- *culturally or gender-specific overrepresentation in office referrals, detentions, and suspensions, and*

- *any identifiable gaps in student achievement.*

Notes:

Other intervention strategies may address teacher needs, e.g., classroom management, parent communication, lesson plan development, instructional design and delivery, developing parent-friendly rubrics, developing effective classroom routines, dealing with confrontational students, etc.

Inclusion: identifying pertinent research, practices, and data, and visiting local and national models that will support successful school-wide inclusion.

Curriculum & Content

One of the key components along the road to excellence is the willingness of teachers and support staff to continually assess, reassess, evaluate, and reevaluate the effectiveness of the school's curriculum and content. Although the text books, core content, and timing of units may be established by the local school board, there is generally great flexibility in the design of thematic and interdisciplinary units, identification of supplemental materials and programs, study trips, guest speakers, the design of at-home study tools, in-school tutorial assistance, and designing instructional delivery that connects content to students preexisting knowledge.

Skill-based After School/Extracurricular Activities: designing activities directed at cultivating social and academic skill development paving the way to student excellence in and preparation for local, state, and national programs, e.g., Odyssey of the Mind, Science Fair, Spelling Bee, Quiz Bowl, National PTA Reflections Competition, Student Newspaper, writing, math, science, and computer programming competitions, etc.

Standardized Test Preparation: developing study guides, parent tips, study groups, test preparation and test taking strategies, and reviewing the core curriculum for alignment with standardized, nationally-normed, end-of-grade tests, or exit exams.

Reading: developing school-wide strategies and identifying innovative models for ensuring that every student is capable of reading at or beyond grade level. Developing/promoting such activities as a *Back Pack Book Club,* Student/teacher book discussion groups, book readings and book talks by authors, parent/mentor reading buddies, developing intervention/prevention strategies, promoting family literacy, establishing student, classroom, and school-wide reading goals, developing monthly reading themes, establishing pre- and post-reading activities associated with guest speakers, study trips, local/national events, and promoting school/community book fairs.

Practical Learning Outcomes: developing innovative programs that connect the curriculum to real-world application of learning outcomes (e.g., publishing books, greeting cards, marketing student art, contributing to research journals, manufacturing products, etc.).

Gang Awareness and Intervention: identifying gang customs, rituals, and initiation rites within the school or surrounding community. Developing a partnership with local law enforcement, juvenile agencies, and intervention programs to provide school-wide awareness, early identification, and effective intervention to reduce gang influence and negative peer pressures. While street gangs, prominent in urban communities, are more easily recognizable, the negative peer culture of ridicule, put-downs, and bullying by groups of suburban students is just as destructive to school climate and culture and to the emotional and mental health of students who are being victimized.

Curriculum Development: reviewing and writing curriculum that meets the unique needs of students and the surrounding community, capitalizes on preexisting knowledge, is reflective of the diversity of the school community, taps into the capacity and unique knowledge-base of teachers, and is relevant to the real world outside of school.

Alignment with the Standards: engaging in the ongoing and critical review of curriculum and content and its alignment with the standards. May include reviewing thematic and interdisciplinary units and their alignment with state/local learning goals, timing of instructional units, and conceptualizing expanded learning opportunities that reinforce state/local standards.

Thematic & Interdisciplinary Units: engaging in the ongoing examination, and development, of thematic and interdisciplinary units that deepen and reinforce learning across the curriculum. Designing interdisciplinary units that enhance the core curriculum, tap into student interests, and result in effective culminating activities, customs, or rituals.

Study Trips: writing curriculum units that prepare students for the exploration, research, and observations to be made on study trips such as:

- *identifying materials,*

- *senses to be stimulated,*

- *observations to be made,*

- *data to be compiled,*

- *methods of publishing data, and*

- *methods of sharing data (i.e., written reports, skits, plays, lectures, videos, etc.).*

Needs-driven Curricula: engaging in the ongoing examination of the school's curriculum and its correlation with student needs, i.e., cultural, community, social, etc. Coordinating the timing and introduction of curriculum units with societal, political, and community activities that correlate to curriculum units, i.e., federal, state, and local elections, Black History Month, Cinco de Mayo, and other ethnic-specific holiday celebrations, local customs/traditions, changes in seasons, etc.

Instruction

Each school community must engage in the ongoing examination and assessment of instructional practices raising such questions as:

1. Are our instructional practices effective?

2. Are they grounded in pertinent research?

3. Are they aligned with the state standards?

4. Are they engaging our students?

5. Are we getting the results that we envisioned?

The *Tennessee Value Added Assessment System* study identified teacher effectiveness as the greatest contributing factor to student success. Increasing teacher effectiveness throughout a school community requires that administrators, teachers, support staff, parents, mentors, and the central office consciously and actively support teachers in providing effective instruction for all children. As a parent, I support my sons' teachers each school year by

providing information pertaining to my sons' learning styles, Multiple Intelligences, best and worst learning situations, best and worst subjects, personality types, etc., anything that will help them to be effective with my children.

Areas abound within a school community to increase instructional effectiveness and deepen student learning:

Teaching Styles/Learning Styles: engaging in the ongoing research, experimentation, and demonstration of instructional strategies that can be consciously directed at multiple learning styles and how students can demonstrate learning. Providing conscious efforts to provide the best match of teaching styles to learning styles.

Cooperative Grouping: engaging in the ongoing research, experimentation, and demonstration of cooperative grouping methodology to enhance learning, i.e., personality types, Multiple Intelligences, learning styles, gender-specific, multi-age/multi-level, homogeneous, etc.

Performing Arts: cultivating excellence within the areas of music, dance, fine/visual arts, theatre, etc. Providing opportunities for students to showcase talents in school/community performances, local, state, regional, national, and international competitions.

Enrichment Programs: cultivating excellence in extra and co-curricular activities such as:

- *athletics,*

- *cheerleading,*

- *band,*

- *chess club,*

- *year book production,*

- *web page design,*

- *book clubs,*

- *boy/girl scouts,*

- *drill team,*

- *double dutch team,*

- *ROTC, or*

- *Color Guard.*

Providing a broad range of exposure and enrichment opportunities in such areas as:

- *aviation,*

- *scuba diving,*

- *surfing,*

- *sailing,*

- *skiing,*

- *landscape design,*

- *political action,*

- *environmental advocacy, or*

- *community service.*

Planning school-wide and classroom study trips that enhance student exposure, reinforce learning outcomes, assist in test preparation, and provide opportunities for student celebrations. Developing pre- and post-study trip instructional activities that connect study trips to student needs, interests, dreams, and aspirations.

Social/Personal Development: working with identifiable student groups (i.e., gender, cultural, ethnic, or socio-economic) to enhance social skills, strengthen academic

Notes:

skills, provide cultural exposure, promote college planning, identify mentors, etc.

Brain-Compatible Instruction: participating in professional development opportunities in the areas of brain-compatible instruction to provide in-school leadership in current brain research and its implications on learning, lesson design, instructional delivery, and student assessment. Reviewing curriculum and content to ensure that lesson design and instructional strategies engage a higher number of each student's 19 senses.

The 19 senses

Senses	Kind of Input
Sight	Visible light
Hearing	Vibrations in the air
Touch	Tactile contact
Taste	Chemical molecular
Smell	Olfactory molecular
Balance	Kinesthetic geotropic
Vestibular	Repetitious movement
Temperature	Molecular motion
Pain	Nociceptive
Eidetic imagery	Neuroelectrical image retention
Magnetic	Ferromagnetic orientation
Infrared	Long electromagnetic waves
Ultraviolet	Short electromagnetic waves
Ionic	Airborne ionic charge
Vomeronasal	Pheromonic sensing
Proximal	Physical closeness
Electrical	Surface charge
Barometric	Atmospheric pressure
Geogravimetric	Sensing mass differences

Professional Development: identifying specialized professional development opportunities that will increase the knowledge base needed to pursue the school's vision.

Teen Parent Support Group: developing instructional activities, coordinating discussion groups and book clubs, facilitating guest speakers and mentors, identifying resource information and coordinating with local social and community services to provide services for young mothers and to ensure headstart opportunities for young children.

Instructional Rubrics: reviewing and writing rubrics for major instructional activities to enhance teacher effectiveness, student performance, and to cultivate parental involvement in and support of academic tasks.

Stakeholder/Teacher Planning: providing leadership on creating stakeholder/teacher planning teams as a means of further achieving instructional goals. May include involving parents in planning disciplinary units, designing rubrics, aligning the curriculum with state/local learning goals, and identifying ways of reinforcing the curriculum at home.

Guest Speakers: identifying guest speakers, lecturers, and disciplinary experts who embody the spirit of the school community and who can provide testimonials, experiences or specific knowledge pertinent to the school's vision, goals, and learning outcomes.

Grading Methodology: engaging in the ongoing review and assessment of grading methodology and its support of school-wide achievement goals. May include evaluating such issues as:

- *Is the grading methodology consistent with achieving the school's overall vision and fulfilling the school's mission?*

- *Is the grading methodology consistent with student and family needs?*

- *Is the grading methodology clear to students and families?*

- *Is the grading methodology consistent, impartial, and equitable?*

- *Does the grading methodology inspire high-level student performance?*

Extended Learning Opportunities: identifying study trips, videos, plays, sporting events, or other special programs that provide students with extended learning opportunities that are consistent with the school's vision and stated learning goals.

Assessment

Assessments must be consistent with the school's vision and established goals. The ultimate goal of assessment is to pave the way to the school becoming a quality school; To provide a barometer that measures progress toward achieving the vision and fulfilling the mission. Assessments will be both quantitative, i.e., academic achievement, standardized test scores, and qualitative, i.e., parent/student attitudes toward the school community, the effectiveness of guest speakers, the esthetic environment, and the prevailing language and behaviors exhibited throughout the school community.

The approach to assessment is:

1.   If it's in the vision, review and assess it.

2.   Develop qualitative and quantitative measurement criteria for assessing the success and effectiveness of programs, initiatives, and operational strategies.

Attitudes, instructional effectiveness, study trips, rubrics, school/home communication mechanisms, thematic and interdisciplinary units, business partners, parent/volunteer involvement, customs, rituals, staff development, utilization of resources, etc. must all be assessed. As previously stated, a school community is a dynamic organism impacted by countless variables each school year. The programs, policies, procedures, and practices must be assessed during and at the end of each school year.

Effective assessment must be driven by two primary criteria:

1.   Is this consistent with our vision?

2.   Is this in the best interests of our students?

School-wide Assessment: engaging in an ongoing data gathering, assessment, analysis, and reporting of the school's progress toward achieving it's mission, vision, and articulated goals.

Component-specific Assessment: engaging in an ongoing data gathering, assessment, analysis, and reporting of the school's progress toward achieving the goals that directly pertain to each of the school improvement components,

Vision, Climate & Culture, Curriculum & Content, and Instruction.

Demographic Assessment: engaging in an ongoing data gathering, assessment, analysis, and reporting of the school's demographic data as it pertains to students, families, and the demographics of the surrounding communities.

Student Achievement Assessment: engaging in the ongoing data gathering, assessment, analysis, and reporting of the school's progress in the specific areas of academic achievement as outlined in the school's vision, i.e., grades, honors/Advanced Placement enrollment, standardized test scores, end-of-grade exams, Talented and Gifted placements, etc.

Staff Development: engaging in an ongoing data gathering, assessment, analysis, and reporting of the school's staff development efforts and its impact on student achievement and the achievement of the school's stated goals.

Stakeholder Surveys: engaging in data gathering, assessment, analysis, and reporting of stakeholder needs and attitudes toward the school community.

Utilization of Resources: engaging in the ongoing data gathering, assessment, analysis, and reporting of the school's utilization of resources and the effectiveness in helping the school to achieve its stated goals.

Each of these, and countless other opportunities, exist within each school community for teachers, support staff, administrators, students, parents, and community partners to participate in cultivating one or more pockets of excellence. These are the building blocks to developing a quality school, closing the student achievement gaps, and meeting the real needs of teachers, support staff, parents, and students.

Discussion Questions

1. Write a personal mission as it pertains to the student(s) you have accepted personal responsibility to ensure his or personal growth and academic success.

2. What strategies can you utilize to meet each need identified in Maslow's Hierarchy of Needs (i.e., physiological, esteem, social, safety, and self actualization) for this student?

3. What strategies can you use to help this student to develop a personal mission designed to lead to their own self-actualizing experiences, personal growth, and academic success?

4. If you are in a middle or high school setting, construct a complete and comprehensive college plan based on this student's interests and/or career aspirations?

5. Identify any weaknesses and/or inconsistencies in the student's behavior, attitude, or work ethic that would hinder he or she from carrying out such a college-bound plan.

6. Match your strengths, talents, abilities, knowledge, experiences, and group affiliations to the student's weaknesses. How will helping the student to overcome his or her weaknesses further refine or redefine your Mission?

7. What staff persons, parents, or community volunteers do you believe possess the skills, interests, or leadership ability to further assist you in fulfilling your Mission as it pertains to this student's personal growth and academic success?

Notes:

Chapter 3

In building shared vision, a group of people build a sense of commitment together. They develop images of 'the future we want to create together,' along with the values that will be important in getting there and the goals they hope to achieve along the way. Without a sustained process for building shared vision, there is no way for a school to articulate its sense of purpose.

Unfortunately, many people still think that 'vision' is the top leader's job. In schools, the 'vision' tasks generally falls to the superintendent, the principal, and the school board. Within a classroom, it may fall to a teacher. But visions based on authority are not sustainable. They may succeed in carrying a school or a school system through a crisis. 'The superintendent wants us all to pull together to get through this budget crunch,' but when the crisis is over, people will fall apart, go back to their fractionalized and disparate hopes and dreams. They will never know the potential that comes from creating a shared vision of what their school, their classroom, and their community might be.

— Schools That Learn

Developing Your Vision

While a school's stated mission outlines its general overriding purpose, i.e., "To create lifelong learners and productive citizens," its vision provides clarity of purpose, focus, and direction in terms of what it intends to achieve, i.e., "To create a safe school community, create a nurturing school climate and culture, provide frequent opportunities to celebrate student achievement, to help all students to achieve proficiency in accordance with state and local standards, to expose students to world class academic, arts, sports, and extra-curriculum programs, eliminate any cultural-, socio-economic- or gender-based achievement gaps, etc."

Your school's vision evolves directly from what you want your students to achieve, e.g., meet state learning goals, help more children reach proficiency, help children achieve their potential, or provide children with actualizing experiences. The vision evolves directly from the stated mission of the school. While many schools have not engaged in the process of developing a clearly-defined vision, nearly every school has an articulated mission, even if it is only a reprint of the district's mission statement. When a school community has not engaged in the process of developing, articulating, and communicating a shared vision, fragmented, individualized visions of teachers and support staff with evolve. For example, when asked the question, "What is the vision of Princeton Junior High?" one teacher responded, "I don't know what the vision of the school is, but my vision is to get them out of here and into high school." Achieving such a vision does not require that students internalize character values, become productive citizens, lifelong learners or achieve state learning proficiencies. The lack of a clearly-defined and commonly-shared school-wide vision may lead many teachers and support staff to narrowly define their vision as "Let's just get them out of here."

The vision of a school community will represent the prevailing values and beliefs of the school community. Developing a shared vision helps to provide focus, clarity, and guide school-wide improvement efforts. It is this shared vision that helps to guide the individual vision of teachers and support staff. When the vision of classroom teachers is to get them to the next grade level, the teacher may not envision teaching life skills, character values or cultivating a put-down-free learning environment as integral to achieving such a vision. When the vision of the school's principal is defined as establishing a disciplined school community, the principal may not envision achieving academic excellence or closing the various achievement gaps between identifiable groups of students within the school as integral to achieving such a vision.

The values, experiences, and beliefs of those participating in school improvement planning will greatly impact upon the language and focus of the mission and vision of the school community. If the stated vision evolving from the school improvement planning process is helping students *achieve* grade level proficiency, achieving such a vision can occur without envisioning developing instructional practices, extracurricular activities, or providing extended learning opportunities that will inspire students to reach *beyond* proficiency levels. The point is, when the focus is on achieving proficiency all goals, resource expenditures, staff development, etc. are driven toward that end. If on the other hand, the mission and vision focused school-wide efforts on helping children to achieve their potential, while quantitative goals may be established that the school community will achieve 100% proficiency, the mission and vision would inspire qualitative goals of providing opportunities for students to soar beyond proficiency to realizing potential.

The school's vision will reflect the values, beliefs, and experiences of the school's stakeholders

Despite whether or not a school community has taken the time to develop a clear vision of what it wants to achieve with students, prevailing school-wide expectations and beliefs create internal visions among teachers, staff, parents, and students. While such internal visions may not be printed or articulated, they will drive school-wide efforts, policies, programs, and contribute to the very culture of the school community.

In my experiences working with the professional and support staffs of low-achieving schools, the greatest obstacle confronting the school's efforts to increase academic achievement is the prevailing belief of the professional and support staff that the majority of their students are incapable of high academic achievement and successful social skill development. Those students who are high academic achievers and well-mannered are considered the exception rather than the rule. In such schools, the staff's attention is focused on the children's deficits i.e., below grade level, living in poverty, history of discipline problems, truancy, lack of at-home support, lack of resources, poor hygiene, underdeveloped language skills, etc. Rather than recognizing and appreciating student strengths in their resilience in overcoming such obstacles, the internalized vision of many teachers and support staff is that students are incapable and that parents don't care about student success.

Such a vision of low achievement becomes a self-fulfilling prophecy as parent involvement ideas and innovative initiatives are shunned as teachers proclaim, "Why bother? These parents don't care. We can't be expected to bring these children up to grade level in just one year. It's not our fault that they don't do the homework. I really feel sorry for these children, but there's nothing that I can do."

In sharp contrast, the Flower City School, #54 (grades 3 through 5) in Rochester, New York, which has a high population of students on free and reduced lunch, has a school-wide vision based on teacher capacity rather than on

Notes:

student deficits. Their vision of student success has kicked off a number of school-wide initiatives which includes taking the entire school to breakfast at local restaurants to support their fight-free, put-down free programs; taking all of the 4th and 5th grade students to visit local colleges and universities; treating students like young men and women capable of dining in fine restaurants by adorning their cafeteria tables with flowers and table cloths; and kicking off their "Back Pack Book Club" *[Building Dreams: K-8 Teacher's Guide]* which received a proclamation from the Mayor of Rochester, New York, in February, 1999.

The Flower City School Back Pack Book Club, and other school-wide reading initiatives, is helping students achieve their vision of 100% proficiency in reading.

The Flower City School, #54 is engaged in the ongoing process of conceptualizing operational strategies to fulfill its vision such as establishing a Flower City School Scholarship Fund to assist Flower City Alumni in pursuing their postsecondary education.

One third grade classroom, having internalized the Flower City vision of high academic achievement, affirmed at their "Back Pack Book Club Kick-off Breakfast" (at which time the entire school had breakfast at the Shoney's breakfast buffet), that they could read over 2,000 books between February and June. By June, they had exceeded their goal as they tallied over 2,500 books. That year, Flower City School was recognized as having the highest increase in reading scores in the district (26%).

Whether internalized or clearly stated for all to see, your school's vision will be an extension of your mission. The operational goals that you ultimately establish will be reflective of your experiences and beliefs. If you believe that you can cultivate a school community in which teachers and students enter each day with passion and purpose, then you will seek out the resources and tools that are needed to solve the myriad of problems that hinder teaching and learning. Ultimately, what you believe will be reflected within your school's printed or internalized vision.

A team of teachers at a middle school in Greenville, South Carolina, gathered together to develop the school's vision. During the discussions one teacher found it impossible to envision lifting students beyond the state proficiency levels. "Mr. Wynn, so many of our students are below grade level in reading that I would be happy if we could just help more of them achieve proficiency. I just can't envision them rising above proficiency. They have so many issues at home outside of our control." The problem confronting many school communities reflect their experience, or history of student achievement; in this case, underachievement. This teacher's experiences were that most of the children entering into this middle school were below grade level in reading. The eighth grade reading scores indicated that the majority of students entering the sixth grade below grade level were still below grade level by the end of eighth grade. As a result of her experiences at the school, it was impossible to believe in the possibility of exceeding the standards. In her mind, meeting the standards itself was an unrealistic expectation. Therefore, exceeding the standards was insanity!

The fundamental principle of establishing your vision is:

Your beliefs (i.e., faith, attitude, etc.), together with your experiences (i.e., education, years of teaching, success/failures, etc.), will determine what you do and subsequently what you aspire to do. This, in essence, will determine the scope of your vision and the ensuing operational goals.

The dynamic of beliefs and experiences is a very powerful one, each influencing the other. Your beliefs will lead you into new experiences as you boldly pursue the unknown. Your successful experiences will expand your beliefs while your failures will challenge them. When new teachers graduate from college and enter school communities, many do so with beliefs that they can make a difference within the lives of children. Because they lack the experiences needed to undergird those beliefs, their first days of school will either strengthen or undermine their confidence. If they enter a school community with support from colleagues, experience success within the classroom, develop positive relationships with students, and are embraced and supported by families, their beliefs will be strengthened and their vision will be reinforced. However, if they enter a school community with little staff support, without a clearly-defined school-wide vision, where students not only are underachieving but who constantly challenge the teachers' authority, and where parents are not partners in their child's learning, the teacher's beliefs will be challenged, if not shattered. This dynamic is one of the greatest contributing factors to staff morale and teacher retention.

When Marva Collins started the Westside Preparatory School on Chicago's impoverished west side, she did so with a belief that she could make a difference in the lives of her students. She had no experience running a school; however, it was her belief that she could make a difference that inspired the students she eventually served, the teachers she eventually hired, and the parents who ultimately entrusted their children to her:

I believe that the classroom of every American school must become the flame that will enlighten the world, fire the imagination, give might to dreams and wings to the aspirations of girls and boys so that they may dare to become literate citizens of their locales, and with equal comfortableness, citizens of the universe. I believe that far too few educators realize that a good, solid education is the parent of progress, the creator of creativity, the designer of opportunity and the molder of human destiny.

[Ordinary Children, Extraordinary Teachers]

Don't Wait on the Principal

Anyone can become a catalyst for change within a school community, whether the change is initiated at a School Board meeting, through a Superintendent's mandate, at a PTA/PTSA meeting, by a classroom teacher committed to turning her classroom into a "Best Practices" classroom, by a parent volunteering within a classroom or by a mentor committed to ensuring that all children learn how to read and comprehend.

Notes:

The power of change is within each of our hands. We can do much more than criticize what's wrong in our schools. We can become a contributing force to ensure that more of what's right occurs each day within our schools.

Each school's Mission, Vision, and Statement of Beliefs must become the guiding documents for staff development, school-wide planning, and student initiatives. Schools of excellence do not happen by accident, but through the passionate pursuit of excellence driven by the school's vision, framed by the school's beliefs and core values, and embodied by each individual within the school community. The mosaic of excellence is painted with broad strokes across the canvas of a school community. One by one, programs of excellence are cultivated, each giving birth to its own customs and rituals.

With a clear vision, the school's principal and the school district's administrators primary responsibility to children is to support and empower teachers, parents, and support staff to engage in the passionate pursuit of their respective pockets of excellence. It is the passionate pursuit of putting a winning team onto the football field; to develop a world class music program; to develop a nationally recognized entrepreneurial program; or to develop a school recognized for academic excellence that is usually led by a handful of individuals who are driven by a personal mission to cultivate a program of excellence.

The clearly-defined, commonly-shared vision provides the guiding light for all of the components that follow. The vision directs allocation of resources, hiring practices, curricular and co-curricular activities, teacher training, study trips, parental involvement, business partnerships, classroom management practices, curriculum and instruction, etc. Unlike the Mission, which provides a broad purpose, the vision outlines the specifics of what the school wants to achieve.

In the *Accelerated Schools Project* from Stanford University, they recount the experiences of North Middle School:

The North Vision Committee took 48 single-spaced pages of written input from parents, students, and staff to create this all-encompassing vision which is posted in every classroom in English, Spanish, and Vietnamese:

> *The North Middle School's Vision*
>
> *We are a community of learners who:*
>
> > *Achieve academic excellence,*
> >
> > *Face life with confidence,*
> >
> > *Appreciate the arts,*
> >
> > *Love learning,*
> >
> > *Value and respect ourselves and others,*
> >
> > *and*
> >
> > *Experience success and fulfill our dreams.*

To make the vision more than a written statement, but a meaningful focus for practices and beliefs, the school sought a number of different vehicles for making its vision readily visible and accessible to all. When school members walk in the front door of the school, they are greeted each morning by a mural of the vision created by the industrial technology and visual arts teachers on one wall and the vision quilt created by students that hangs on the other. The school's vision quilt represents the hopes and dreams of the entire school community. Each classroom designed a square that best represented the different parts of the school's vision and with the help of teachers and support staff, a classroom representative sewed his/her class piece into the larger design. While the quilt was taking shape, a number of classroom teachers created lessons centered around the vision, giving students an opportunity to create poems, drawings, and skits to signify what the vision meant to them. In this way, the school

Notes:

started to bring the vision to life and continues to do so through numerous classroom activities and school-wide initiatives.

In the book, *Shaping School Culture: The Heart of Leadership,* the authors outline how the quest for a driving vision paved the way to higher student achievement:

The principal began by engaging faculty, parents, staff, and students in extended discussions regarding the kind of school they hoped Stevenson might become. Throughout the dialogue, he made a conscious effort to provide participants with the information they needed to arrive at informed decisions about future directives. He shared research on effective schools, gathered information on the academic performance of top schools in the state, compiled data on Stevenson students, and presented countless examples of how the school fared in comparison with others. Gradually, consensus emerged as to what Stevenson High School might become. A vision statement was written, endorsed by all parties, and adopted as Board policy.

The authors went on to note that, "the vision statement provided a blueprint for the school's improvement efforts."

While it [the vision] provided a general direction for improvement, the principal attempted to sharpen the focus by engaging the faculty in a series of questions. He asked the faculty to move beyond the affirmation of the belief that 'all children can learn' to address such questions as, 'What do we expect all students to learn in each of our courses? How will we respond to students who do not initially achieve the intended learning? How can we provide these students with more time and support for their learning? What collective commitments must each of us make to ensure that all our students learn? What criteria do we use in assessing students' work? What are our strategies for improving upon the results we are getting?'

When forced to answer such questions, stakeholders within a school community must confront the issues, obstacles, and attitudes which stand in the way of the school that is envisioned and the current reality of the school. The faculty at Stevenson, as in any school, discovered that preexisting beliefs, expectations, and assumptions may no longer be appropriate and that new beliefs, expectations, and assumptions are needed to develop the programs and partnerships that are consciously designed to help students meet high academic standards. The hiring practices at Stevenson changed as the school recognized that it needed teachers who had a clear sense of what they were trying to accomplish and who were willing to become part of a team in the pursuit of a collective vision. They consciously sought teachers with experiences and interests reflective of their students and who accepted as part of their assignment the need to motivate and inspire students to believe in and apply themselves.

To validate their success and measure their journey, the principal reviewed their data and searched constantly for evidence of improvement—grade distributions, reduced failure rates, improved attendance, higher levels of student or parent satisfaction. He looked for gains on standardized achievement tests, increases in the number of students exceeding state standards on state tests, reductions in suspensions, and so on. His reports to faculty offered more longitudinal data, comparisons, and trends to demonstrate that the collective efforts of the staff were making an important difference. These efforts eventually led Stevenson to being recognized as one of the top high schools in the nation, the first school in the county to receive the United States Department of Education Excellence in Education award, the first school in the state to receive the award a second time, and one of only ten schools nationally to receive the award a third time.

Notes:

Focused Staff Development

Identifying and understanding the unique challenges confronting a school community that ultimately impact student achievement helps to create a mental picture of the school we envision. The pursuit of solutions to those challenges will frequently take the form of professional development. Rather than a one-size fits all approach, teachers and support staff should be directed toward the professional development opportunities that specifically provide the experiences and learning outcomes needed to overcome the unique challenges confronting the school community and achieve the school's vision.

For example, it is impossible to engage students in rigorous classroom instruction within a school community of high office referrals. Each time a student misbehaves in a classroom:

- the teacher must take away from instructional time to deal with the respective behavior.

- if an office referral is warranted, the teacher must stop instruction to write the referral and, in most cases, either escort the student to the office or contact the office to request an administrator or security personnel to come and get the student.

- time-on-task is lost to the student being referred to the office as well as all of the other students in the classroom.

- leadership time is lost to the administrator who must now defer duties dedicated to pursuing the school's vision, e.g., meeting with potential business partners, interviewing new teachers, meeting with school improvement planning committees, etc., to deal with the student being referred to the office.

If disruptive classroom behaviors represents one of the challenges confronting the school community, one of the goals evolving from the school's vision must be **zero** office referrals. Establishing such a goal would lead to professional development in such areas as:

- dealing with confrontational students;

- developing effective cross-gender, cross-cultural, cross-socioeconomic, cross-generational, and non-verbal communication;

- implementing intervention strategies for students with chronic discipline problems;

- creating more engaging classrooms;

- creating more time-on-task activities;

- creating more effective cooperative grouping;

- creating in-class conflict resolution strategies;

- cultivating parental involvement and creating effective home-school communication strategies;

- developing relationships with students and families to proactively avoid classroom disruptions; and

- developing effective discipline policies and other support mechanisms.

Office referrals reflect a breakdown in relationships between students and teachers and between students themselves. The ultimate goal of staff development as it relates to this one challenge must be assist to teachers in strengthening these relationships by providing teachers with the tools and techniques, and enhancing their understanding of how to cultivate a nurturing collaborative classroom climate and culture.

In all of the challenges confronting the school community, proactive and responsive staff development must be done in a manner consistent with the school's vision, and guided by effective data gathering and assessment.

Focused, effective staff development requires that we effectively gather, analyze, and objectively report the data pertaining to each component of the school's vision.

Staff development that is driven by effective assessment will result in such initiatives as:

- sending small teams of teachers to workshops and seminars with an action plan and timeline for applying the knowledge gained.

- identifying teachers who aspire toward "Best Practices" status and developing a long-term professional development strategy to ensure that they acquire the desired knowledge base.

- effectively gathering, reviewing, and analyzing data with individual teachers, department chairpersons, and subject area or grade level teams to identify specific staff development needs.

I recently spoke to the teachers and support staff at an elementary school in Philadelphia, Pennsylvania. They dragged into the room at the end of the school day in a typically exhausted fashion. Few teachers brought paper or pencil. There was, generally, little enthusiasm demonstrated toward this, another ritualistic staff development.

My opening remarks to the staff were as follows:

I have had an opportunity to sit with your principal and review your student achievement data. I have a good sense of the issues that you are confronted with in your school community. There are numerous strategies that I have written about, that I could demonstrate, and that I could share with you directly pertinent to the issues that you are confronting in your school. However, my experience is that this would do little good without knowing what the vision is for your school community. I'd like everyone to take out a sheet of paper. Those of you who don't have paper please raise your hand and we will provide you with paper and pencils. I'd like for you to write down the vision for this school as you know it.

Some teachers began writing while others stared at their sheets of paper. "If you don't know what the school's vision is simply write down, 'I don't know.'"

After you write down the school's vision I'd like for you to write down your grade level vision.

Finally, I would like for you to write down three goals that you have for this school year that you believe are necessary in order for you to achieve your grade level vision and subsequently the school's vision. This is where I will direct my comments.

As you might guess, most teachers wrote, "I don't know what the vision of the school is." Without a clearly-defined vision it is impossible for any vision to be commonly shared. Subsequently, it is impossible for each grade level to have a vision that is in support of the overriding school's vision. Notwithstanding, without a clear focus of what we wanted to achieve, and a clear understanding of the challenges confronting us, the staff development time and money could not be focused on developing meaningful strategies and solutions for increasing student achievement.

The caveat is that the principal had a clear vision as many principals do. However, the principal could not teach every class; could not hold every parent conference; could not deal with every classroom disruption; could not attend every professional development conference or professional development session with her teachers; and could not deliver every instructional lesson. The only way to ensure that our efforts are focused is through the development of a clearly-defined, commonly shared vision to guide us.

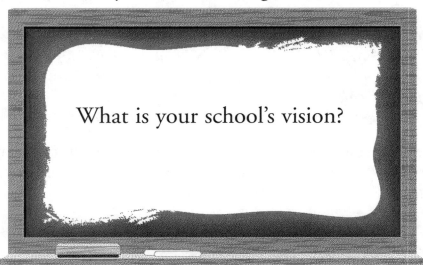

What is your school's vision?

Examples of Excellence Abound

Whatever the current achievement level of your school, anecdotal evidence suggests that even low-achieving schools, which frequently lack effective school-wide strategies and programs, will experience pockets of excellence.

For example, some schools that achieve local, state or national recognition through such academic activities as Odyssey of the Mind, State Science Fair, Micro Society or the National Spelling Bee, may not achieve excellence in their athletics, marching band or theater programs, while other schools with low-academic achievement receive local, if not national recognition, for their athletic teams, marching bands, and other non-academic programs. And yet, before an argument can be made that excellence cannot co-exist within non-academic and academic programs, we find high schools, scattered throughout the United States, who have done just that. They have championship football teams AND Rhodes Scholars. Within such schools, their pockets of excellence are varied and broad reaching. Lead by individuals, ingrained in a school-wide culture and traditions, and driven by a school-wide vision, the pursuit of excellence is as normal as the opening and closing of each school day.

I have been in many academically low-achieving high schools where the expectations of athletic excellence permeate throughout the community. As you drive up to the school, there is a banner that touts state championships in basketball, football, track or other sports. As you enter the school, there are huge trophy cases that proudly display their impressive athletic achievements. Photographs of athletes adorn their wall of fame. Their coaches are idolized within the local community and may even eat free at local restaurants. Despite achieving athletic excellence these schools continue to experience low academic achievement, largely because no one is paying attention to the example that the athletic program has put forth for all to see:

- There is a clearly-defined vision internalized by players, coaches, and the surrounding school community.

- There is a climate and culture of teamwork, school spirit, high expectations, internal and external support mechanisms.

Notes:

- Visual images are utilized to reinforce expectations (e.g., banners, trophies, pennants, t-shirts, bumper stickers, jerseys, flyers, etc.).

- Customs and rituals are developed to kick off the season, recognize athletes, thank patrons, and celebrate success.

- The curriculum and content successfully utilizes interdisciplinary (i.e., physical development, mental clarity, work ethic, collaboration, effective cooperative grouping, identification of individual strengths and weaknesses, effective intervention strategies, and teaching to multiple learning styles) and thematic units (history, rules and regulations, goal setting, etc.).

- The instructional approach nurtures relationships and taps into each player's intrinsic areas of motivation.

- There is an ongoing assessment of performance data (e.g., tackles, passing/running yardage, third down efficiency, special teams performance, fourth quarter performance, etc.).

- The instructional programs (via game film) of other schools are constantly used to measure and fine-tune their strategies and planning efforts.

147

Many scoff at the idea that the process of creating world class academic achievement can be broken down into components as simplistic as those incorporated into the process of creating world class athletic achievement. Yet the examples are there for all to see. Good coaches are good teachers and the best teachers are more often than not, good coaches:

- *Good coaches build good players despite the circumstances and situations outside of their control (i.e., single parent households, parents who may not support academic tasks, parents who may not even attend athletic events, players who come from poverty households, etc.); so, too, do good teachers.*

- *Good coaches begin with the end in mind (i.e., Vision); so, too, do good teachers.*

- *Good coaches cultivate a climate of cooperation, collaboration, personal responsibility, fairness, and trust; so, too, do good teachers.*

- *Good coaches push, lead, and inspire players to stretch toward their personal potential within a framework of contributing their individual talents and abilities toward a collective goal; so, too, do good teachers.*

- *Good coaches proudly display their player's collective and individual achievements; so, too, do good teachers.*

Notes:

How successful your school community is at fulfilling its mission is directly dependent upon your successfully developing solutions to and implementing strategies for the unique challenges that you face (e.g., gangs, drugs, teen pregnancies, minority student underachievement, high ESL population, student/parent apathy, teacher ineffectiveness, truancy, transient student population or teacher-parent-student attitudes toward the school community). Every staff meeting, staff development, parent conference or other school-related activity must be driven by your vision and consistent with fulfilling your mission. In essence, every endeavor within a school community must begin with the end in mind.

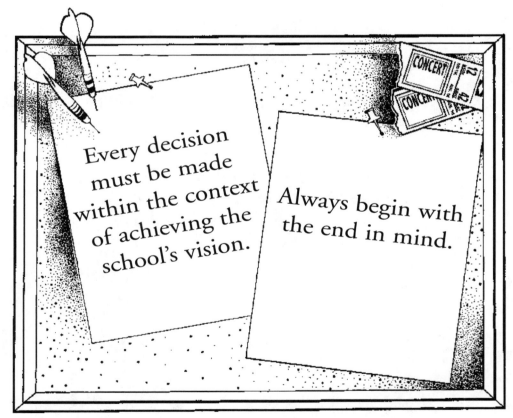

The challenges that you face in fulfilling your school's mission are numerous. They include, but are not limited to:

- increasing student performance on standards-based testing;

- inspiring students to engage in academic rigor;

- cultivating parental support;

- engaging students in a meaningful, relevant curriculum;

- reducing classroom disruptions;

- increasing attendance;

- reducing tardiness;

- increasing student retention of what is taught within the classroom;

- developing effective teacher teams to conceptualize solutions to the many unique problems within each school community;

- ensuring the academic success of students who begin the school year below grade level in reading or mathematics;

- reducing class size; and

- hiring effective teachers and increasing teacher retention.

This is the short list. Whatever the issues confronting your school community, you cannot effectively, holistically, or systemically plot your course without a clearly-defined vision. Notwithstanding your local or state accountability standards, as a school community, you must measure yourself against the standard, "How prepared will our students be to become successful within this society once they leave our school?" All students must be measured against this standard; not the ones who come "ready to learn" or the ones who are "at grade level" or the ones who look like, think like or share your teachers' values. The vision of your school community must be to educate ALL of its students. Parents don't keep their best at home and send you the rest. What they have is what you get.

Notes:

Vision: The clearly-defined, commonly-shared vision of a school provides the guiding light for all of the components that follow. The vision provides the framework for allocation of resources, hiring practices, curricular and co-curricular activities, teacher training, study trips, parental involvement, business partnerships, classroom management, curriculum and instruction, etc. Unlike the Mission which provides a broad purpose, the vision outlines the specifics of what a school community wants to achieve.

Developing Your School's Vision

If you have ever engaged in discussions of what the perceived problems are within your school community, you have probably experienced little difficulty in identifying the many challenges and obstacles to increasing student achievement. In fact, so many problems can usually be identified that the process itself can be distressing. Large group discussions are often side-tracked and frequently fail to lead to systemic or sustained change. The meetings are frequently heated, rarely productive, and generally leave staff persons depressed or disheartened.

The process of problem identification and problem solving are, and must be, entirely different processes. Furthermore, they should never occur within the same session. Problem identification must be exclusively devoted to identifying all real and perceived problems while making no attempt to solve or analyze the problems as they are being identified.

For example:

Problem:

We have low parental involvement and participation in school-wide events.

Analysis:

Our parents don't care about their children.

Statements to support the analysis:

We do all that we can and no one supports our efforts.

The last time that we had an assembly program no one came and our children were so disappointed.

We don't bother hosting curriculum nights anymore. It's just a waste of teachers time.

Our parents only come when we have food, then they leave as soon as they eat.

In a large group setting, once the problem is identified, (i.e., lack of parental involvement), any attempt to analyze the problem at this time is simply counterproductive. If this is not avoided, one statement can sidetrack the discussion for 30 minutes or more with each person voicing his or her opinion about what is wrong with the parent population at the school.

The approach should be: *What is the first issue hindering student achievement?*

First person to respond: *We have a lack of parental involvement and a lack of support of school-wide events.*

Facilitator: *Thank you, what is the next issue?*

The goal of problem identification must be to encourage the input from the varying perspectives and experiences of the school's stakeholders regarding the totality of the issues and obstacles hindering student achievement. Keep in mind that this part of the process has a specific purpose: To develop our school-wide vision. The goal at this time is not to analyze the problems, discuss the problems, evaluate whether or not the problems are real or to solve the problems.

Begin the process of developing your vision by:

• gathering together all pertinent stakeholders (i.e., teachers, parents, support staff, business partners, community representatives, etc.) for the purpose of engaging in a candid and open discussion of all of the issues perceived to be hindering student achievement. All stakeholders must have an opportunity to articulate their concerns and their perceptions, whether real or imagined.

Pre-discussion activity:

At the beginning of the first meeting, each individual should develop a "Comprehensive Screen" or perspective regarding the issues within your school community. They should proceed through the following questions by noting the first things that come into their minds. Allow no more than twenty minutes to complete the activity.

A. What are your major concerns regarding student achievement in this school?

B. What are your major concerns regarding

safety issues in this school?

C. What are your major concerns regarding student behavior in this school?

D. What are your major concerns regarding teacher and staff behavior in this school?

E. What are your major concerns regarding parent and community involvement in this school?

F. What are your first concerns each school day?

G. What confuses you most about this school community?

H. If you could make three changes tomorrow in this school, what would they be?

I. If you could make three changes by the opening of school next year, what would they be?

J. If you could make three changes before you retire, what would they be?

What issues do you believe are hindering our efforts to increase student achievement?

Notes:

The Comprehensive Screen is designed to help you see the "big picture" from your perspective regarding your school community. The purpose of not allowing any more than twenty minutes to complete the activity is to understand the issues that "most concern" you. These are the issues in the forefront of your mind that must be factored into the discussion that follows pertaining to developing the school's vision.

Facilitate this process by:

- placing easels and chart paper around the room;

- initially asking each person to take a moment to reflect on what he or she perceives to be the problems hindering student achievement;

- having each person take a sheet of paper and write down each of their concerns;

- having each person articulate one of the concerns they have identified;

- noting each concern on one of the chart pads and continuing person-by-person until each person in the room has had an opportunity to articulate one concern; and

- continuing the process of asking each person to articulate another concern until each person in the room has had an opportunity to articulate each concern that they have noted.

Thank everyone for their participation and schedule another meeting to review the first draft of the school's vision.

Draft Your Mission and Vision

Establish a Verbal/Linguistic M.I. Team (see the Appendix) to undertake the responsibility of drafting the school's vision. Provide this team with the chart paper containing the concerns articulated in the meeting. Additionally, provide this team with:

- the other pertinent educational vision statements relating to your local schools:

  A. Mission and Vision on the federal level.

  B. Mission and Vision on the state level (be sure to include learning goals, state guidelines, etc.).

  C. Mission and Vision for your school district.

With this information, this team should attempt to:

- develop a one line statement that states your school's Mission;

- group the concerns from each of the sheets of chart paper into general categories (e.g., school safety, student achievement, school-community relationships, resource needs, etc.); and

- working from the concerns, draft statements that provide the reciprocal of the categories of concerns identified as hindering student achievement. It is assumed that solutions to these issues would result in increased student achievement. This in essence is your school's Vision.

  For example: the reciprocal of *student apathy* is a vision of inspiring student achievement; the reciprocal of *lack of parental involvement* is a vision of developing strong home-school-community relationships; the reciprocal of *lack*

Notes:

of resources is a vision of effective school-business partnerships, etc.

Keep in mind that the goal, at this time, is not to solve the problems or to evaluate whether or not the problems can be solved. The goal is to provide a vision of what the school community would look like if successful solutions to the problems were, in fact, identified and implemented.

- Finally; draft your Vision (it must be consistent with, and guided by the Federal, State, and local guidelines).

Compare each of your Vision Statements on the federal, state, and local level with the Vision of your school. The Vision of your school must be in support of the Mission/Vision for your local school district, which should be in support of the Mission/Vision of the State Department of Education, which in turn should be in support of the Mission/Vision articulated by the Federal Department of Education.

While the Vision of your school community may be much more ambitious than what has been articulated by your local school district or by the State Department of Education, it should not be in conflict with the mission/vision of the local and state levels. Also, achieving your school's Vision should reflect the state learning goals and be consistent with local district guidelines.

Circulate Your Draft and Revisit the Problems

To become the driving force behind the necessary school-wide and systemic efforts, your Vision must be defined,

What is your vision for our school?

effectively communicated, and commonly shared. There is no time limit on drafting, revisiting, redrafting, and revisiting your Vision. The purpose for allowing each person to articulate his or her respective concerns, no matter how insignificant others may perceive them to be, is to lead each person into becoming a participating member in the change process. The final draft of your school's Vision must be reflective of the needs, hopes, and dreams of your entire school community. Only then will it have the power to shape all discussions, frame all decisions, and drive all of your school improvement efforts.

Following are the steps for using your draft of the school's vision to receive stakeholder input and solicit stakeholder buy-in.

1.   Date the current draft of your school-wide Vision and circulate it throughout your school community.

2.   Provide a mechanism for receiving stakeholder input (i.e., suggestion boxes, team meetings, town hall styled meetings, PTA/PTSA, classroom meetings, etc.).

3.   Establish a deadline for submitting feedback.

4.   Review the feedback, date, and redraft the vision.

Notes:

5.   Circulate a final draft and establish another cut-off date for feedback.

6.   Publish the final, dated draft of the school's Vision.

The discussions for shaping the school's Vision are designed to provide an opportunity for participants (who should be a representative group of the school's stakeholders) to articulate their perceptions regarding the issues confronting, and the future focus of, the school community. Participation in this process nurtures the needed emotional investment of participants. Developing the school's vision can be a long, arduous process that is essential to the work ahead. The components of school climate and culture; curriculum and content; instruction; and assessment will all be driven by your school's Vision and the operational goals that are established as a result of that Vision.

Drafting Your Grade Level or Special Program Vision

While the school's vision provides a compass that guides the school's direction toward creating higher student achievement and cultivating a socially and emotionally nurturing school community, what about your classroom, subject area, or program?

- What is your vision as a kindergarten teacher?

- What is your vision as a sixth grade teacher?

- What is your vision as an eighth grade Algebra teacher?

- What is your vision as an eleventh grade honors Biology teacher?

I recently sat down with Barbara Hires, principal of Maximo Elementary School in St. Petersburg, Florida; the Title I Lead Teacher, Betsy Cambut; and a fifth grade student, Lorenzo

Hogans. Maximo Elementary was about to become a Micro Society School. The teachers were actively engaged in selecting the ventures that they would facilitate (i.e., Post Office, Technology, Banking, School Store, etc.). Our discussion centered around conceptualizing the vision for a publishing venture. Lorenzo, a fifth grade student, has a passion for writing and dreams of publishing his poetry and short stories. He was invited to participate in the discussion to help ensure that our vision was reflective of his dreams and aspirations.

We need to meet with the elementary school teachers and outline how they can help children in the primary grades develop the skills that they will need to be successful in our AP classes. Our vision is to close the achievement gap and have equal representation from our student body in our honors and AP classes by 2005.

Notes:

After much discussion, debate, and deliberation, the objectives of the publishing venture were:

1. Integrate student writing activities, i.e., poetry, short stories, raps, lyrics, essays, etc., into the core curriculum.

2. Guide student writing activities toward actualizing events, i.e., published books, book marks, book fairs, poetry recitals, etc.

3. Identify business partners, mentors, and other disciplinary experts who can provide exposure and expanded expertise to nurture students in such trade areas as layout, design, editing, marketing, sales, printing, binding, distribution, packaging, and displays.

4. Integrate the publishing venture into other micro society ventures, i.e., advertising, graphic arts, technology, distribution (Post Office), art (illustration and cover design), etc.

5. Create a non-profit foundation to solicit donations, grants, and business contributions to underwrite publishing ventures, authors-in-residence, study trips, etc.

6. Create a series of study trips designed to expose students to the multifaceted dynamics of the publishing industry, i.e., the Library of Congress, printing facilities, advertising agencies, bookstores, binderies, graphic arts agencies, book fairs, etc.

7. Create a writing club comprised of students who demonstrate higher level abilities or interests in pursuing writing as a profession who would edit, judge, and coordinate the publishing efforts of other students.

8. Develop integrated thematic units as a means of incorporating creative writing time as part of the core curriculum.

9. Create customs, rituals, ceremonies, awards, and recognition for celebrating writing and publishing.

10. Coordinate theme writing units with teachers and identify student compositions to be included in an annual school anthology.

11. Expose students to the technology that is utilized in the publishing industry, i.e., scanners, computers, desktop publishing software, layout and design software, digital cameras, fonts, and typography.

12. Coordinate school-wide writing contests, e.g., poetry, essays, short stories, local events, and curriculum themes.

13. Gather data, perform an ongoing analysis, and develop a writing curriculum that outlines the process of creating a publishing venture and the venture's impact on student achievement.

14. Provide staff development and student training for other schools interested in creating publishing ventures and exposing students to a wide range of writing opportunities.

15. Create a specific mission, vision, core values, and guiding beliefs for the publishing ventures' facilitators, business partners, mentors, and students.

16. Utilize disciplinary experts for special-focus tutoring, in such areas as editing, conceptualizing stories, brainstorming, creating storyboards, packaging, pricing, marketing, distribution, and product display.

17. Develop partnerships with other schools (i.e., middle, high, college, trade) to assist students in developing long-term plans, identifying scholarship sources, special camps, etc.

18. Review each of the writing activities for alignment with the state standards.

19. Publish student work for sale in the school bookstore, book fairs, art shows, and through local school-related events.

20. Develop a resource library of the publishing industry and writer's resources, reference books, videos, magazines, periodicals, national and international meetings and contests, and supplemental materials.

With discussion points guiding their efforts, a group of teachers and support staff drafted a student-friendly mission statement for the publishing venture:

The mission of the Mariner's Publishing Corporation is to write and report stories, edit and publish, advertise ventures and help other students write by publishing a magazine and an anthology and renting writers and authors in order to achieve our goal of being journalists earning money and having a ball!

On the following page is a letter from the lead teacher, Betsy Cambut, outlining how their efforts have inspired their students.

MAXIMO ELEMENTARY SCHOOL

4850 - 31st Street South
St. Petersburg, Florida 33712
Telephone: (727) 893-2191

BARBARA HIRES
Principal

FELITA LOTT
Assistant Principal

March 13, 2002

Dear Mr. Wynn,

I thought it was time for me to give you an update on our writing venture here at Maximo. After your visit, Mrs. Hires asked me to coordinate this activity.

Three other teachers, two hourly teachers and I created a plan for this year. We advertised for interested fourth and fifth graders who had a passion for writing and then had those students submit writing samples along with their application. At our first meeting, we wrote a mission statement (attached) and decided to work first on a news magazine. Payroll was set up, each child designed his/her own business card, and a "rent–a–writer" enterprise was started. Since we have more than one on–going business, we are called the Mariners' Publishing Corporation.

The result of our first effort is included in this letter. We will now begin planning our second edition and are discussing an anthology.

It has been a real learning experience for ALL of us; the children have been enthusiastic and delightful to work with! Several teachers have told us that our "employees", who have never enjoyed school, are eager to come to our venture.

Thank you for all the inspiration and help you gave us to get started. I truly feel that many of these students are gaining more from this experience than just seeing their names in print!

Sincerely,

Betsy Cambut

Mrs. Betsy Cambut

Notes:

The continued discussions between teachers, parents, support staff, and students will lead to developing a clear vision for the future of the publishing venture and how it will impact upon student achievement. Following is an example of how the venture's vision might be stated based on the venture's stated mission and accompanying goals and objectives.

Our vision

- **Create a non-profit foundation for the specific support of publishing-related ventures, i.e., book publishing, study trips, authors-in-residence, etc.**

- **Integrate student writing activities, i.e., poetry, short stories, raps, lyrics, essays, etc., into the core curriculum.**

- **Guide student writing activities toward actualizing events, i.e., published books, book marks, book fairs, poetry recitals, theater productions, etc.**

- **Develop stakeholder collaboration that will nurture and expose students to every facet of the publishing/writing industry.**

- **Integrate the publishing venture with other micro society ventures so that students may share and appreciate the wide range of skills and abilities required to develop a successful business.**

- **Provide plentiful and meaningful opportunities for students to utilize and apply a wide range of technologies.**

- **Write, publish, and train others in the curriculum areas developed.**

- **Create a seamless matriculation of students from the Maximo Elementary School Publishing Venture into middle school, high school, and a four year college or university with a writing/publishing focus.**

- **Engage students in instructional activities that will result in superior performance on state and national performance-based exams.**

Taking the time to discuss, debate, and deliberate what you envisioned will guide your efforts in developing a mission and vision that provides focus and clarity. Your mission and vision provide a framework for engaging in the arduous process of ordering materials, identifying space requirements, identifying technological needs, identifying resources, identifying opportunities for meaningful parent involvement, soliciting community and business partnerships, identifying the needed curriculum components and staff development, and establishing stakeholder teams to conceptualize the necessary operational and implementation strategies.

Clarity of our Mission/Vision allows us to prepare for our journey, coordinate our efforts, and set sail with confidence that we can achieve our destination.

Notes:

Discussion Questions

1. What is the vision of your school, where is it posted, and how is it communicated throughout the school community?

2. Under the captions: *Climate and Culture*, *Curriculum and Content*, and *Instruction* list the data that is being gathered (or the data that needs to be gathered) and reviewed to assess your school's ongoing progress toward achieving your vision.

3. What is the vision of your athletic program, grade level, subject area, classroom, department, extracurricular activity, or assembly program?

4. How has your vision (i.e., grade level, subject area, departmental, etc.) been communicated to students and families?

5. What qualitative and quantitative goals have been established, and what data is being gathered and reviewed to assess your ongoing progress toward achieving your vision.

6. List three groups of people, other than students, whose support you need to help you to achieve your vision, e.g., colleagues, business partners, tutors, parents, etc.

7. What formal mechanisms have you put into place to:

    • communicate your needs to each of these groups of people; and

    • specifically outline in sufficient detail what you need for each of these groups of people to do to help you to achieve your vision?

Chapter 4

Our efforts at educational improvement often do not work to guarantee good schools for everyone. Reforms that focus only on changing structures or school governance will never succeed in building positive organic forms that will serve all students. Reforms that bring new technologies or higher standards won't succeed without being embedded in supportive, spirit-filled cultures. Schools won't become what students deserve until cultural patterns and ways are shaped to support learning. Leadership from throughout the school will be needed to build and maintain such positive, purposeful places to learn and grow.

— *Shaping School Culture*

A Research Framework

Even after a school proceeds through the painstaking efforts of clarifying its mission and vision, it must then conceptualize the strategies needed to fulfill its mission and achieve its vision. As Ron Edmonds stated, "We know all that we need to know to effectively educate children." Our problem is not "knowing." Our problem is "using" what we know as a foundation to engage in the process of doing. Relevant research should always represent one of the primary components of the school's vision. In fact, a focus on research should happen within two distinct places: First, at the beginning (Vision) as a framework for focusing our efforts and resources; secondly, at the end (Assessment) as a measure of our efforts and the utilization of our resources. The

Notes:

problem in many school communities is that it doesn't happen at all. Subsequently, when our efforts at reform fail, we play the blame game. "We didn't have enough money. We had too many restrictions. Parents didn't support our efforts. Children were unmotivated. We didn't have enough planning time. Our books and materials were outdated. Our school day was too long or too short or too something!" Stop the insanity and develop a strategy-focused team to identify the research that is relevant to your school and relevant to your vision of the school that you are attempting to develop. In addition to the framework that research studies provide, each school community must also engage in its own ongoing in-school data gathering, analysis, evaluation, and assessment.

"Rather than being driven by stereotypes, mis-perceptions, or the history of our school, lets look at the data."

Research is essential to depersonalizing problems, thereby focusing on the problems and not on the people. For example, common to low-achieving schools are high numbers of discipline problems (i.e., fighting, vandalism, disrespect for authority, and disregard for school policies) and office referrals. In such schools, a review of the demographic and statistical data frequently reveals that:

- a disproportionate percentage of office referrals and suspensions are African-American or Latino males who live in poverty; and

- a disproportionate percentage of those office referrals are made by white, middle class, female teachers.

  Student's perspective: *She doesn't like me and she is always trying to embarrass me in front of my friends.*

  Teacher's perspective: *These children have no respect for authority.*

The obvious challenge facing such school communities is to depersonalize the problem and focus on the data rather than playing the blame game.

By focusing on the data rather than blaming the people we are more likely to conceptualize staff development needs for teachers and intervention strategies for students.

Teacher needs:

- *Cross-gender, -cultural, -socioeconomic communication techniques.*

- *Techniques for dealing with confrontational students.*

- *Classroom management.*

- *Creating more on-task time within the classroom.*

- *Building relationships within the classroom.*

- *Developing effective cooperative grouping.*

- *Understanding children living in poverty.*

Notes:

Student needs:

- *Developing positive relationships with adults and other students.*

- *Becoming connected to the school community, e.g., sports, clubs, student government, before/after school programs, etc.*

- *Developing effective home-school communication.*

- *Developing a long-term context to process current decisions.*

- *Learning how to productively and proactively manage behaviors.*

A proactive approach to cultivating more positive and less confrontational student behaviors might lead to developing intervention strategies for students, and utilizing relationships between students and other teachers, mentors, coaches, administrators, counselors, business partners, and parents to encourage more positive self-directed behavior within the classroom.

Create staff discussion groups as a means of exploring ideas and strategies to help you to achieve your vision.

Finally, we might establish a book club that provides a forum for teachers to read and discuss the issues and intervention strategies pertinent to those students most likely to be referred to the office and/or suspended from school:

- *Empowering African-American Males to Succeed: A Ten Step Approach for Parents and Teachers* [*Wynn*]

- *The Eagles who Thought They were Chickens* [*Wynn*]

- *Inspired to Learn: Why We Must Give Children Hope* [*Peters*]

- *A Framework for Understanding Poverty* [*Payne*]

- *Why Are All of The Black Children Sitting Together in The Cafeteria?* [*Tatum*]

Whether these, or other strategies are employed, the focus must shift from the people to the problem. Pertinent data must be gathered, appropriate training and/or resource materials must be identified, and pertinent research must be identified to help develop proactive strategies.

Formal research, such as the following summary of the *Texas Successful School-wide Research Study* and the *Urban Schools Research Study* can provide a valuable barometer to measure your school's current practices, culture, programs, and policies. While the data gathered in both research studies came from largely high poverty schools, the conclusions of the studies represent practices and strategies appropriate for all schools interested in high student achievement.

At the end of each school year we must plan to gather and evaluate all of the pertinent data which impacts upon our school community. Our in-school data, together with valid research studies, should be used to guide our pre-planning efforts. As a matter of course, the end of each school year

Notes:

should conclude with a critical assessment and evaluation of our policies, programs, and practices. The questions that must be raised are:

1.   Were our policies, programs, and practices effective?

2.   Did they assist in our efforts to fulfill our mission and achieve our vision?

3.   Were they consistent with relevant research (whether national or in-school studies)?

The Texas Research

The *Texas Successful School-wide Research Study* is an excellent barometer to measure a school's efforts toward increasing student achievement.

How many of the seven themes commonly shared by the high achieving schools identified in the study are currently existing within your school?

The first commonly-shared theme outlined in the study deals with the mission/vision of the school:

A focus on the academic success of every student was articulated through a fundamental belief that they (teachers) could succeed with every child, 'These schools did not simply have mission statements, their sense of mission was articulated in every aspect of their planning, organization, and use of resources.'

An examination of the seven themes that are reflected within the Texas research study provides an invaluable frame of reference for developing strategies and implementation approaches for any school community. As you review the research that follows, place a check next to those themes that you believe are currently reflected and in practice within your school.

Research Summary

Successful Texas School-wide Programs: Research Study Results
The Charles A. Dana Center, University of Texas at Austin (1996)
(Dr. Laura Lein, Dr. Joseph F. Johnson, Jr., Mary Ragland)

In the 1994-95 school year, over 50 schools with over 60% of children on free or reduced lunch (most with over 75%) were identified among the highest achieving schools within the state. The schools received Title I funds and were at various stages of implementing Title I school-wide programs.

In the Spring of 1995, in each school, at least 70% of their students passed the reading and mathematics sections of the Texas Assessment of Academic Skills (TAAS). At the time of the study, few Texas schools had reached this level of academic achievement. Of the over 50 schools, 26 in diverse settings, from 18 educational regions within the state were selected for the research study which included interviews and observations with school personnel, parents, community members, and students.

Before describing what we found, it is probably important to describe what was not found. First, if there is a magic formula, a simple prescription or a miracle program that makes all the difference, we did not find it. We found more differences than similarities in the instructional programs and approaches used in the 26 schools.

Some schools used whole language approaches, while others focused on phonics. Some were making cutting edge uses of instructional technology, while in others, computer technology was virtually absent in instruction. Some of the schools had joined Henry Levin's Accelerated Schools Project. Some were becoming engaged in the Success for All Program from John Hopkins University. Some were using Reading Recovery approaches. Others seemed to take pride in not having a clear allegiance to any specific program or methodology. Following are the common characteristics, or themes, of the schools studied:

Notes:

Theme 1: Focus on the Academic Success of Every Student.

Many studies of effective schools emphasized the extent to which successful schools shared a common mission [Texas Education Agency, 1989]. A study of 12 successful Title I school-wide projects [U.S. Department of Education, 1994] found that the schools had an agreed-upon vision for all students that was based on higher academic standards.

In all of the 26 schools studied, there was a strong focus on the academic success of every student.

- *These schools did not simply have Mission Statements, their sense of mission was articulated in every aspect of their planning, organization, and use of resources.*

- *Almost every decision about the selection of instructional materials; staff development; use of resources; scheduling of the school calendar; assignment of teachers, support personnel, and volunteers; and use of space was guided by a focus on the mission of ensuring the academic success of every student.*

- *Instructional approaches were chosen because they believed that the particular approach would be effective in meeting the specific needs of their students and in utilizing the unique strengths of their staff and community.*

- *Formal and informal methods were used to collect and analyze information regarding the policies, programs, and practices most likely to result in improved academic achievement.*

- *"What's best for kids?" was heard repeatedly as a benchmark for making decisions.*

- *Teachers planned lessons with a focus on getting each and every student to succeed academically. Teachers were attuned to the special ways in which individual students learned best.*

- *A conscious effort was made to align the curriculum with the objectives of the TAAS. Teachers knew the objectives and identified the most effective instructional approaches.*

- *Teachers felt supported with adequate instructional materials and relevant staff development.*

- *Everyone had a role in actualizing the school's mission.*

Notes:

Theme 2: No Excuses.

These schools did not accept excuses for the failure of any student. Educators at these schools tended to believe that they could succeed with any student. Ultimately, there were no excuses for low performance. Teachers never accepted that the difficult situation (of students) was a reason to lower their academic expectations, but instead, engaged in creative efforts to respond to the unique situations of students:

- *Calling students' homes to provide wake-up calls.*

- *Allowing students to take extra portions of lunch home so that they would have dinner.*

- *Teaching parents how to read to their children.*

- *Developing partnerships with businesses and community services.*

- *Establishing priorities in respect to expenditures to ensure that scarce resources were focused on student achievement.*

- *Rules and policies were continually assessed and re-assessed for their impact on student achievement.*

- *There was a continual focus on improvement rather than assigning blame.*

- *High student expectations were accompanied by high teacher expectations.*

- *Everyone internalized as their "job" to ensure student success.*

Theme 3: Experimentation.

Educators felt such strong responsibility for ensuring the academic success of students that they eagerly sought ways to improve teaching and learning. As teachers and administrators engaged in experimentation, they also encouraged students to experiment and to identify new ways to accomplish tasks. If an approach was not working with one student or any group of students, teachers were allowed, encouraged, and even expected, to try different approaches. Thus, experimentation flourished as individual teachers, grade-level teams, site-based decision-making teams, and entire school staffs considered new ways to stimulate the achievement of students:

- *Teachers performed pilot tests of materials or strategies before adoption by the entire school.*

- *Teachers experimented with the organization of the school day, use of technology, use of intersessions, and the assignment of support staff.*

- *Teachers encouraged student experimentation and innovation.*

- *Students were taught that failure is just a step that sometimes precedes success.*

Notes:

Theme 4: Inclusion.

Everyone is a part of the solution. In the schools we studied, it seemed that everyone who came in contact with a student was a partner in ensuring that student's academic success (i.e., regular/special ed. teachers, nurses, counselors, bus drivers, administrators, custodians, office staff, cafeteria workers, instructional aides, librarians, parent volunteers, part-time personnel, community leaders, and other students). Everyone who worked at the school, attended the school or who sent children to attend the school had a strong sense of ownership:

- *Everyone was recognized as a part of the team to ensure student success.*

- *The broadly-defined roles allowed many individuals to assume leadership roles.*

- *Multi-faceted outreach was developed to make parents partners in their child's success.*

- *Open-door policies and open-door attitudes were common.*

- *School personnel assumed responsibility for creating an environment in which parents wanted to become involved.*

- *Students were involved in cooperative learning or peer tutoring strategies in which they worked together to facilitate their learning.*

Theme 5: Sense of Family.

Overwhelmingly, the most common metaphor observed in the schools was the school as a family. Statements such as, "We're a family here," or "These are all my children," were heard frequently. The actions of teachers, principals, students, parents, and other members of the school community frequently reflected the concern, dedication, involvement, respect, and love that one would expect to find in the healthiest of families.

- *Students were treated with respect and concern.*

- *Teachers were concerned with the child's total development beyond the performance on the TAAS (e.g., music, art, physical education, etc.).*

- *Attention was given to children's social and emotional needs.*

- *School activities, bulletin boards, and curriculum materials were consciously directed at reflecting and celebrating the cultural and*  *linguistic diversity of students.*

- *Hallways, classrooms, doors, and ceilings were used to display student work.*

- *Academic and non-academic accomplishments were consciously celebrated.*

- *School climate was consciously cultivated to provide a safe place for growing and learning.*

- *Adults behaved in ways that communicated that they were happy that the students were there.*

Notes:

- *Discipline was enforced consistently, quickly, fairly, and in a manner that demonstrated respect for the the individual student.*

- *Staff consciously minimized the use of labels.*

- *Special programs were located or organized in ways that minimized the separation or stigmatization of students.*

- *Parents were greeted warmly and provided with a special place to make them comfortable in the school.*

- *Parent communication consciously took into account parents' languages, dialects, and backgrounds.*

- *All school personnel, regardless of position or tenure, were perceived as important members of the school family.*

- *Schools consciously sought ways to utilize the personal and professional strengths of staff members, beyond their traditional job descriptions.*

Theme 6: Collaboration and Trust.

Openness, honesty, and trust characterized most of the interaction among school personnel. School personnel openly shared concerns and successes with each other. Teachers seemed to prefer working in teams and did so frequently.

- *Teachers provided assistance to each other and learned from each other.*

- *Schools cultivated an atmosphere where teachers felt free to express their concerns about ideas or actions without fear of reprisal.*

- *While schools worked together as teams, they respected the rights of individuals to disagree.*

- *Teachers felt comfortable sharing their weaknesses.*

- *The collaboration extended across subject areas, "If you can help me with my math lessons, I'll help you with social studies."*

- *Teachers collaborated with other grade levels (even when that grade level extended to a different school) to develop an understanding of each other's curricula and expectations.*

- *Formal and informal forums were established to discuss policies and programs.*

- *Planning time was consciously developed to achieve the mission.*

Notes:

Theme 7: Passion for Learning and Growing.

Although schools clearly took time to celebrate their successes, there was almost an immediate redefinition of higher goals. In these schools, there is continuous seeking of new horizons, new opportunities, new ways of operating. The process of discovery and learning on the part of all participants is considered the central business of the school.

- *Professional development was not an event at these schools, it was a part of the culture, a part of the way of life.*

- *Teachers were constantly attempting to lift greater numbers of students to higher achievement levels.*

- *The pressure to achieve was almost entirely self-imposed.*

- *Learning activities were continually aligned with school improvement plans.*

- *Staff members attended conferences, visited effective schools, and observed promising programs.*

- *Teachers shared journal articles and discussed educational literature that enriched their discussions about how to improve.*

- *The frequent analysis of data led to the adoption of new approaches that built upon the successes of individual teachers or groups of teachers.*

- *Teachers were learning as much about teaching as their students were learning about reading and mathematics.*

- *Parents and students were partners in learning and demonstrated an eagerness to grow intellectually.*

- *There was constant reaffirmation, support, and validation of learning throughout the school community.*

Many of the Texas themes are echoed within the school communities studied in the *Hope for Urban Education: A Study of Nine High-Performing, High-Poverty, Urban Elementary Schools.*

We must pay particular attention to the common strategies that are reflected within the attitudes and behaviors of the administrators, teachers, and support staff within those schools studied.

Research Summary

Hope for Urban Education:
A Study of Nine High-Performing, High-Poverty, Urban Elementary Schools

This report is about nine urban elementary schools that served children of color in poor communities and achieved impressive academic results. These schools have attained higher levels of achievement than most schools in their states or most schools in the nation. They have achieved results in reading and mathematics beyond that achieved in some suburban schools.

All nine schools used federal Title I dollars to create Title I school-wide programs and shared the following characteristics:

- The majority of students met low-income criteria. In some of the schools, at least 80 percent of the students met low-income criteria.

- The school was located in an urban area and did not have selective admission policies.

- Student achievement in mathematics and reading was higher than the average of all schools in the state (or higher than the 50th percentile if a national-normed assessment was used). At least three years of assessment data were available to gauge the school's progress.

- There was no evidence that the school exempted large percentages of students from participation in the assessment program because of language proficiency or disabilities.

- The school and district leaders consented to participation in the study in a timely manner.

The nine schools, representing nine states, were different in important ways. These differences suggest that many urban elementary schools serving poor communities can achieve high levels of student achievement. Also, the differences suggest that schools may be able to achieve academic successes through different means. Some of the differences observed included the following:

Notes:

- *Student enrollment ranged from 283 to 1,171.*

- *Although all of the schools served elementary grades, they had different grade level configurations, starting as early as pre-kindergarten and ending as late as grade eight.*

- *Student demographics varied. At six of the nine schools, most students were African-American. At one school, most students were Hispanic, and at another most were Asian-American.*

- *Only two of the schools used nationally-known comprehensive school reform models; one used the "Accelerated School Program" and another used "Success for All."*

- *Even though none of the schools would have been considered high-performing based on achievement data from five years ago, some of the schools made dramatic improvement over a three or four-year period, whereas others took five years or longer before experiencing dramatic gains in student achievement.*

- *In a few cases, the district office played a major role in the school's improvement efforts. In contrast, there were other cases where the district played a modest role in the improvement process.*

- *A few of the schools managed to make dramatic improvements without great turnover in teaching personnel. In contrast, some schools experienced substantial teacher turnover during the reform process.*

Common Strategies

Beyond these differences, there were important similarities in the strategies used to improve academic achievement. The following strategies were used by many of the nine schools:

- *School leaders identified and pursued an important, visible, yet attainable, first goal. They focused on the attainment of this first goal, achieved success, and then used their success to move toward more ambitious goals.*

Notes:

- *School leaders redirected time and energy that was being spent on conflicts between adults in the school toward service to children. Leaders appealed to teachers, support staff, and parents to put aside their own interests and focus on serving children well.*

- *Educators fostered in students a sense of responsibility for appropriate behavior and they created an environment in which students were likely to behave well. Discipline problems became rare as the schools implemented multi-faceted approaches for helping students learn responsibility for their own behavior.*

- *School leaders created a collective sense of responsibility for school improvement. The shared sense of responsibility was nurtured by joint planning processes and reinforced by efforts to involve everyone in key components of the school's work.*

- *The quantity and quality of time spent on instructional leadership activities increased. Principals spent more time helping teachers attend to instructional issues and decreased the time teachers spent on distractions that diverted attention away from teaching and learning. Also, principals put other educators in positions that allowed them to provide instructional leadership. School leaders constantly challenged teachers and students to higher levels of academic attainment. They used data to identify, acknowledge, and celebrate strengths and to focus attention and resources on areas of need.*

- *Educators aligned instruction to the standards and assessments required by the state or the school district. Teachers and administrators worked together to understand precisely what students were expected to know and be able to do. Then, they planned instruction to ensure that students would have an excellent chance to learn what was expected of them.*

- *School leaders got the resources and training that teachers perceived they needed to get their students to achieve at high levels. In particular, school leaders made sure that teachers felt like they had adequate materials, equipment, and professional development.*

- *School leaders created opportunities for teachers to work, plan, and learn together around instructional issues. Time was structured to ensure that collaboration around instructional issues became an important part of the school day and the school week.*

- *Educators made efforts to win the confidence and respect of parents, primarily by improving the achievement of students. Then educators built strong partnerships with parents in support of student achievement.*

- *School leaders created additional time for instruction. In some cases, efforts focused on creating additional time for attention to critical instructional issues during the school day. In other cases, efforts focused on creating additional time beyond the regular school day.*

- *Educators persisted through difficulties, setbacks, and failures. In spite of challenges and frustrations, school leaders did not stop trying to improve their schools.*

The successful approach to cultivating sustained, systemic increases in student achievement must take into account all available effective schools research. Yet, despite the plethora of current research of what leads to high achieving schools, teachers, administrators, support staff, and parents must engage in the process of conceptualizing strategies which respond to the unique needs of each school community. There are no cookie cutter formulas, no one-size fits all, no quick fixes, and no short cuts.

While the research may guide your way, the final ownership of the mission, vision, beliefs, implementation strategies and strategic plans of each school community rests with the teachers and support staff in partnership with parents, mentors, business partners and the students themselves, who, ultimately, must take ownership of their own learning.

Notes:

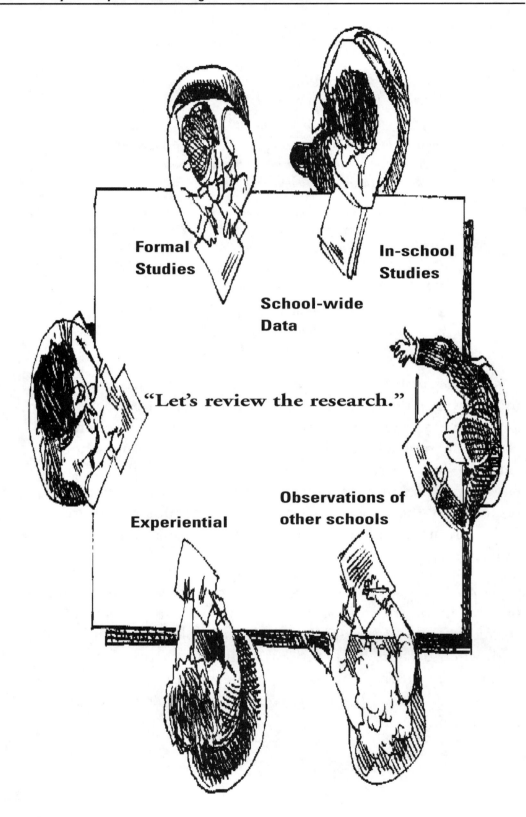

Discussion Questions

1. Review the seven themes common to the high achieving schools outlined in the Texas Successful School-wide Research Study (p. 173) and discuss which themes are currently reflected in your school-wide practices and are internalized as part of your school's culture and/or core values.

2. Which one of the seven themes represents the strongest theme in your school? Which represents the weakest?

3. Review the common practices in the Hope for Urban Education Research Study (p. 184) and discuss which practices are currently reflected in your school, grade level, subject area, department, or extracurricular activity.

4. In the Hope for Urban Education Research Study it was noted that schools identified an achievable first goal. What would be the achievable first goal that you would like for your school, grade level, department, or program to establish?

5. What strategies can your team, department, or program conceptualize, take ownership of, and operationalize to ensure that this goal is achieved?

6. How will you monitor your progress and assess your success?

7. Identify opportunities to engage your student in assisting or supporting these efforts.

Chapter 5

Statements about vision incorporate the values and commitments that guide the system as well as beliefs about structure. These statements appeal to hearts as well as to minds; they command loyalty and emotional attachments and provide orientation for specific action. Vision statements, if they are important, are not intended to be realistic but to be inspiring. They describe conditions to be realized and give a basis for determining the merit and worth of particular missions, the desirability of particular goals, and morality of particular actions. Vision is important, but without deeply held and well-articulated beliefs, it is "as sounding brass, or tinkling cymbal."

— Inventing Better Schools

Beliefs, Values, & Guiding Principles

Now that your Mission and Vision have been written, what are your beliefs? Your statement of beliefs must articulate the core values or guiding principles needed to pave the way toward achieving your vision and fulfilling your mission. The research on high achieving schools will prove a valuable resource in shaping the core values and guiding principles of the school community. Are the beliefs, core values, and guiding principles of your school community reflective of those beliefs which are common in high achieving schools? Are your core values consistent with what will be needed to achieve your vision and fulfill your mission?

Stephen Covey, in his book, *Principal-Centered Leadership*, states:

Principles are not invented by us or by society; they are the laws of the universe that pertain to human relationships and human organizations. They are part of the human condition, consciousness, and conscience. To the degree people recognize and live in harmony with such basic principles as fairness, equity, justice, integrity, honesty, and trust, they move toward either survival and stability on the one hand or disintegration and destruction on the other.

Core Values or Guiding Principles should be those words or phrases that are embodied within your Statement of Beliefs.

Review the listing of common core values (pages 195-197) and identify those values that embody the guiding principles that would provide the compass for creating your school's or classroom's statement of beliefs. Such guiding principles might be stated as:

- Each stakeholder within our school community must be **accountable** for student achievement.

- Each stakeholder within our school community must demonstrate the **courage** needed to become an advocate for our students.

Covey goes on to comment:

Correct principles are like compasses: they are always pointing the way. And if we know how to read them, we won't get lost, confused, or fooled by conflicting voices and values. Principles are self-evident, self-validating natural laws. They don't change or shift. They provide 'true north' direction to our lives when navigating the 'streams' of our environments.

Many of the needed core values or guiding principles are probably implied, if not explicitly stated, in your statement of beliefs. Some of the language that may find its way into your statement of beliefs are:

Notes:

- *courage*

- *collaboration*

- *compassion*

- *honesty*

- *trustworthiness*

- *integrity*

- *respect*

- *responsibility*

Core values or guiding principles provide a consistent compass despite adversity and hardship.

Your statement of beliefs should contain language that can be used to shape your discussions, guide your actions, and cultivate an ethical school community.

Every school community (and classroom within each school community) must develop a set of core or ethical values that define how people and ideas are to be treated. These core values or ethical standards must exist to frame the ensuing discussions, share opinions, and engage in the rigorous debate of the strategies and solutions needed to increase student achievement and cultivate an emotionally- and socially-nurturing environment for students and teachers.

I believe that the greatest of all core values as it relates to the education of our children is *Courage*. I believe that the greatest of all guiding principles related to the transformation of school communities on behalf of our children is *Collaboration*.

The phrase that embodies the spirit of collaboration is, "How can I help?" One of the themes previously outlined in the *Texas Successful School-wide Research Study* was, "Collaboration and Trust." This theme was found to exist within each of the high achieving schools studied. Sustained, systemic, and holistic school transformation is impossible without it. As you structure teams and empower individuals to focus their energies, creative, and intellectual capacities toward solving the complex problems confronting your school community, the phrase, "How can I help?" must be heard more commonly than, "Why do we have to do that?" or "Why are you suggesting that we do it that way?" You might consider posting the phrase, "How can I help?" throughout your school community. Cultivating the spirit of collaboration and trust is integral to successfully developing and implementing solutions to the challenges ahead.

How can I help?

On the following page are the core values, from a curriculum entitled, *The Eagle Team: A Leadership Curriculum,* designed as a specific intervention strategy to cultivate leadership skills within both high and low academically achieving students. The values taught to students through the curriculum provide an excellent framework for initiating discussion of the core values to be articulated and embraced by your school community. Avoid the tendency to assume that students, parents, and the surrounding community shares certain values. Also, avoid the propensity to assume that the negative values demonstrated through the behavior of students implies that positive values haven't been taught at home.

The core values or guiding principles of each school community provides a reference point for the school as the United States Constitution provides a reference point for the nation. No matter which political party is in control, no matter which direction public opinion is leaning, no matter how heated the discussions and vehement the disagreements, the United States Constitution provides a compass for where

Notes:

we are going and how we are to conduct ourselves as a nation; not always perfect, not always just, but always providing a reference point to measure our direction and to provide us with a compass to guide our way. Always to be measured by, "Is this in the best interest of the American people?"

Core Values & Guiding Principles

Accountability. *To be accountable and to accept responsibility for ones conduct or actions.*

Citizenship. *Performing the duties and responsibilities in accordance with the rights of a person recognized as a member (citizen) of a community or government.*

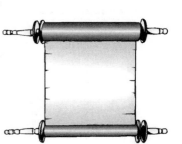

Collaboration. *To work together toward some common goal or objective.*

Commitment. *To accept responsibility and apply oneself to the successful completion of a task or action.*

Community Service. *To make a valuable contribution to uplifting, edifying or supporting the quality of life for others.*

Compassion. *To demonstrate human kindness toward the plight and needs of others.*

Conscience. *The sense of moral goodness regarding one's own conduct, intentions or character, together with a feeling of obligation to do right or to be good; a sensitive regard for fairness or justice.*

Consequences. *The resulting effect of one's choices or actions.*

Courage. *Firmness of mind and spirit in the face of great difficulty. The mental or moral strength to persevere in the face of opposition, danger, fear, or hardship. To stand firm for one's principles or beliefs despite criticism, difficulty, or opposition.*

Determination. *To demonstrate firmness of purpose and to display personal resolve at completing a task or reaching a decision.*

Dignity. *To carry oneself with honor and respect.*

Diligence. *The steady, careful, and persistent effort that one devotes to his or her work, duties or responsibilities.*

Fairness. *To demonstrate a sense of justice that is impartial, free of favoritism or bias that is consistent with rules, logic, or ethics.*

Notes:

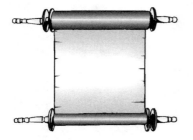

Fortitude. *The ability to exhibit courage in the midst of great pain or adversity.*

Honesty. *To demonstrate fairness, justice, and truthfulness in character and behavior.*

Initiative. *To demonstrate the ability to take action, begin a task, or create a plan on one's own accord without being directed by others.*

Integrity. *To adhere to a code of moral or artistic values. To demonstrate language and behaviors that are guided by honesty and the quality of incorruptibility.*

Justice. *To demonstrate the fundamental principle of moral rightness in attitude or actions. To uphold what is just and in accordance with honor, standards, or the law.*

Kindness. *To demonstrate affection, helpfulness, or sympathy toward others.*

Perseverance. *To remain steadfast in the pursuit of one's goals or a particular course of action, belief, or purpose.*

Persistent. *To refuse to give up or let go of one's goals and objectives. To obstinately endure despite challenges and obstacles.*

Reflection. *The honest, inward focus and evaluation of one's actions, behaviors, and experiences.*

Resilience. *The ability to continue toward a goal or objective in spite of challenges, obstacles, misfortune or circumstances beyond one's control.*

Respect. *To demonstrate appreciation for, and consideration of others. To demonstrate conduct toward another that conveys a high sense of moral value or appreciation.*

Responsibility. *To accept accountability for one's conduct and actions. The ability to make moral or rational decisions and to be answerable for one's behavior.*

Restraint. *To demonstrate the ability to intelligently and responsibly control one's actions.*

Trustworthiness. *Actions and mannerisms that inspire the confidence of others in one's reliability. Deserving of the trust of others.*

Truthfulness. *Being sincere in actions, character, and what is being stated; a conscious attempt to honestly state or acknowledge the truth.*

The Ethical Standard of Excellence

You cannot cultivate a school of excellence without having the passion to do so. The pursuit of excellence will cause you to confront the issues within your school community that are hindering student achievement. The honest and passionate pursuit of developing effective strategies and solutions requires that you factor yourself into the equation. You cannot attribute all failings on the school board, superintendent, central office, principal, classroom teacher, parents, students or the society at-large. While there are certainly issues that can be attributed to each of these areas or individuals, the creative capacity to solve many of the problems lies within each of us.

Whether you are the principal, classroom teacher, parent or student, are you doing all that you can to help your school become a school of excellence?

You cannot pursue excellence without honesty and integrity. For many, this will be a painful experience. You will be forced to confront your own biases, stereotypes, and long-held beliefs regarding why children are failing, why classrooms are out of control, why parents don't want to become involved in the school, and why there are such negative discussions in the teacher's lounge. This experience is so painful that many people within school communities refuse to look at the data or publicly share the data.

Once you objectively look at the data and engage in an assessment of the issues and obstacles unique to your school community, you realize that these children are not failing in all schools. So why are they failing in your school?

In 1998, at a county-wide meeting of Pinellas County Schools (Florida) administrators, I responded to a question from a principal in which he asked, 'How can we increase minority student achievement without increasing parental involvement?' In my response to the question, I stated that in my experience, whenever we raise the question, of increasing parental involvement, we rarely mean meaningful parental involvement.

Therein lies much of our problem. Parents are interested in becoming partners in their child's success. However, in many school communities we are not seeking partners.

I gave the example of my attempt to become a partner with my son's fifth grade teacher, a white female, who, from my observations, could use better classroom management and cooperative grouping, particularly given the fact that the majority of her office referrals were African-American males.

I went on to outline how I volunteered to provide a classroom demonstration of cooperative grouping based on Myers-Briggs personality type preferences during which the teacher graded papers rather than observe the demonstration. I also commented that I had provided his teacher with resource materials and agreed to meet and discuss possible strategies to increase student achievement, particularly the achievement of minority boys, none of which she appeared particularly receptive to.

I went on to comment that my son was the only African-American male enrolled in the fifth grade Talented and Gifted program, and, the only African-American male to consistently qualify for the Honor Roll in her classroom.

Many of the administrators in attendance were outraged that I had shared the real data and articulated the honest perspective of a parent being served by the district. Thusly, the core value of Honesty was not one which was highly-valued by many of those in attendance. And, after experiencing a large number of administrators who approached me to indicate their support of my comments, they themselves, did not have the Courage to articulate what they themselves know to be a systemic failing throughout the district to move more African-American children into Talented and Gifted programs and the deplorable numbers of African-American children who were routinely placed into special education.

Despite their outrage, when my son graduated from the fifth grade, his elementary school lost 100% of its African-American male representation in the fifth grade Talented and Gifted program. Without clear core values or guiding principles it is impossible for a school or school district to move beyond the rhetoric of "talking about student achievement" to implementing plans and practices to actually "increase student achievement." Until such values as courage, integrity, honesty, and truthfulness guide the school toward reviewing instructional and classroom management practices, and gathering and assessing achievement and discipline data, it is unlikely to engage in the process of conceptualizing operational strategies that will lead to measurable progress toward closing the respective achievement gaps.

The state of North Carolina was one of only two states in the country in 2001 to measurably close the achievement gap. Two of the eleven recommendations from the state task force on closing the achievement gap specifically outlined a focus on measurably increasing culturally- and economically-specific groups in higher level classes and decreasing their representation in special education.

The North Carolina Commission on Raising Achievement and Closing Gaps stated:

> **Recommendation One:** *that the state take steps to reduce, then eliminate the disproportionate number of minority students assigned to special education programs. As a part of the ABCs reporting process, require that schools provide descriptive data, in table format, that will allow for comparisons between the percentage of students assigned to the various categorical special education programs in school districts with state averages in those same categories, and with the rates of incidence of the various handicapping conditions in the general population of our nation.*

> **Recommendation Two:** *that the state recognize its obligation to ensure that students have an equal opportunity to learn by promoting, encouraging, and funding instructional approaches that expose minority students currently functioning at or near grade level to advanced content, challenging strategies, and quality work, thus increasing the number of minority students to perform at the highest levels on standardized and end-of-grade tests.*

[First Report to the State Board of Education]

To meet these recommendations schools will be forced to embrace them in their mission and reflect them in their vision. In this way they will be guided to gather and assess all pertinent data and earnestly listen to the opinions of the school's stakeholders. You cannot embrace the mission of educating children and avoid the data or be offended by the opinions of stakeholders within your school community. With proper core values and guiding principles to guide their way, teachers and administrators will no longer be outraged that parents point out the achievement gaps, but will be outraged that there is a gap to be pointed out.

The Statement of Beliefs

The school's statement of beliefs provide the standards by which the school proceeds toward fulfilling the mission and achieving the vision.

Statement of Beliefs: This statement may also be guided by the district's or State's Statement of Beliefs. The statement of beliefs should be the barometer against which all discipline decisions, peer mediation, staff-administration interaction, and student-teacher-parent interactions are measured.

Examples of school-wide belief statements:

We believe:

> *in respect for the individual and for the rights and property of others within our school community;*

> *in school-wide collaboration and that all policies, programs, procedures, and decisions must be measured against, 'Is this in the best interests of our students?';*

> *that effective school-community partnerships are needed to ensure that we acquire the necessary resources to ensure the highest levels of student achievement; and*

> *in holding students, teachers, and support staff to the highest standards and that our motto is 'Excellence without compromise!'*

Notes:

A school's core values and guiding principles provide a framework for discussing, debating, deciding, and determining how the school navigates its way along the educational continuum toward fulfilling its mission.

On the following pages are examples of some of the statements of beliefs and guiding principles that schools have developed in support of their respective missions/visions.

The Harry Daniels Primary Center

Notes:

Our Beliefs

We believe that it is our collective responsibility to motivate, encourage and support children; and to create a positive and productive learning environment conducive to achievement of skills essential to constructive living.

Mt. Bethel Elementary School

Our Beliefs

- The learning environment will be a place of mutual respect.
- Our students are entitled to a highly challenging curriculum tailored to meet their innate abilities.
- The staff, parents, students, and involved community members are best qualified to plan the implementation of an appropriate educational program.
- Teachers, administrators, and staff have the obligation to stay abreast of the research concerning children, how they learn, and what they need to know.
- The materials and methods will be responsive to the needs, interests, abilities, and talents of the students.
- Parental involvement in the planning, implementation, and assessment of the educational program is vital.
- A consistency of expectations between home and school is necessary.
- The allocation of resources and choice of materials, curriculum, staff development, and scheduling will be done with the specific needs of Mt. Bethel's population as the determining factor.

Notes:

John Hopkins Middle School

Our Beliefs

- **We believe that our efforts must be guided by the JHMS Vision and that every decision must ultimately be measured against, 'Is this in the best interests of our students?'**

- **We believe in respect for the individual.**

- **We believe in a safe school community that promotes positive and constructive behavior.**

- **We believe in fostering a climate of collaboration, communication and compassion for each individual within the JHMS community.**

- **We believe in seeking every opportunity to recognize, validate and celebrate the achievements of our students and staff.**

- **We believe in the right of every individual to be nurtured and encouraged in the pursuit of his or her dreams and aspirations.**

Once the beliefs are stated, each school is challenged with making them operational. This can only occur when they are constantly referred to in discussions of strategies, in debates of issues, and during the enforcement of discipline policies. "Are the policies that we're implementing or the decisions that we're making consistent with our stated beliefs?" Teachers, administrators, and support personnel must continually reference the school's stated beliefs until they are ingrained within their consciousness. Only at that point will the stated beliefs become operational and the school community become ethically driven and principle-centered.

Discussion Questions

1. What are the beliefs, core values or guiding principles that support your school's vision?

2. Where are they posted, how are they taught, and what customs, rituals, and traditions reinforce them?

3. List three core values that define your current school-wide climate and culture.

4. List three core values that define each of the following: teacher-student; teacher-parent; teacher-teacher; and staff-administrator relationships.

5. What are the current current cultural norms or values communicated within your department/ program that pertain to academic achievement?

6. Discuss the values, beliefs, and expectations that you would like to define your school, department, program, and/or activity.

7. Discuss the customs, rituals, and traditions currently existing, or that should be created, to communicate and reinforce these values.

8. List the major curriculum components, thematic units, grade-level, or school-wide practices that are utilized to teach these values.

9. What three values do you believe have reached a level of consciousness within your school community that they are unconsciously referred to when making decisions regarding students and families?

Notes:

Chapter 6

Strategy does not (or should not) stand as a management process. A continuum exists that begins in the broadest sense, with the mission of the organization. The mission must be translated so that the actions of individuals are aligned and supportive of the mission. A management system should ensure that this translation is effectively made. Strategy is one step in a logical continuum that moves an organization from a high-level mission statement to the work performed by front-line and back-office employees.

— *The Strategy-Focused Organization*

From Plans to Practices

The five previous chapters have outlined philosophical and practical approaches to establishing goals and developing solutions to the unique needs of any school community. Each school travels along the educational continuum, albeit high or low performing, rural or suburban, serving affluent children or children who live in poverty. However, once the Mission, Vision, Statement of Beliefs, and Core Values are developed, the challenge that a school now faces is, "How do we make them operational?"

There is no shortage of paper within school communities throughout the country. There are, and have been, all types of initiatives and new directives from the school board or the superintendent. There have been School Improvement Plans, Curriculum Initiatives, Staff Development, Business partnerships, and annual themes. School districts' missions have hung prominently in front offices and yet, school communities have been unsuccessful at achieving the goals outlined in their respective School Improvement Plans or at embodying their missions within school cultures, relying on it as a framework to guide their efforts. Why will this time be any different?

If you want to fulfill your mission and realize your vision, you must:

- learn as much as you can about the students and the communities you serve;

- take this information into account as you establish qualitative or quantitative goals for each component of your vision; and

- develop a Strategy-Focused Team for each component of your vision, charged with *conceptualizing and implementing* the necessary operational strategies.

Who are the Students and Communities You Serve?

Poverty is no excuse for failure. Every school community is challenged with identifying, understanding, and preparing to serve the real needs of students and families. In one school community, student issues revolve around mental health concerns such as anxiety disorders, anorexia, high divorce rates or absentee fathers who are white collar workers, who put in long hours or travel frequently. In another school community, students are confronted with gangs, violence, families living in poverty, and large numbers of students living in female-headed single parent households. In another, students are not native speakers of English, families are transient, and parents are migrant workers.

Notes:

An analysis of the data and demographics of each school community would reveal that some schools are experiencing:

- low standardized test scores;

- low ACT/SAT scores;

- low percentage of students who pass the end-of-grade assessments;

- high numbers of students who are below grade level in expected academic achievement;

- low high school graduation rates; and

- a high number of teen pregnancies.

On the other hand, other school communities have a high percentage of students graduating from high school and performing well on standardized testing. However, their issues are:

- substance abuse;

- suicides;

- depression;

- anxiety-related disorders; and

- such a rigorous academic focus that students are precluded from participation in extra and co-curricular activities or engaging in community/ service projects.

If our intent is to identify and understand the unique needs of each school community and the unique demographics of the children and families served by each school community, our data gathering, problem identification and analysis, and implementation strategies will create a better chance for truly serving children.

Parents don't keep "Their Best" at home. Whomever they have is who they send to school. Parents don't get to choose which child learns easily and which one struggles. They have to love and teach them both. So, too, do we.

Do You Understand Poverty?

The Center for the Study of Poverty at Columbia University reports that in 1996, one out of four individuals [one in three Latino children] under the age of 18 was living in poverty. As the student populations of schools become more and more impoverished the teacher population becomes more and more middle class. As the student population becomes more and more reflective of children of color, the teacher population becomes more white. The problems within the schools that I visit is that teachers are more and more disconnected from children and their families, i.e., teachers operate from white middle class values and belief systems and the children and their families operate from African-American, Hispanic, migrant group, and other cultural values and beliefs which also frequently reflect the social and cultural implications of living in poverty.

In many school communities, there is a recognizable socio- economic- and cultural-disconnect between teachers, students, and the families they serve. Despite the fact that schools qualify for special local, state, and federal funding for serving children who live in poverty, many teachers don't understand poverty. The catch-all phrase used by those who teach in high poverty schools to explain the dismal levels of student achievement is, "A high percentage of our students are on free or reduced lunch." Throughout the country, in many of the schools that I've visited, my introduction to the schools was nearly the same. Despite the part of the country where the school resides, I was greeted by the principal, assistant principal or school counselor, "Good morning Mr. Wynn, welcome to our school. We're so happy that you could spend time at our school and speak with our students and staff. You know, Mr. Wynn, 90% or our children are on free or reduced lunch."

What's being implied is that we are what we are because of the children and families we serve: "The children are to blame for the problems in our school, particularly in the areas of discipline and achievement."

In my book, *Follow Your Dreams: Lessons That I Learned in School,* I addressed the issue of poverty from my perspective, being born into poverty in Pike County, Alabama, and growing up in poverty on Chicago's south side:

People talk a lot about poor children. They feel sorry for them and assume that they're stupid. I know a lot about poor. I was born poor, I grew up poor, I went to college poor, and I began my first job out of college, poor. My biological mother was poor. My adoptive parents were poor. Most of my relatives and all of the people I grew up with were poor. Yes, I know a lot about being poor.

I meet a lot of teachers who feel sorry for poor children. I don't. I was poor and I didn't need anyone to feel sorry for me. I needed people to help prepare me to compete. I needed people to help me discover the potential that I didn't realize that I had. I needed people to help me to discover my dreams and to develop a plan for how to achieve those dreams. I needed someone to help me to develop my 'game.'

School communities where the teachers and staff define their school by how many children are on free or reduced lunch or by how many come from single-parent households are deficit-focused. Poverty is a reality of families, not an excuse for low achievement of schools. Having large numbers of students who live in single parent households requires that we provide more effective instruction in the classroom and rely less on a parent's ability to devote long hours to helping students with homework.

If the demographics of your school indicate that you serve children and families who live in poverty, then you need to help your administrators, teachers, and support persons understand poverty thereby moving your focus from the deficits of students to the capacity of teachers.

Notes:

Ruby Payne, in her book, *A Framework for Understanding Poverty*, writes:

To better understand students and adults from poverty, a working definition of poverty is "the extent to which an individual does without resources." Such resources would be:

- *Financial: Having the money to purchase goods and services.*

- *Emotional: Being able to choose and control emotional responses, particularly to negative situations, without engaging in self-destructive behavior.*

- *Mental: Having the mental abilities to acquire skills (reading, writing, computing) to deal with daily life.*

- *Spiritual: Believing in divine purpose and guidance.*

- *Physical: Having physical health and mobility.*

- *Support Systems: Having friends, family, and backup resources available to access in times of need.*

- *Relationships/Role Models: Having frequent access to adults who are appropriate, who are nurturing to the child, and who do not engage in self-destructive behavior.*

- *Knowledge or Hidden Rules: Knowing the unspoken cues and habits of a group.*

Typically, poverty is thought of in terms of financial resources only. However, availability of financial resources, while important, does not explain the differences between the success of individuals who leave poverty and those who remain in poverty. The ability to leave poverty is more dependent upon other resources than upon financial resources.

Developing the operational strategies that will best serve the children and families within your school community requires that you understand the students and families which your school serves. Children in poverty need more than simply an education measured by standardized test scores; they need to know how to emancipate themselves from poverty. Ms. Payne goes on to note:

Hidden rules exist in poverty, in middle class, and in wealth, as well as in ethnic groups and other units of people. Hidden rules are about the salient, unspoken understandings that cue the members of the group that this individual does or does not fit. For example, three of the hidden rules in poverty are the following: The noise level is high (the TV is always on and everyone may talk at once), the most important information is non-verbal, and one of the main values of an individual to the group is an ability to entertain. There are hidden rules about food, dress, decorum, etc. Generally, in order to successfully move from one class to the next, it is important to have a spouse or mentor from the class to which you wish to move to model and teach you the hidden rules.

Children living in poverty need mentors who can help them to understand the hidden rules of the middle class.

Subsequently, schools that have a deficit-focus fail to value student's survival skills and appreciate their resilience in the face of seemingly insurmountable obstacles. A further failing is that teachers, who operate from middle class norms and values, fail to teach children living in poverty the hidden rules of the middle class, and school counselors fail to

Notes:

provide students and families with clear action-plans which frequently are based on middle class norms and values. These norms and values are not taught in the textbooks, are rarely discussed in classrooms, and yet are relied upon to shape policies, decisions, student placement, and student evaluation. For many families living in poverty, by the time they begin to understand the hidden rules, many of their children have developed discipline records and experienced such low academic achievement levels that they are excluded from certain academic courses, special programs, magnet schools, and extracurricular activities.

Changing this dynamic requires that we once again raise the questions, "What is our vision?" and "What is in the best interests of our students?"

Driven by the demographics of a high poverty student population, and guided by these two questions, I have successfully worked with the ninth grade classes at several high schools to teach students what *I*, was never taught while growing up in poverty attending the Chicago Public Schools.

I believe that any school can use the following steps as a framework for helping high poverty student populations to replace their hopelessness with hope, and for teaching them the norms and values of the middle class as a stepping stone to their emancipation from poverty.

1.   Engage students in a series of instructional units entitled, *"Follow Your Dreams and Define Your Future"* designed to be introduced in homeroom, social studies, reading, and language arts classes.

2.   Reinforce the program through visuals posted throughout the school that promote the slogan and raise such questions as:

"Have you discovered your dreams?"

"Are your attitude, academic achievement, discipline records, and actions consistent with pursuing your dreams?"

"What do you know about your dreams?"

"Who do know who is living your dreams?"

"What do you dream of doing?"

"Where do you dream of going?"

"Where do you dream of living?"

"What do you dream of changing?"

3.   Invite guest speakers to share with students and parents the norms and values of the middle class. The "How To" lessons of discovering and pursing your dreams for both parents and students.

Engage students in creating "Follow Your Dreams!" visuals to promote the events and guest speakers, e.g., banners, posters, pennant flags, flyers, brochures, etc.

4.   Provide opportunities for students to meet with speakers in a more informal setting outside of the school-wide or grade level assemblies. Provide for a formal sign-up procedure via a contract of participation, signed by a parent or a guardian:

Contract of Participation

I am interested in joining our school's Dream Team.

I understand that I will have to make a commitment to participate in the Dream Team meetings and activities during the school year.

_____

Student Name   Grade/Homeroom

My child has my permission to participate in the Dream Team activities. I understand that guest speakers will speak to students during the school year and that a series of parenting seminars entitled, *"Ten Steps to Helping Your Child Succeed in School"* will be offered to parents.

I understand that in order for my child to participate in the Dream Team activities, I must commit to attending at least half of the parenting sessions.

I further authorize the school to photograph or video tape the student and parent meetings and to use the images as needed to further promote the Dream Team program.

_____

Parent or Guardian   Date

5. Require students who sign up for the Dream Team to read and discuss such books as, *Follow Your Dreams: Lessons That I Learned in School.*

6. Open the first meeting with a presentation by a guest speaker who can make a connection with students, someone who has lived in poverty, has learned the hidden rules of the middle class, and who embodies the values that you are attempting to teach your students. Arrange for an interactive session between students and the guest speaker.

7. Provide an opportunity to deepen learning by providing lunch and engaging students in informal discussion groups culminating in the creation of "Dream Portfolios." Video tape and photograph the day's activities.

8. Identify areas of responsibility, e.g., group facilitators, hosts, hostesses, creating flyers, greeting guest speakers, creating logos, filming, photography, etc and provide sign up sheets.

9. Provide student participants with paraphernalia to support and promote the program, e.g., t-shirts, pins, posters, pencils, rulers, books, etc.

10. Provide a dream theme for each meeting together with student areas of responsibility, e.g, designing flyers, greeting speakers, etc.

11. Schedule a series of parenting seminars surrounding each of the student themes. Involve students in sharing their experiences through oral presentations, poetry, essays, skits, and video clips from their interactions with guest speakers and dream-building activities.

Notes:

12. Plan a culminating activity where students and parents receive certificates, planners, scrapbooks or photo albums to celebrate their involvement. Students should clearly understand middle class norms and values and develop an action-plan for pursuing their respective dreams and aspirations.

This operational strategy evolved from understanding the demographic data and unique needs of a high poverty student population and was designed to achieve such goals as:

• helping students to focus on their long-term dreams and aspirations;

• teaching students some of the "hidden rules" of those persons who are living their dreams and aspirations;

• helping students and parents understand some of the goals that they must establish and the strategies that they must implement that are consistent with pursuing their respective dreams and aspirations;

• providing students and parents with the knowledge needed to pursue their respective dreams and aspirations; and

• cultivating positive relationships and connecting students and parents to the school community.

What are Your Goals?

Establishing relevant goals is no small task. Avoid the temptation to write volumes of school improvement data that no one is going to refer to, let alone follow. Also, avoid establishing goals where percentages are simply pulled out of the air, e.g., 10% reduction in office referrals, 15% increase in reading scores, 90% attendance, etc. Whenever schools establish such goals, they can be traced back to a lack of clarity in the school's vision. For example, when the vision is to engage students in a rigorous academic curriculum, it follows that the goal must be zero office referrals, not a 10% reduction. "Engaging students in a rigorous academic curriculum," requires that we do not lose any instructional time to scolding students, writing office referrals, escorting students to the office, explaining why they have been sent to the office, distracting the principal from important instructional issues or interrupting class as the students are eventually sent back to the classroom.

Establishing a goal of zero referrals would lead us to the following types of actions:

1. Engaging in an effective analysis of when, where, and why students misbehave.

2. Identifying which teachers require staff development in understanding poverty, dealing with confrontational students, classroom management, cultivating a positive classroom climate and culture, and building effective parent partnerships.

3. Developing an interdisciplinary, instructional approach to teaching students the expected behaviors during the first days of school.

4. Analyzing disciplinary policies for their effectiveness and age-appropriateness.

The process for establishing the school's goals would involve such actions as:

1.   Gathering the school's guiding documents, i.e., Mission, Vision, Statement of Beliefs, Guiding Principles, and/or Core Values.

2.   Gathering student demographic data.

3.   Identifying all of the relevant academic, social, and emotional problem areas, i.e., standardized test scores, discipline issues, suicides, depression, anxiety disorders, attendance, tardies, etc.

4.   Developing a "Wish List" that pertains to the problem areas.

5.   Reviewing the Wish List and eliminating any wishes that don't directly pertain to the school's Mission/Vision.

6. Categorizing the remaining wishes into such areas as:

- academics,

- standardized testing,

- social,

- emotional,

- school spirit, and

- other (areas that relate to one or more components of the school's vision).

7. Establishing one goal per committee (Strategy-Focused Team).

8. Engaging each committee in developing action plans that are driven by the school's guiding documents, taking into account student demographic data, and rooted in relevant research.

9. Establishing a three to five year plan for each goal, e.g.,

- *year one: gather data and develop customs and rituals;*

- *year two: introduce mentoring component and recognition programs;*

- *year three: establish comparable components with feeder schools.*

10. Documenting the research, meeting minutes, contacts, communications, action plans, etc. from each committee and incorporating them into the school-wide action plan.

Notes:

Moving from Discussions to Solutions

After engaging in the process of identifying the multitude of issues and obstacles confronting your school community, you must consciously work to avoid the pitfalls experienced by school communities each year. Largely, within school communities throughout the country, we develop task forces, committees, and hold public meetings to endlessly discuss the problems. Following such discussions, we typically tinker around and are frustrated by our continuing inability to bring about systemic and sustained changes to the dynamics within a school community that lead to measurable increases in student achievement.

In many school communities, it has become a rite of passage to join any number of *school improvement* committees; meet and discuss the problems over the course of an entire school year; after a number of frustrating (often heated) meetings the committee breaks into smaller working committees; these committees occasionally discuss solutions or bring recommendations back to the total committee; the small group recommendations are further discussed, debated, or discarded; eventually (if you're lucky), the larger committee adopts a resolution and makes a formal recommendation to the school's principal and waits for the principal to take action on one or more of the committee's recommendations. The principal, bless his or her heart, was not in the meetings; did not participate in the discussions that led to the recommended solutions; did not establish the implementation timeline; and does not have the budget, manpower, and in some cases, willpower to implement the multitude of ideas being thrown at him or her. Subsequently, all such recommendations are tossed or in some cases laid to rest in the principal's recommendations folder.

How is it that enlightened, well-intentioned, intelligent, caring people engage in this insanity in thousands of schools each year throughout the United States? We must stop the madness!

The principal doesn't need more recommendations, he needs people who, being driven by the school's vision, will accept the responsibility of implementing their ideas and measuring their results.

Synergy

Synergy comes from the Greek word *sunergos*, meaning "to work together spontaneously." Synergy indicates the working together of different agents, individuals or entities so that the total effect is greater than the sum of the individual parts. Our bodies represent a synergistic system. We sweat when we're too hot. We shiver when we're cold. Our brains release adrenaline in situations of danger or when we need an extra boost of energy. Our brains release endorphins in situations full of joy, fun, and celebration to help us achieve ecstasy.

My wife, who has had a dream of entering into competitive bodybuilding, has learned of the synergy involved in the sport. Ultimate muscular development and body sculpting occurs under the guidance of a professional

Notes:

trainer who develops a balanced diet of carbohydrates, fats, proteins, and water consumed at specific intervals throughout the day. The workout regimen focuses attention on specific muscle groups, at a predetermined time, on specific days of the week (e.g., Monday: chest; Tuesday: legs; Wednesday: back; Thursday: shoulders; Friday: biceps and triceps, etc.). The actual training involves specific muscular movement, weight, reps, sets, and rest intervals. The cardiovascular program is specifically designed to burn fat, increase heart-lung capacity, and minimize muscle loss. Each evening requires a prescribed period of rest for maximum muscular building and rejuvenation. The final product on competition day represents the result of the effective synergistic system of diet, strength training, cardiovascular work, rest, and mental clarity.

Within organizations, synergy represents the focused, combined efforts of many individuals or departments working toward a predetermined outcome requiring the give-and-take between individuals.

Whatever the difficulties we mush continue pressing forward. The alternative is unacceptable.

Some of the reasons that synergy can be difficult to cultivate within a school community are:

1.   The school lacks a clearly-defined vision that mobilizes individuals toward clearly-defined and commonly-shared goals.

2.   When committees are established (although well intentioned) the committees, themselves, lack a clearly-defined vision of what they were established to accomplish.

3.   The committees are rarely empowered to move through the entire process of establishing the committee's vision, identifying the problems, conceptualizing strategies, and implementing solutions.

As a result, the committees don't take ownership of their own recommended solutions, don't directly control the implementation of their ideas, and rarely create a work product (i.e., research, implementation strategies, time lines, cost, etc.) that future committees can benefit from. This is not to imply that school-based committees aren't important, just that within thousands of schools throughout the country they have operated in a largely ineffective manner. This is also not to infer that principals shouldn't delegate more responsibility to school-based committees, just that until the committees are effectively established, clearly focused, and empowered to implement their ideas and solutions, more autonomy isn't the answer.

So, how do we proceed? First, assess the effectiveness of your current school-based committees by answering the following questions:

1.   Is each committee driven by your school's mission and vision?

2.   Has each committee developed its own mission/vision in support of the school-wide mission/vision (i.e., what is our purpose and what do we want to achieve?)?

3.   Has each committee been empowered with the authority (within certain guidelines) to both conceptualize and implement needed strategies?

4.   Has each committee established measurable qualitative or quantitative goals based on the committee's articulated vision?

5.   Has each committee been responsible for documenting its meetings, identifying relevant research, developing operational strategies, assessing the utilization of resources, developing action plans, and establishing implementation time lines?

School-based committees have been ineffective for so long and have such negative stigma attached to the name, itself, that I would suggest adopting the name *Strategic-Focused Teams*. Such teams would be formulated with the aforementioned five questions in mind. Their purpose would be to provide a mechanism for conceptualizing and carrying out action plans and implementation strategies within the clearly-defined, succinctly stated mission/vision of the committee. Teams would be responsible for such issues as:

- Conceptualizing and implementing component parts of holistically-conceived strategies (e.g., visuals, communication, logistics, cultivating relationships, etc.);

- Working with small groups of people engaging in the effective identification of pertinent data, analyzing such data, conceptualizing solutions based on such data, and carrying out implementation strategies based on those solutions;

- Identifying the needed resources and expertise to successfully carry out implementation strategies;

- Cultivating broad-base support and involvement from the school's stakeholders;

- Performing a continuing re-assessment of problems and solutions; and

- Being driven by the passionate pursuit of excellence within the narrowly-defined problem solving areas assigned to the group.

While various methodologies can be utilized to structure these teams, preexisting teams can be called upon to carry out certain tasks, e.g., grade level teams, subject area teams, school improvement council, school advisory council, PTA/PTSA, etc., My experience is that teams formed based on Multiple Intelligences Theory (M.I. Teams) provide the most powerful, productive, and synergistic problem solving framework possible.

For solutions to have a chance at being systemic and sustainable, they must be holistic (made up of many small pieces) and driven by small teams. These teams must be empowered to make decisions, and are held responsible for implementing the strategies which they conceptualize.

The mission can only be fulfilled and the vision achieved when the strategic plan and organizational framework are conceptualized in a way that enables and empowers teachers, parents, business partners, and support staff to effectively execute the action plans. The role of the principal is to empower the individuals with the tools, resources, and organizational structure needed so that they can effectively achieve their tasks, and also to provide a centralized communications center for disseminating information regarding what is going on within the school.

Notes:

The benefits of this approach are clear:

1.   Stakeholders become passionate participants in achieving the school's vision.

2.   Stakeholders make the needed emotional investment in achieving the school's goals and objectives.

3.   Stakeholders invest the time, energy, resources, and creative input needed to fulfill the necessary daily tasks.

4.   Stakeholders develop sustaining relationships with other stakeholders (including students) that cultivate school spirit and pride.

5.   The school becomes self-evolving and is less dependent on the principal for its successful daily operation.

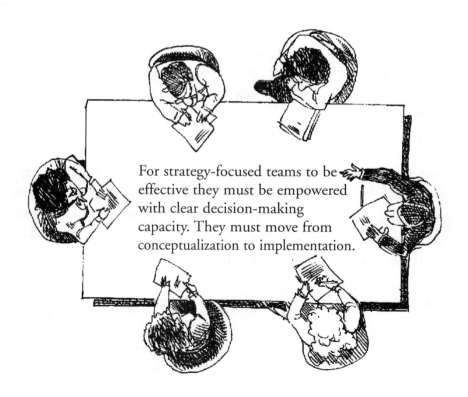

For strategy-focused teams to be effective they must be empowered with clear decision-making capacity. They must move from conceptualization to implementation.

Multiple Intelligence (M.I.) Teams— Operational Strategies

Traditional school teams, i.e., grade level, subject area, School Improvement, etc., are insufficient to create a Strategy-Focused School. Their operational objective is too narrowly defined. Grade level teams deal primarily with curriculum and instruction. Subject area teams are self explanatory. School Improvement Teams provide more overriding than operational strategies. While each of these teams and the work they they do can be beneficial to your school community, their efforts must be supplemented by strategy-focused teams, or they must develop strategy-focused teams within their existing structure which embody an M.I. framework.

M.I. Teams provide a strategic focal point through which all issues related to the respective intellectual domain must pass to ensure the holistic, systemic approach needed for sustained school improvement. Each team must be empowered to create their own mechanisms to facilitate change and to effectively communicate between teams.

While the concept of M.I. Teams (see Appendix) provides a framework for problem solving, to ensure that solutions are holistically conceived, strategy-focused teams must evolve into operational units within each school community. Each team should be comprised of individuals who have strengths within the intellectual domains being relied upon for decision-making and for carrying out action plans. Such teams are likely to be made up of a cross section of the school community, e.g., mentors, business partners, teachers, paraprofessionals, cafeteria workers, students, counselors, parents, and community representatives. Business/community partners might include graphic arts studios, architectural firms, public relations firms, senior citizen homes, and churches.

Notes:

Depending upon the needs of your school community, the M.I. framework can be integrated into your current school improvement-related committees. After engaging in the analysis of the current M.I. strengths of each committee, it can help to focus recruitment efforts for additional committee members.

Following is a list of M.I. Teams and the areas of responsibilities which should be assigned to each team:

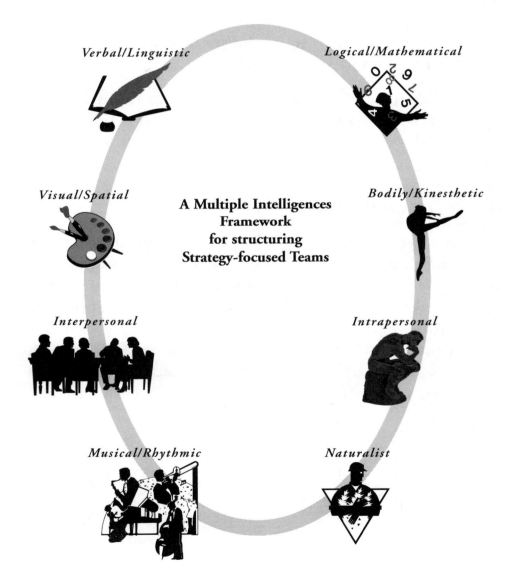

Verbal/Linguistic

Logical/Mathematical

Visual/Spatial

A Multiple Intelligences Framework for structuring Strategy-focused Teams

Bodily/Kinesthetic

Interpersonal

Intrapersonal

Musical/Rhythmic

Naturalist

Scheduling (Logical/Mathematical Intelligence)

Ideal team leader: Math or Science teacher, principal, or assistant principal

The Scheduling team is responsible for the ongoing review of school processes which would include such areas as:

- Student movement
- Assemblies
- Block or daily schedules
- Logistics of guest speakers
- Study Trips
- Special events
- Meeting agendas
- Yearlong timeline of rituals/ceremonies
- School opening/closing
- Logistics of communication
- Data gathering and analysis
- Charts, graphs, and demographics
- Budgets

Notes:

Curriculum and Communication (Verbal/Linguistic Intelligence)

Ideal team leader: Language arts teacher, curriculum writer

The Curriculum and Communication team is responsible for ongoing assessment of curriculum models and communication strategies which would include such areas as:

- Developing instructional units to teach the school's Mission, Vision, Statement of Beliefs, and Core Values

- Developing thematic whole-brain units

- Developing instructional units regarding school history

- Developing instructional units to involve students in the school-wide planning efforts (e.g., painting, drawing, presenting, discussing, researching, school newsletter, reporting school events, etc.)

- Performing a language audit to ensure that the mission, vision, statement of beliefs, core values and guiding philosophies are incorporated into all school-related correspondence, e.g., student planner, school brochures, student orientation letters, welcome letters for new teachers, press releases, etc.

- Becoming curriculum experts in areas of innovation pertaining to the school's vision

- Performing an ongoing evaluation of the rubrics and curricula being used and their effectiveness at achieving the learning goals as outlined in the vision

- Reviewing all school-related correspondence for consistency, editorial content, and grammatical correctness, e.g., press releases, parent letters, referral forms, flyers, meeting notices, etc.

Relationships (Interpersonal Intelligence)

Ideal team leader: Parent, support staff, teacher

The Relationship team is responsible for conceptualizing and coordinating activities and events designed to strengthen relationships throughout the school community such as:

- Town Hall meetings
- Back to school and end of school activities
- Teacher, student, community activities, events, rituals, ceremonies, and appreciation programs

- Recognition awards and programs
- Visitor, parent, and volunteer procedures
- Business/community partnerships
- New/retiring teacher rituals and ceremonies
- Staff retreats and team-building programs
- Ensuring that school-wide events are people and family friendly e.g., curriculum night
- Birthday, anniversary, graduation, recognition of students, staff, business/community partners

Spirit/Pride (Intrapersonal Intelligence)

Ideal team leader: Parent, student, support staff, teacher

The Spirit/Pride team would work closely with the Relationship Team. There is a spirit and pride component to each relationship-building area. For example, while a school dance might be scheduled to build stronger relationships between students, a teacher sock hop, balloons representing school colors, and a special principal's dance would be spirited components.

In addition, to support the efforts of the Relationship group, this group would be responsible for the rituals and ceremonies designed to cultivate school spirit, pride, and staff, and community morale which might include such areas as:

- Developing promotional items such as buttons, balloons, banners, t-shirts, bumper stickers, note pads, folders, pennant flags, calendars, and pins

- Coordinating Monday morning staff coffee or Friday afternoon "Thank God it's Friday" staff get-togethers

- Developing school spirit rituals, ceremonies, and special events

- Coordinating school-wide decorations for school opening, closing, and thematic units

- Coordinating opening and closing rituals at staff meetings

- Developing school spirit and recognition programs

Imagery (Visual/Spatial Intelligence)

Ideal team leaders: Art teacher, student, teacher, support staff, parent, business-community partner, mentor

The Imagery team would be responsible for the images throughout the school community that reinforce the mission, vision, beliefs, and core values. This team would also work closely with all of the other teams to conceptualize and develop the images to support their efforts:

- Images posted throughout the school community, e.g., signage; flyers; brochures; flags; posters; the mascot; school colors; core values, beliefs, vision, and mission banners

- Recognition images, e.g., awards, certificates, trophies, yearbook, ribbons, school letters, promotional items (i.e., cups, mugs, book marks, pennant flags, etc.)

- T-shirts, logos, graphics, and illustration designs

- Photographs, video, and multimedia productions

- Directional signs

- Bulletin boards and theme walls

- Corridors, cafeteria, media center, and architectural designs

- Business/community partnerships with graphic design studios, advertising agencies, printers, silk screen manufacturers, artists, galleries, framers, laminators; Art Colleges, banner companies, and publishers

Notes:

Athletic Performances (Bodily Kinesthetic Intelligence)

Ideal team leader: Dance teacher, gymnastic teacher, cheer leading coach, P.E. teacher

The Athletic Performances team is responsible for student presentations involving athletic, dance, cheerleading, marching, gymnastics, step shows, etc. This team interacts heavily with any team planning formal programs, assemblies, rituals, and ceremonies, works closely with the Musical Performances team, and is responsible for such areas as:

- The physical performance component in the rituals, ceremonies, events, assemblies, and pep rallies

- Developing gymnastics, tumbling, and cheerleading routines to communicate school spirit and pride

- Field/health and fitness days and programs

- Dance components to thematic units, particularly in the area of social studies

- Rock climbing, scuba diving, sailing, rafting, study trips and retreats

- Health and fitness awareness

- Nutrition and exercise programs to support academic achievement and testing

- Health related team-building activities

- Business/community partnerships with fitness centers, sports franchises, personal trainers, body-builders, choreographers, dance schools, professional dancers, Olympic and professional athletes

Musical Performances (Musical/Rhythmic Intelligence)

Ideal team leaders: Music, band, orchestra teacher

The Musical Performances team is responsible for all student related performances in the area of musical composition. This team would heavily support the efforts of the Athletic Performance team and all school related events, rituals, and ceremonies by performing or coordinating such tasks as:

- Writing/performing the school song, identifying or developing opening and closing themes, special events, assembly, rituals, and ceremonial themes

- Developing/performing special programs, composing theme music

- Developing business/community partnerships with recording studios, producers, symphonies, professional musicians, special event venues, and playhouses

Notes:

Environmental (Naturalist Intelligence)

Ideal team leader: Custodian, landscaper, student, parent, teacher, support staff

The Environmental team would be responsible for ensuring that the interior and exterior of the building is consistent with the core values, mission, and vision of the school. This team would interact heavily with the Imagery team to ensure excellence in imagery and landscaping throughout the school community.

Such responsibilities might involve:

- outdoor landscaping and gardening

- indoor landscaping themes

- thematic units in such areas as rain forests, geographical terrain, etc.

- nature walks, bird watching, butterfly watching, maintaining an environmental watch, endangered species lists, and the study of nature within the school community

- business/community partnerships in the areas of horticulture, farming, landscaping, gardening, meteorology, fishing, sailing, hiking, rock climbing, zoos, aquariums, animal stores, veterinary clinics, etc.

M.I. Theory in Practice

At the John Hopkins Middle School in St. Petersburg, Florida, we began by identifying a diverse group of stakeholders to engage in the process of conceptualizing the school's vision (i.e., administrators, teachers, parents, business partners, central office personnel, support staff, etc.). This group met one day per month for three months, one day per week for eight weeks, and every day after school for one week. After engaging in several months of dialogue leading to identifying the major components to be articulated within the school's vision, a M.I. team highly developed in Verbal/Linguistic Intelligence was established to draft the school's vision. Once the draft of the school's vision was written, it was circulated throughout the school community. After receiving feedback from parents, teachers, support staff, and other stakeholders, the final draft of the John Hopkins Middle School Vision was written.

Vision

The Vision of John Hopkins Middle School is to create a school climate and culture of:

- **High academic achievement and performance-related outcomes.**

- **A safe, risk-free school community evidenced by high attendance rates and appropriate student behavior.**

- **Respect for the individual and value of the inherent diversity of the JHMS community.**

- **Relevant and practical learning outcomes of all for academic and elective curriculum.**

- **Effective collaboration between all JHMS stakeholders for opportunities that will enhance JHMS students in the discovery, exploration and pursuit of their respective dreams and aspirations.**

- **An inviting learning environment where all JHMS stakeholders feel that they are valued members of the JHMS family.**

The Verbal/Linguistic team went on to write the John Hopkins Middle School Statement of Beliefs.

Statement of Beliefs

- **We believe that our efforts must be guided by the JHMS Vision and that every decision must ultimately be measured against, "Is this in the best interests of our students?"**

- **We believe in respect for the individual.**

- **We believe in a safe school community that promotes positive and constructive behavior.**

- **We believe in fostering a climate of collaboration, communication, and compassion for each individual within the JHMS community.**

- **We believe in seeking every opportunity to recognize, validate and celebrate the achievements of our students and staff.**

Using the Mission, Vision, and Statement of Beliefs as the guiding documents, the question was raised, "What is the first opportunity that we have as a school community to begin the process of fulfilling our vision and communicating our beliefs?" After some debate, one of the administrators commented, "Well, I think that the school's opening is our first opportunity to cultivate the type of school community that we envision, and to share with parents and the surrounding community what we believe." An analysis of the previous years' school opening revealed that little was done consistent with the newly articulated school's vision. The school opening had always been planned by the administrative team, highly developed in Logical/ Mathematical Intelligence. The school was opened, the principal gave his "Code of Conduct" speech. Students were herded off to class, many without schedules, except for the seventh graders. In the state of Florida, you cannot begin school in the seventh grade without proof of state mandated immunizations. Subsequently, year after year, in this 1500-student middle school, over 200 seventh graders were herded into the gymnasium to await their parents. Countless other students stood in long lines throughout the day awaiting their class schedules. There was a great deal of anxiety among students, parents, teachers, administrators, and counselors.

Armed with our vision and beliefs we engaged in a mind-mapping activity of school opening strategies pertinent to each of the M.I. domains (see illustration on the page 243). What resulted was an operational strategy, driven by the school's vision, that resulted in a pre-school opening celebration entitled, "Trojan Preview Day," which occurred the Saturday before the official county-wide school opening.

Following this discussion, the planning team was separated into smaller M.I.-specific teams (i.e., Verbal, Logical, Interpersonal, etc.). Each team identified a team leader and began the process of conceptualizing strategies and formulating action plans within the confines of its narrowly-defined focus. Each team began soliciting input from other teachers and support staff with talents and interests in its unique intellectual domain (e.g., art teachers, music teachers, curriculum planners, etc.). Rather than being side-tracked by discussions outside of its intellectual domain (i.e., the Visual Team debating budgets, the Verbal Team debating logistics, the Logical Team debating signage, etc.) notes were passed between teams. The Logical Team requested that the Verbal Team write the parent correspondence and press releases. The Visual Team requested a budget from the Logical Team for purchasing signs and banners. The Interpersonal Team requested permission from the Logical Team to open the school for classroom tours to be facilitated by the Student Council,. The Intrapersonal Team requested that Mr. Green, the School Safety Officer and physical fitness buff, dress up as a Trojan and take pictures with parents, particularly the single parents!

Notes:

The result was a synergistic and holistic action plan. Sixth grade parents and their children were welcomed into the school community. Returning parents were welcomed back in an orderly and high-spirited way. Students demonstrated leadership skills by conducting tours and answering questions. Over 1400 student schedules were distributed, ensuring a smooth school opening. Bay Front Medical Center was on site to provide immunizations, ensuring that fewer students would be herded into the gymnasium on the first day of classes. Community and social service agencies were on site, providing valuable information to families. The school-wide clubs were represented. The PTSA signed up parents and sold t-shirts. The cheerleaders cheered. The steel drums played. A spirit of camaraderie and school pride was fostered that paved the way for not only the best school opening in the school's history, but to recognition of John Hopkins Middle School for the best school opening within the state of Florida.

The role of the school's principal is to ensure that school-wide efforts are directed toward fulfilling the mission and achieving the vision. As long as strategy-focused teams are operating within this framework the principal must support their efforts in conceptualizing and implementing operational strategies that will enable the school to fulfill its mission.

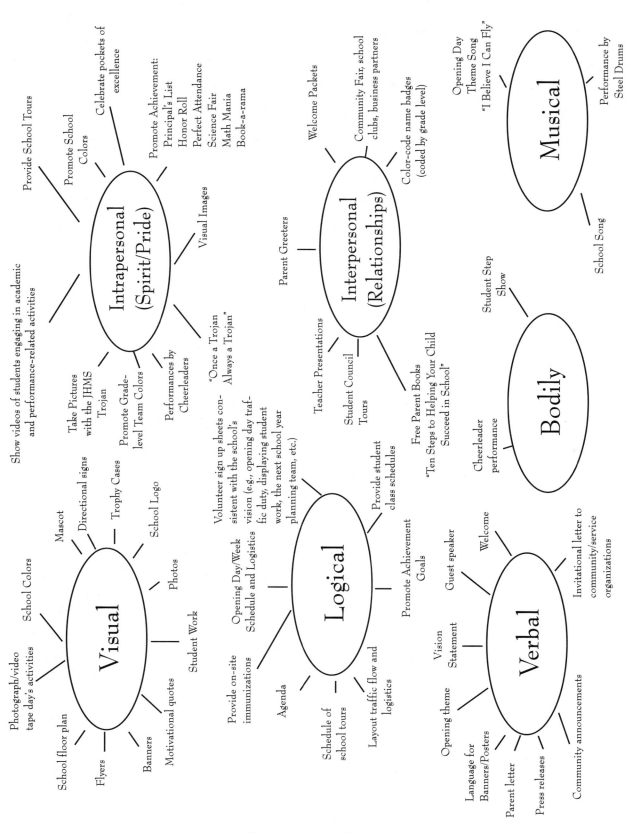

Notes:

Gardner's research indicated that each of us has and relies upon all of the intellectual domains, however, no two people utilize the same combination of intelligences in exactly the same way. Also, each person is more highly proficient in some of the eight intellectual domains and less highly in others.

The challenges we face in establishing strategy-focused school-based teams are:

1. Identifying problems or groups of issues and focusing each M.I. team on conceptualizing strategies which lie within its intellectual domain.

2. Merging the respective strategies from each M.I. team into an holistic strategy.

To apply the M.I. framework to problem-solving within a school community, consider doing the following:

1. Review the Multiple Intelligences Summary in the Appendix and list your intelligences in order from one to eight (one being the most highly developed and eight the least developed in terms of how you solve problems).

    Many people will have difficulty quantifying their choices because, frequently, some intelligences are equally well developed. However, please do your best to list them in descending order.

2. List the eight intellectual domains on a sheet of chart paper for the benefit of the entire group.

3. Go through each of the eight intellectual domains and ask for a show of hands of those persons who identified that domain as their number one or most dominant intelligence. Ask for people to limit themselves to a single number one choice.

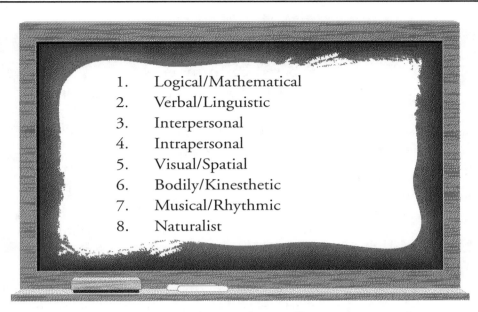

4. Tally the number for each intelligence on a chart pad and have someone create a list of the names of each person represented within each intellectual domain.

5. Identify the problem, e.g., changing student schedules.

6. Group individuals interested in conceptualizing strategies and developing action plans into M.I. groups, i.e., Logical/ Mathematical, Verbal/Linguistic, Visual/Spatial, Interpersonal, Intrapersonal, etc.

7. Have each group work independently and conceptualize strategies that utilize its unique intellectual domain. As previously mentioned, some or all of the following M.I. teams might be developed:
   • Communications (Verbal/Linguistic)
   • Logistics/Procedures (Logical/Mathematical)
   • School Spirit/Pride (Intrapersonal)
   • School-wide Signage, Images, and Environment (Visual/Spatial, Naturalist)

Notes:

- Staff Morale, School-Community Relationships (Interpersonal)
- School-based Performances (Musical/Rhythmic, Bodily/Kinesthetic)

8. Have each group write up and make a group presentation of their strategies.

9. Combine the write-ups from each group and develop a holistic action plan with each group maintaining the responsibility for implementing their ideas.

Through my experiences, these types of M.I. teams provide extremely effective holistic approaches to problem solving. In staff development sessions with teachers, M.I. grouping creates naturally diverse cross-gender, cross-socioeconomic, cross-cultural grouping for focused problem solving. The special focus nature of the problem-solving efforts helps to keep teams from straying off on tangents and empowers them to conceptualize, strategize, and implement solutions.

The interaction between groups further helps them to developed an appreciation for each group's specialized skills.

For example:

- Procedural Teams (Logical/Mathematical) prepare agendas that are fast moving, relieve boredom, and are logistically well conceptualized.

- Imagery Teams (Visual/Spatial) support the efforts of all teams with signage, flyers, banners, graphic arts, and printed programs.

- Curriculum and Communication Teams (Verbal/Linguistic) ensure that the school's mission, vision, statement of beliefs, and core values are integrated into meetings, assemblies, and school-wide communications.

- Other teams focus their work on building relationships, enhancing school spirit, and creating a nurturing school environment consistent with the school's mission, vision, beliefs, and core values.

With such teams in place, the principal may perform in the role of strategic coordinator and concentrate his or her efforts on ensuring that each team has the needed planning time, access to facilities, and resources to successfully implement their strategies.

In the book, *The Strategy Focused Organization*, the authors note:

A study of 275 portfolio managers reported that the ability to execute strategy was more important than the quality of the strategy itself. These managers cited strategy implementation as the most important factor shaping management and corporate valuations.

More recently, a 1999 Fortune cover story of prominent CEO failures concluded that the emphasis placed on strategy and vision created a mistaken belief that the right strategy was all that was needed to succeed. 'In the majority of cases—we estimate 70 percent—the real problem isn't bad strategy but bad execution.'

While this example refers to portfolio managers within the private sector, it applies directly to the processes inherent within a school community's journey toward fulfilling its mission. Strategy-focused teams provide the best opportunity for shared ownership in the school-wide focus of achieving the school's vision.

Discussion Questions

1.   Review the Multiple Intelligence teams (p. 230). Identify the team(s) where you can make the greatest contribution to conceptualizing and operationalizing school-wide strategies.

2.   Develop a demographic profile of your lowest achieving students (profile both deficits and assets). Based on student demographics, list deficits that must be addressed and assets that can be utilized to increase academic achievement levels.

3.   Develop a demographic profile of your highest achieving students. Based on student demographics, list ten high priority needs that must be addressed to provide exposure to enrichment opportunities, local/national competitions, and/or more engaging instruction.

4.   What are the assets and deficits of the student whom you have accepted responsibility for?

5.   Discuss ways in which your M.I. Team can develop strategies, opportunities, or programs designed to build stronger relationships and provide greater enrichment opportunities to connect your students and the surrounding community to your school.

6.   List the student or school-wide needs that your M.I. Team can immediately impact based on the current sphere of influence of your team members (e.g., school bus, cafeteria, department, classroom, athletic program, extracurricular activity, before/after school program, tutorial assistance, mentoring, special interest area, etc.).

Chapter 7

We need to be acutely aware of and concerned about our children, speaking of them as a whole. I worry about the millions who come into the world with handicaps, seemingly impossible to overcome—children whose lives are blighted by neglect and abuse, children who have limitless capacity but almost no opportunity. In the long term, this may well be the most serious problem facing our nation because its consequences multiply and reach forward through generations.

— *Standing for Something*

Creating a Core Team

School communities stand on the foundation of relationships and, thus, their road to excellence is interwoven through the fabric of those relationships. The network of relationships between small groups of people, whether it be teacher/teacher, teacher/student, teacher/parent, administrator/parent, administrative/business partners, counselor/mentors, school bus driver/student, custodian/teacher, athletic coach/alumni, etc., leads to the many pockets of excellence that exist within virtually every school community. Whether it is the drama club, band, football team, speech and debate club, chess club or other co-curricular or extracurricular activities, excellence is cultivated by small groups of people. Ideally they work in collaboration with the rest of the school community. However, most often they work in isolation. Through a core team, we can begin to create an inter-connected web of relationships between these groups and individuals.

Steps to creating the core team

The Core Team is perhaps the most important of the strategy-focused teams. The Core Team may be developed to create the school's guiding documents (i.e., Mission, Vision, Core Values, Guiding Principles, etc.), to provide necessary leadership in developing operational strategies, or to provide the opportunity for individuals or groups who are actively cultivating pockets of excellence within the school community to meet and discuss their strategies within the larger context of school-wide success.

Following are some of the steps to developing your Core Team:

1. Identify those people who are passionately involved with, or who have expressed an interest in, some aspect of pursuing excellence within your school community, albeit athletics, academics, student government, intervention programs, or curricular and co-curricular activities. This may include coaches, teachers, custodians, cafeteria workers, bus drivers, mentors, parents, or volunteers.

   This group might include lead teachers or team leaders, a PTA/PTSA representative, a SAC member, the principal, assistant principals, parents and community representatives, business partners, students, and any other stakeholders who have been active in your school reform/planning efforts or who have been active in cultivating pockets of excellence within your school community.

2. Identify a group facilitator. Ideally, this should be someone from outside of the school who can offer an unbiased and objective voice to facilitate the group's discussions. It is preferable

that this person has expertise in the school improvement planning process and in facilitating group discussions.

3. Extend invitations outlining that this group will be gathering to engage in a discussion of the issues confronting your school community.

4. Provide a binder, hereafter referred to as "The School Improvement Planning Manual" to everyone attending your Core Team meeting that includes the following information:

- An illustration of the Educational Continuum;

- A copy of the Texas Research and Urban Schools Research studies, and any other research pertinent to your school community;

- The state learning goals;

- The district's Mission, Vision, Core Values, Statement of Beliefs, and learning goals;

- The School Improvement Plan; and

Notes:

- The school's demographic and segregated achievement data (i.e., racial, gender, socioeconomic) including, but not limited to:

  - *standardized test scores*

  - *end-of-grade level test data*

  - *state, district ranking*

  - *Talented and Gifted enrollment*

  - *honors/Advanced Placement class enrollment*

  - *special ed./needs placement*

  - *office referrals and suspensions*

  - *free and reduced lunch*

- A listing of your school's current committees, organizations, clubs, business-partnerships, and other pertinent stakeholder groups (e.g., curriculum, departments, school improvement, school advisory council, booster clubs, PTA/PTSA, parent support groups, foreign language clubs, chess club, math club, etc.); and

- Supplies should include: a three hole puncher, divider tabs, post-it notes, three-hole punched paper, pens, and pencils.

The complete demographic, achievement, discipline, test, and class and special program enrollment data is useful in helping Core Team members broaden their perspectives of the totality of needs within the school community. It helps the football coach, music teacher, and chess club facilitator to develop a bigger picture of how the excellence which they've achieved within their special focus activities can become a part of the school-wide collaborative effort needed to foster excellence throughout the school community.

5. Engage participants in:

    •   identifying the current pockets of excellence within the school community, e.g., football team, state Science Fair winner, National Quiz Bowl champions, Teachers with National Teacher Certification, etc.

    •   a roundtable discussion of the current level of student achievement as indicated by your aggregate data.

    •   reviewing the themes outlined in the Texas Successful School-wide Research Study and any other pertinent research that will guide your efforts. Discuss which themes or components are currently existing and/or missing from your school community.

6. Engage each person attending this meeting in the exercise of developing a personal Mission

Notes:

Statement and in identifying what they perceive their assignment to be in assisting the school in fulfilling its overriding mission (or to clarify one if one hasn't been developed).

Have each person place their personal Mission Statement in the front of their binder.

7.   Solicit from this group a commitment of those persons who are willing to meet regularly over a pre-determined period of time to participate in and facilitate the efforts of developing the school's Vision.

The Core Team is critical to providing the necessary leadership in developing sustained systemic and holistic school improvements strategies. Each school community must cultivate the expertise to and nurture the relationships that will ensure continuity. Too many schools ride the tide of principals and superintendents. When the principal leaves, the school is lost. When a new superintendent is hired, the school awaits new directions. The Core Team ensures continuity through intimate involvement in developing the school's Vision, Mission, and Statement of Beliefs. They become active participants who drive the school-wide efforts that lead to sustained systemic levels of high student achievement. They, in essence, become the driving force behind the school becoming self-evolving.

Core Team members have already demonstrated their passionate commitment to student achievement through their efforts toward cultivating excellence within their respective spheres of influence. Additionally, Core Team members will have an emotional investment in the success of the processes that lie ahead.

Responsibilities of the Core Team:

1. Make a year-long commitment to the strategic development process.

2. Assume a leadership role within at least one of the transformation components.

3. Be willing to serve as a small group facilitator for one or more of the Strategic-Focused Teams.

4. Cultivate relationships within their spheres of influence which will support the work that follows (e.g., Booster Club, grade-level teams, business partnerships, special-focus groups, and community organizations).

School's have begun to engage in a cursory approach to teaching the values and behaviors needed within a school community to help the school achieve its vision. Many schools post Character Values, Core Values or Life Skills posters. Some schools even engage children in discussing the values indicated on the posters. However, few schools have integrated the values articulated into the fabric of school climate and culture.

All schools are continually maneuvering along the educational continuum and, as such, must conceptualize action plans and develop strategies for dealing with the complex issues unique to the school community. Schools with high academically achieving students and high standardized test scores or those with tragically underachieving students and disappointingly low standardized test scores, are continually undergoing change.

It is not whether your school will undergo trans-formation, but rather, whether the Core Team that you have developed will take a proactive role and guide your school through the transformation continuum. The multiplicity of issues that will confront your school community in its goal of becoming a school of excellence or closing any respective achievement gaps can be forecasted with absolute certainly. These issues began revealing themselves the day that you opened your doors up to children.

Use the Research

I had the opportunity to present the closing keynote address at the North Carolina Education Association's Annual Conference. During the conference, I had an opportunity to speak at length with an elementary school principal. During our conversation she outlined what she perceived to be the problems in her school:

- *Low teacher expectations.*

- *High numbers of children on free or reduced lunch.*

- *Lack of parental involvement.*

- *Student apathy toward the learning process.*

- *High numbers of students below grade level in reading and mathematics.*

- *High numbers of office referrals.*

- *High incidents of fighting and suspensions.*

The principal stated, "I've tried everything and nothing appears to be working with these children." She then went on to ask, "What would you recommend?" As a consultant, I hear this question often. Before I could answer, another principal interceded, "I was thinking about getting together with some of the other principals in my district. We could, perhaps, get together for "Happy Hour" on Friday evenings to discuss some of the things that each of us is doing in our schools." While I would never condemn getting together with colleagues to discuss strategies, I would question Friday evening when everyone is burned out from the struggles of the week or whether getting together during "Happy Hour" would provide for any real type of strategic discussions? The other principal went on to further comment that all of the schools in her district were struggling, so the Friday evening gathering would most likely become a pity party rather than a strategic planning session.

In my response to the principal's initial question, I raised the following questions:

1.   What is the mission for your school?

    Her response was, *"I want my students to become lifelong learners."*

2.   What is your vision for your school?

    Her response was, *"You know, most of my students are on free or reduced lunch. I just want for them to take school seriously."*

3.   What research are you using to guide your efforts to increase student achievement within your school?

    To this she responded, *"I'm not really using any research. We have a reading program."*

I went on to ask if she was aware of the *Texas School-wide Research Study of High Achieving Schools,* which appeared to reflect schools that were very much like hers, i.e., high minority student populations, over 60% of the children on free or reduced lunch, and a history of underachievement. She was unaware of the research, so I shared the seven themes outlined in the research. I shared with her how I have used the research study as a catalyst for discussion with teachers regarding whether or not the themes common to high achieving schools were currently reflected in their school communities. However, midway through this dialogue, the principal interrupted me to say that she "felt" that she should

Notes:

look for a self-esteem building program before she involved her teachers in looking at any research.

This was not the first time that I have had a conversation with a teacher or a principal who was "experimenting" with children. Unlike the research theme of experimentation (i.e., focused experimentation), usually the experimentation is not focused, has no research foundation, and is analogous to a mechanic who says, "I don't know what's wrong with your car, but I'm going to put any part on and hope for the best!"

Experimentation should be focused and it should be research-based, even if it is only anecdotal evidence. You need some evidence. Furthermore, if you have not established your mission and have no clearly-defined vision it is impossible for your experimentation to have any meaningful research foundation whatsoever. Almost anything will do, because you don't really know where you're going!

Despite my best efforts, the principal was not at a point where she was able to expand her thinking or shift her paradigms. Oftentimes, the principal within a school or teacher within a classroom is unable or unwilling to consider the change components and explore strategies that may provide real solutions to their problems. She was convinced that she would "try" a self-esteem program before attempting anything else.

While there are any number of research studies that outline how schools have successfully resolved the many issues and obstacles that they are confronted with in solving the student achievement puzzle, I suggest that you identify research that is pertinent to the unique needs of your school community. I frequently refer to the Texas research because I believe that the seven themes outlined in the study provide a valid barometer for school communities to measure their efforts against. Marianne Hickman of the Leadership Academy in the Charlotte-Mecklenburg Schools (Charlotte,

NC) first shared the Texas study with me and I have referred to it often since.

Here is how I suggest you use the Texas research (or any other research that you are using) to guide your efforts:

1. Make a copy of the research summary and distribute it to every teacher within your building (this is what I did at my son's middle school).

2. Tell the recipients, "Please review this research study identifying the types of themes common within high achieving schools and place a check next to those themes which you believe are reflected in our school community."

3. Identify one theme to be discussed at each of seven consecutive staff meetings and ask teachers to give examples of how the theme is currently being exhibited within your school community.

4. Share the research with other stakeholders within your school community and ask for their objective input as well.

5. Host a Town Hall meeting with parents, community representatives, students, and staff and discuss the themes as they relate to your school community.

6. Incorporate the research into your School Improvement Manual or into your Classroom Procedures Manual. Use this and other research to guide your discussions pertaining to issues regarding student achievement.

The importance of using this and other research to guide your efforts cannot be underscored. If you have a solid research foundation to guide your efforts, it instills confidence throughout the school community that your opinions and beliefs are based on some real-world examples of how others have solved the student achievement puzzle. It also provides a reference point from which to engage in discussions regarding new ideas or strategies that you conceptualize.

Implement Change through the Curriculum

Whenever the opportunity presents itself, integrate your strategies into the fabric of the curriculum. My rule of thumb is, "Whenever you can integrate a strategy into the fabric of curriculum, you stand a tenfold increase of becoming successful." Whenever a task exists outside of the normal routines of the school, which largely center around curriculum and instruction, you significantly decrease the likelihood of sustained implementation. On more than one occasion, teachers and administrators have sat in meetings attempting to solve problems when someone proclaimed, "We did x-y-z once and it really seemed to work," or "We had an assembly for our students and they left more focused and more motivated." Then everyone sits around the room wondering why they stopped doing something that by all accounts worked?

If it's not a part of the normal ongoing routines, daily operations, or part of the curriculum it will probably be delegated to one person. That person may or may not fulfill their task. They may retire, leave, get fired or simply become disgusted with the seeming lack of support for this, yet another task, "On top of everything else that I have to do."

No matter where your school is located, it is reasonable to assume that your teachers are expected to teach and your students are expected to learn. Yet, when it comes to implementing the multitude of ideas and strategies that are required to pave the way toward higher student achievement and creating an socially and emotionally nurturing school community, we assign this monumental task to a few individuals who, typically, will need to work after school, during their planning times, weekends, and holidays to implement just a small fraction of the strategies. Historically, those people get burned out or just fed up. Whatever their altruistic motivation in the beginning, they eventually find the demands on their time and their personal lives to be too much to continue this insanity. Good for them! If more people realized that this approach to school-wide problem solving is insanity, then we would consider the following approach, which makes a lot more sense:

1. Look for an instructional tie-in to every strategy that is conceptualized. If it requires researching, writing, presenting or computing, identify the subject areas where students can become involved in the process.

    In case you aren't aware, in a typical school community, students outnumber adults by a ratio of 10 to 1. In some schools, it may be as high as 20 to 1. They represent a tremendously underutilized resource in facilitating systemic change.

2. Keep in mind that the vast majority of the strategies that are conceptualized involve valid workplace skills, e.g., painting a mural, writing a press release, filming a presentation, creating a brochure, making signs, preparing refreshments for a meeting or collating binders.

    Not only do students benefit in a very relevant and practical way from their meaningful involvement, but they become active participants in the transformation of their schools. After all, it is their school. They are not cattle to be herded through it, but artists, thinkers, problem solvers, and architects in its very design.

Notes:

3.   Each strategy that is integrated into the fabric of curriculum gets students involved in the process. Parental involvement increases each time that students are involved in the process.

4.   Each strategy that is integrated into the fabric of curriculum is sustaining. The continued evolution of the school community should not be dependent upon the principal, teachers, staff, or students. Curriculum integration ensures that the school becomes self-evolving.

5.   Each strategy that is integrated into the fabric of curriculum is taught, whereas, each strategy that is conceptualized outside of the curriculum is "talked about."

There are many opportunities through the curriculum for actively engaging students in the process of supporting school-wide efforts, e.g., creating brochures, press releases, web pages, flyers, newsletters, corresponding with potential business partners, speaking to local civic and community organizations, etc.

The Reality of Your School Community

Nearly every school community in America is concerned with "Increasing Student Achievement" or "Closing the Achievement Gap," whether they are white children from the trailer parks in Texas and Florida, Appalachian children in the Kentucky and Tennessee mountains, Native American children on the reservations in Arizona, the Latino children in the barrios of New York or African-American children in rural and urban communities throughout America. Newspapers publish stories and editorials, School Boards hold meetings, federal and state agencies establish task forces, teachers are held accountable, and yet, each day the achievement gap widens. In many school communities, people are losing hope that it's possible to successfully help all children to become socially and academically successful in school. With all of the social issues confronting principals, teachers, families, and our children each day, schools have become depressing places to be. With gangs, graffiti, yelling, fighting, cursing, broken toilets, drugs, and guns, "Increasing Student Achievement" may be what America wants, but within many school communities, the most pressing issues on the minds of principals and teachers have nothing to do with increasing student achievement.

Even if your school is not as overwhelmed with these issues and actually has a focus on increasing student achievement, you must contend with increasing student attendance, increasing parental involvement, increasing teacher effectiveness, increasing teacher hiring and retention, increasing student performance on standard testing, increasing English proficiency, increasing school safety, and reducing discipline problems and classroom disruptions. It's a little distracting for the classroom teacher if children are yelling and screaming in the corridors long after the tardy bell has rung. The issues of student apathy, disrespect and disregard for authority, students' unwillingness to consistently participate in the academic process, teacher apathy, teacher

Notes:

ineffectiveness in matching teaching styles to learning styles, parental apathy and lack of parental support for academically-related tasks, lack of resources, and violent and disruptive students provide continuing distractions from our focus on increasing student achievement. We must not forget the parents who come into the school during the school day cursing, threatening or physically assaulting staff members. These are the "real" issues confronting a school community. It is no wonder that schools find it difficult to navigate the complex maze of obstacles that hinder achieving their goals, much less, the many federal, state, and district mandates.

The historical approach to implementing a new "Program" to reduce violence, develop character, inspire respect, foster parental involvement, and increase reading and math scores has obviously not resolved the complex student achievement problem. In fact, the best reading program is still contingent on teachers teaching it. The teacher's effectiveness in teaching a group of misbehaving, uninterested and unmotivated students is contingent on effective classroom management strategies. Ultimately, student achievement is contingent on whether students are inspired to want to learn what we are teaching. In essence, the best programs cannot teach themselves. All programs require clearly-conceived and effectively-implemented processes with clearly-defined and measurable goals, objectives, and time lines.

Each school community is comprised of stakeholders who represent a broad range of interests, professional experiences, resources, talents, and abilities. Avoid the pitfalls experienced by many school communities wherein they fail in their efforts to cultivate the synergy needed to increase student achievement as a result of predetermining the talents, abilities, attributes, and expertise to be valued. Subsequently, in such school communities only those individuals reflective of the limited set of attributes which they value are "invited" to participate in their school improvement planning efforts, thereby limiting the pool of creative energies available to lead the school into the ranks of excellence and ensure that all students are succeeding.

There are two points for consideration that must guide your efforts whether school-wide, grade level, subject area, classroom or home/community:

1. Assume that the ideal discussion and planning group will demonstrate a broad range of talents, interests, abilities, personality types, temperaments, and strongly-held opinions about what is wrong and what is needed. The group should represent the complete spectrum of gender, ethnic, educational, and socioeconomic levels within the home/school community.

2. You cannot effectively guide the discussion and subsequent efforts of such a group without an effective, independent facilitator who has a clear focus and a clear vision of what is to be achieved.

Most efforts at school improvement get bogged down in details and run off into the sunset on any number of tangents initiated by strong-willed people. Egos, personal agendas, professional and political ambitions, long-held resentment toward staff members, biases, and individual prejudices are just some of the issues that will impact these discussions. Nevertheless, this is a microcosm of the very issues that accompany the communities served by the school. This is not a reason to turn tail and run or abandon the work that lies ahead. It is prudent, however, to factor these variables into the equation of cultivating the needed synergy to be developed.

Who should not Facilitate this Meeting:

- **The principal**. It is important for the principal to participate in the process and to provide an objective validation of opinions. The principal is probably aware of the egos and hidden agendas of individuals who will be participating in this process.

- **A teacher**. Well-respected teachers are needed to provide a calming and objective voice during the discussions which oftentimes become heated. Also, the perception of bias can also hinder open and candid discussions.

- **Anyone from central office**. Central office personnel are often perceived to lack understanding of what the needs of the school community are (real or imagined). Their involvement is much more valuable as participants who can assist in identifying the resources needed to fulfill strategic plans.

The ideal facilitator is a consultant, parent, mentor or business partner who has the confidence of the participants to effectively facilitate the discussions. The facilitator must have the appearance of impartiality, yet have a vested interest in the success of the school community.

Facilitator Responsibilities

1. Begin the process with a clear vision of the task at hand and what the discussions are designed to achieve.

2. Keep discussions focused on the pertinent issues and the stated goals of each meeting.

3. Provide a validating voice to help each participant feel that his or her opinion and ideas are valued and appreciated.

4. Keep discussions from going off on tangents or from being dominated by strong-willed people.

5. Keep discussions focused on developing solutions to the problems and away from attacks on individuals.

6. Keep discussions focused on the group's sphere of influence and away from issues that the group doesn't have the power to directly impact (e.g., negative media images, federal bureaucracy, established school board policy, etc.).

7. Draw all participants into the discussion.

Notes:

It is important that the facilitator familiarize him or herself with each of the eight Multiple Intelligences domains previously outlined (see Appendix). The dominant intelligences required by the group facilitator are *Logical/Mathematical* (attention to the process) and *Interpersonal* (a good understanding of the people). Through these two intellectual domains, the facilitator is able to successfully stay focused on each meeting's agenda and solicit input from all of the participants. A further understanding of M.I. theory allows the facilitator to provide a validating reaffirmation of the intellectual contributions of group members beyond their established educational levels or professional positions.

Furthermore, an understanding of M.I. theory helps the facilitator to understand how people process information and how to lead the group toward holistic solutions rather than the typical, "All we need to do is:"

- *implement a stricter discipline policy;*

- *develop more parental involvement;*

- *align the curriculum with the state learning goals; and*

- *have better preparation at the middle school level (or elementary, or preschool, or whatever the case may be).*

Who to Invite

While the Core Team, as previously discussed, is often comprised largely of people who have been actively involved in various school improvement processes and/or who have a personal interest in student success, at this point we must now solicit stakeholder involvement from throughout the school community:

- Who are the immediate stakeholders within the school community (e.g., administrators, teachers, support personnel, after/before school program representatives, and students)?

- Who are the extensions of the immediate stakeholders (e.g., parents, staff spouses, pastors, community representatives, etc.)?

- Who are stakeholders within the surrounding community (e.g., law enforcement, property/business owners, gang leaders, community services, etc.)?

- Who are the district and local governmental stakeholders?

- Who are the school-related organizational representatives (e.g., PTA/PTSA, Booster clubs, alumni associations, mentoring groups, business partners, etc.)?

- Who are the extra- or co-curricular activity representatives?

Notes:

The purpose of bringing together as diverse a group of stakeholders as possible is to cultivate the synergy and expand the creative and intellectual capacities required for holistic problem solving. The very strategies that are ultimately conceptualized will be done so through the prism of the ingrained beliefs and life experiences of the members of each strategy-focused team.

For example:

- We have lived in the world of personal computers for nearly two decades. Yet, with the internet revolution over the past five years, many teachers and administrators have never used E-mail, performed a web search or worked on a laptop computer. Subsequently, they are unable to conceptualize strategies that utilize such technology.

- Adults often know very little about what is going on in and around the school community, whereas, students know what is going on and directly determine what can go on. Refusal to bring them into the discussion on some level is to refuse to acknowledge their role as influential stakeholders within the school community.

- Despite the "separation of church and state," pastors exert great influence in school communities, particularly in the area of parent and community involvement within the school.

The synergy of new ideas, innovation, and experiences, in essence, new ways of thinking about teaching and learning is arrived at through the synergistic dynamics resulting from the broad range of experiences that a diverse group of stakeholders bring into the discussions.

It is undeniable that people bring their respective beliefs and opinions regarding those issues which passionately concern them into discussions.

For example, I believe that schools should become places of passion and purpose and that students should become engaged in the active pursuit of their respective dreams and aspirations through the curriculum. In this way, the curriculum itself, and subsequent learning outcomes are the most meaningful and engaging. Whenever I am a part of a school's planning efforts, my beliefs are interjected into the discussion. Subsequent to my involvement in my son's former elementary school, ranked in the top ten in the state of Georgia, the school has used a dream-related theme each year for the past five years.

Teachers concerned with parental involvement and central office support will introduce their concerns into the discussion. Administrators concerned with discipline and attendance will introduce their concerns into the discussion. School security personnel, passionate about safety and the logistical movement of students, will introduce their concerns into the discussion. Music and Art teachers may be more concerned about study trips and arts-related exposure and expenditures, while subject area teachers may be more passionate about the block schedule and allocated planning time. All stakeholders have valid and valuable perspectives that are important to shaping synergistic and holistic action plans and operational strategies.

Notes:

Common Questions
Confronting a School's Core Team:

Why are we wasting time discussing the school's Mission/Vision? Isn't the Mission/Vision the same for all schools?

Attached is an illustration of the Educational Continuum, outlined in the book, *Increasing Student Achievement: Volume I: Vision.*

Illustrated are the five major components common to the school improvement efforts and, ultimately, the education of students, within all schools (*Vision; Climate & Culture; Curriculum & Content; Instruction; and Assessment*). Within each of these components are many subcomponents such as: staff development, parental involvement, student code of conduct, discipline policies, instructional practices, learning goals, and assessment mechanisms.

Our purpose is to review our school's mission, vision, statement of beliefs, and guiding principles to ensure that they provide a sufficient compass to guide our school improvement efforts on behalf of our students.

Will I have to make a long-term commitment?

The Core Team is a strategic discussion group. As such, many members may be unable to make it from meeting to meeting as a result of their busy schedules. The ongoing commitment will be made by those members who become a part of the necessary functioning committees.

If I am not an expert at school improvement, how can I help?

Each of us has life experiences, skills, abilities, and interests that give us a unique perspective on the issues and of our school community and the students and families whom we serve. The underlying mission, vision, statement of beliefs, and guiding principles for our school community are simply words unless they are defined and embraced by all of the stakeholders, which will include our students.

The purpose of these initial meetings is to develop a Mission, Vision, Statement of Beliefs, and Core Values that will be used as a framework for the ensuing discussions. Only after these documents have been developed can the discussions pertaining to staff development, workshops, parenting seminars, curriculum, study trips, classroom instruction, intervention strategies, extended learning opportunities, behavioral expectations, utilization of resources, business-community partnerships, etc., be placed into the proper perspective as pieces of the overall puzzle of student achievement.

Meeting Strategies

Begin with a meeting-specific vision and goals that outline what is to be achieved at each meeting.

For example:

> *Our vision:*

> > *Our vision is to bring together a group of people who are concerned about the achievement of our students, to review the pertinent data, and to engage in a discussion of the unique challenges of our school community.*

> > *From that discussion, we hope to ensure that our stated Mission, Vision, Statement of Beliefs, and Core Values are sufficient to guide our strategic problem-solving efforts.*

Notes:

Our goals:

1.   *Review student achievement data.*

2.   *Identify the unique issues and obstacles pertinent to our school community.*

3.   *Develop a Mission, Vision, and Statement of Beliefs to guide our efforts in developing viable solutions to the issues and obstacles unique to our school community.*

4.   *Identify a research-based approach for developing long-term plans and strategies for increasing student achievement within our school community.*

5.   *Ensure that all decisions made within our school community are measured against the statement, "Is this in the best interest of our students?"*

Chapter 8

In our work, we often hear African American parents expressing the hope and desire that their children will achieve at the highest levels academically. What we also hear from these parents, though, is that one rarely sees in the media examples of young Black males who are achieving academically, being rewarded for those achievements, and feeling good about being smart. Even among advantaged African American families, we find that young males are heavily influenced by the popular culture that discourages pride in high academic achievement, demands that young Black males present a hard veneer to the world, and provides numerous opportunities for these young males to become involved in a world of crime and drugs.

— Freeman A. Hrabowski [Beating the Odds]

Closing the Achievement Gap

Throughout the process of constructing the school's guiding documents and structuring strategy-focused teams, I have made no distinction between the processes and approaches to be utilized by high versus low performing schools. The process is true and the continuum is constant, despite the geographic location or demographic make-up of the school. However, since many schools throughout the country are struggling to close identifiable achievement gaps, I would like to provide a specific example of how a low performing school or one that simply has high numbers of low performing students, would be driven by a clearly-defined mission/vision toward conceptualizing the operational strategies needed to lift more students into the ranks of high academic achievers.

Some of the issues common to low-performing schools are:

- *low teacher morale;*

- *high teacher turnover;*

- *ineffective classroom instruction;*

- *ineffective classroom management;*

- *disrespectful behavior exhibited by students, parents, teachers, and support staff;*

- *uninvolved parents;*

- *families living in poverty;*

- *transient or migrant families;*

- *low test scores;*

- *high number of children below grade level in academic areas;*

- *high absenteeism;*

- *high office referrals;*

- *high suspensions;*

- *high placement of children of color and children living in poverty into special education classes; and*

- *achievement gaps between identifiable groups of students (i.e., children of color and white students, boys and girls, middle class children and children living in poverty, etc.).*

These and the many other issues which are contributing factors to low performing schools can be considered the school's circles of influence. The illustration on the following page shows how the influences from the larger society impact families and communities. The influences of families and communities impact school climate and culture. The influences of school climate and culture impact classroom climate and culture, which ultimately impacts instruction, learning, and the attitudes of individual students within the classroom.

However distressing the influences might be, they represent the reality of many low performing schools. The challenge confronting schools being faced with such issues is to move beyond the enormity of the issues and remain true to the process of developing the school's mission/vision. These issues, no matter how depressing, must not be ignored. Understanding these influences helps to shape our vision of what is needed to increase student achievement and to close the respective achievement gaps.

Circles of Influence

Societal [Media Images]

Promotes Violence as a Means of Problem-Solving

Glorifies Profanity and Sarcasm

Negative Images Pertaining to Race, Gender, Religion. Socioeconomic Status, etc.

Sexually Explicit Programming

Glorifies Athletic/Entertainment over Academic Achievement

Perpetuates Gender/Race Biases and Stereotypes

Home/Community

Lack Adequate Study Time/Location

Lack of Parental Involvement in Academic Tasks

Lack of Positive Mentoring

Lack of Self-Control/ Self-Discipline

Requires Before/After School Care

Underemployed or Unstable Household

Limited Exposure to Successful Adults

Lack Financial Resources

Extended Family/Foster Care

Single-Parent Households or Lack of Positive Male/Female Influence

Low Household Goals/ Lack of Planning

Community/Household Void of Inspiration and Positive Images

Holds Teachers in Low Regard

Negative Role Models

Lack Academic Reinforcement

High Amount of TV Viewing

Lack of Spiritual Foundation

Negative Peer Pressure

Negative Peer Values

High Percentage of Free/Reduced Lunch

Many Teenage Pregnancies

Negative View of Women

Verbally/Physically Aggressive

Uses Violence to Resolve Conflicts

Negative Experiences with Law Enforcement

Firsthand Experience with Abuse

Victim or Perpetrator of Violent Crime

Medical/Dental Care

Lack of

Limited English or non-English Speaking Households

Poor Diet

Unorganized Households

Illiterate or Marginally Literate Family

School

Low Teacher Expectations

Low Teacher Morale

Frequent Referrals/Suspensions

Low Attendance

Frequent Tardies

Verbal/Physical Confrontations

Lack of Respect for School Property

Negative Teacher Attitudes Toward Students

Frequent Classroom Disruptions

Students Disruptive in Large Groups

Students Frequently Unprepared

Transient Student Population

Lack Adequate Supplies and Materials

Incomplete or Unfinished Homework

Individual

Negative Verbal/NonVerbal Communication

History of Discipline Problems and Low Academic Achievement

Lack of Respect for Individuals and Authority

Lacks Positive Focus/Direction

Violent Outbursts

Lacks a Middle/Upper Class Mentor

Low Self-Esteem

Apathy

Exhibits Self-Destructive Behaviors

Few Long-Term Goals

Uses Violence as a Means of Problem Solving

Lacks Meaningful Relationship with a Caring Adult

Does Not "Connect" Content to Outcomes

Lacks Nutrition

Poor Grooming & Personal Hygiene

Unrealistic Expectations

The following strategies reflect a focused approach to increasing student achievement based on the types of influences outlined on the Circles of Influence.

Our Mission

Our mission is to cultivate excellence in instruction, in learning, and in the application of the core knowledge as outlined in our State Standards.

Notice that it doesn't state, "create productive citizens" or "lifelong learners." This mission focuses on what we, as a school community, are going to be held accountable for, i.e., educating our students with the core knowledge as has been prescribed by our state and enabling them to demonstrate learning that meets our State Standards. The vision, and the operational strategies that evolve from it, may actually create productive citizens, lead students beyond the state standards, and create lifelong learners. However, our mission is one sentence, focusing on instruction and learning, and setting the benchmark, "State Standards."

In our school community, we have an identifiable achievement gap. The demographic data of our students is typical of low performing schools, i.e, low parental involvement, children living in poverty, high teacher turnover, ineffective classroom instruction, etc. Many students will enter school below grade level, from households in poverty, will lack at-home support mechanisms, and will initially struggle within any number of content areas, but the primary mission of the school remains constant, "to cultivate excellence in instruction" that is driven by a secondary mission to "provide frequent opportunities for students to acquire and apply the core knowledge as outlined in the State Standards."

From that guiding mission we can establish the following vision.

Our Vision

Our vision is:

- **to develop a school community of the highest academic, social, and professional standards that enables each student to exceed state and local learning goals as they journey toward realizing their God-given potential;**

- **to develop a safe, risk-free environment that recognizes and celebrates the inherent diversity of our school community;**

- **to develop a principle-centered school community guided by our stated Core Values;**

- **to help each student pursue his or her respective dreams and aspirations as he or she reaches the level of self-actualization through practical and relevant learning outcomes;**

- **to develop effective stakeholder teams for conceptualizing action plans and implementing strategies that provide continuing opportunities for our staff and students to discover, explore and pursue their respective dreams and aspirations; and**

- **to establish academic, co-curricular, and extracurricular programs that are driven by valid research, and/or the belief that they are in the best interests of our students.**

The components of such a vision outline what is necessary to fulfill the mission. The important themes, i.e., professional standards, instructional excellence, students and teachers being inspired to develop their dreams, providing self-actualizing opportunities driven by valid research, developing effective stakeholder teams, and being guided by our core values, all are reciprocal to the issues that would typically be identified in a vision development session.

Each of these components must evolve into operational strategies and implementation plans. The dialogue, discussions, debates, and disagreements to be encountered in our efforts to devise the necessary school-wide strategies that will lead to fulfilling the mission and achieving the vision must be guided by our core values and guiding beliefs:

Our Core Values

- **Compassion**

- **Collaboration**

- **Courage**

- **Integrity**

- **Resiliency**

- **Responsibility**

- **Respect**

- **Service**

Notes:

Our Guiding Beliefs

We believe that:

- **each teacher, support staff, and school stakeholder should identify at least one pocket of excellence in which he or she will volunteer to support.**

- **each teacher will thrive to be recognized as a "Best Practices" instructor in at least one area of the core or elective curriculum.**

- **each parent will contribute at least 10 volunteer hours in support of our school-wide or classroom efforts.**

- **every decision that is made will be done so within the framework of: "Is it consistent with our vision, and is it in the best interest of our students?"**

With the Mission, Vision, Core Values, and Beliefs as the guiding documents of a school community we are prepared to move on toward developing the needed strategy-focused teams that will be responsible for developing and implementing the necessary operational strategies to close the achievement gap.

Following are some of the steps that we may now take to begin the process of moving from the rhetoric of our guiding documents to developing operational strategies and implementation plans:

1. Every stakeholder within the school community (i.e., teachers, administrators, support staff, parents, mentors, business partners, school bus drivers, custodians, etc.) will receive a three-ring binder labeled, "School Improvement Planning Guide."

2. Every stakeholder will receive a copy of each of our guiding documents and will be encouraged to look for ways of pursuing our mission and communicating our beliefs within their sphere of influence, i.e., on the school bus, in the cafeteria, in the before and after school programs, through our custodial services, in the front office, and within the classroom.

3. Any ideas of action plans developed by any of our stakeholders will be submitted to the administrative office, typed, and distributed to each stakeholder as a School Improvement Planning Manual update.

4. Each decision that is made regarding the utilization of resources, teacher planning, professional development, student assignment, curriculum, staff, families, and students must be made in a way that is consistent with the stated mission, vision, core values, and beliefs.

5. Each grade level, subject area, and school activity must develop a Mission/Vision that is in support of the overall school mission/vision.

6. The Mission/Vision must be used to guide all debriefing and pre-planning efforts.

Notes:

Now that our school community has a compass to guide our way (mission, vision, core values, and beliefs), we may begin to identify the areas and individuals who can provide leadership in making our vision operational.

State/Local Goals

Preparing our students to *exceed* state and local learning goals is predicated upon our understanding of what those goals are. Only then can we ensure that we align our curriculum, thematic units, and instructional methods with those standards so that our students are prepared to perform well on the various state and nationally-normed tests. They will be held accountable for demonstrating proficiency.

Closing the achievement gap and conceptualizing strategies that relate to the real needs of our students requires that we establish goals and operational strategies for such areas as:

1. **Subject Area Standards:** Subject Area Teams would be responsible for identifying the key learning outcomes by subject area that will enable students to demonstrate proficiency in accordance with the state/local learning goals.

   A. Develop a matrix for each subject and align the units of study with the state standards, sequenced in a manner consistent with the district calendar of standardized and end-of-grade testing.

   B. Identify key interdisciplinary and thematic units of study that are timed and aligned with the testing calendar and state learning standards.

   C. Publish a parent-friendly newsletter of at-home tips that will reinforce key concepts as they are covered throughout the school year.

D. Ensure that unit tests, quizzes, and exams are aligned with the state standards.

E. Create an annual time line for instruction and reinforcement of those key areas which children are being held accountable for knowing.

2. **Grade Level Standards:** Grade Level Teams will be responsible for identifying the key learning outcomes by grade level that will enable students to demonstrate proficiency in accordance with state learning goals. Strategies, indicated previously, will apply.

3. **State Gateway Standards:** A Strategy-Focused Team will be responsible for identifying each State End-of-Grade or Gateway Standard.

A. Each End-of-Grade or Gateway Standard will be compared against each subject area and grade level to ensure continuity of instruction and lesson plan development.

B. An assessment schedule will be developed to ensure that students are progressing in a manner consistent with meeting the Gateway Standards.

C. Appropriate intervention programs will be developed to ensure that all students successfully meet the Gateway Standards.

D. Students who are not on schedule to meet the Gateway Standards will be identified and entered into the appropriate intervention programs.

Notes:

E. Each department will be responsible for devising a mission statement and course syllabus which outlines the state standards and how the coursework is designed to help students meet the standards.

4. **Nationally-normed Testing:** Strategy-Focused teams will develop test preparation strategies for school, home, after school programs, mentors, and tutors.

   Parents will receive a K-12 action plan that outlines the impact of standardized testing on course selections and student placement in middle and high school classes, and in college admissions selection.

5. **Gifted Ed Criteria:** A Strategy-Focused Team will be developed to create classroom and home strategies to help more students develop the skills needed to qualify for Talented and Gifted programs.

   The team will also be responsible for developing an in-depth understanding of instructional practices, at-home support strategies, and alternative forms of assessment which will provide for more children to meet Gifted selection criteria.

6. **Inclusion Standards:** A Strategy-Focused Team will be developed to ensure research-based practices to help special education students have access to the mainstream curriculum, co-curricular, and extracurricular activities.

   This team will further be responsible for ensuring that students have not been mis-diagnosed for special education and that each student has an action plan that will allow them to move out of special education if they have the ability to do so.

7. **Professional Development:** A Strategy-Focused Team will be established to assess our success at helping students meet the state standards. They will be responsible for coordinating professional development activities that are directly related to areas of weakness and for ensuring that our professional staff remains on the cutting edge of research-based teaching strategies, instructional delivery, lesson design, and effectively engaging students in the areas of learning deemed essential to achieving standards.

8. **Honors/Advanced Placement:** A Strategy-Focused Team will be responsible for developing a matrix to outline the classes, grade point averages, and test scores required to qualify students for Advanced Placement and honors classes in middle and high school.

School Goals

Evolving from each component of our school's vision will be any number of operational components, each of which will require appropriate operational strategies. The operative phrase is, "If it's in the vision, then it must be assessed." A qualitative or quantitative goal must be established for each operational component evolving from our school's vision. This is the only way to ensure that the vision moves beyond rhetoric to systemic and sustainable practices.

Notes:

The following operational components reflect those areas directly related to closing the achievement gap:

1. **High Student Achievement:** With the books [Increasing Student Achievement, Volumes I-V], as a resource guide, each department will be responsible for creating the appropriate departmental, subject area or grade level mission/vision together with an instructional action-plan for ensuring increased student achievement.

   Such an action plan might include:

   - a schedule of assemblies, guest speakers, study trips, and expanded learning opportunities to reinforce the core knowledge being taught.

   - consistent practices and expectations within all classrooms by subject area and grade level, e.g., heading papers, quizzes, tests, grading rubrics, at-home rubrics, and reinforcement within the before and after school programs.

   - research-based, effective instructional approaches, i.e., brain-compatible instruction, building upon preexisting knowledge, using peers as tutors and coaches, sequencing of lessons, etc.

   - opportunities to recognize, celebrate, and validate student achievement.

   - study groups, academic clubs, tutors, mentors, and opportunities to compete in academic competitions.

   - a resource center that offers research materials that assist with organization, test preparation, time-management, note-taking skills, presentation skills, writing research papers, as well as other appropriate reference materials.

- before and after school programs that relate directly to student social and academic needs.

- student planners as an integral part of the curriculum and academic communications tool.

- each department and subject area being responsible for compiling a list of necessary supplies, resources and resource materials, and expanded learning opportunities.

2. **Celebration of Diversity:** Based on the demographic analysis of the student population we will ensure that:

- there is a thematic unit that culminates in a culturally-relevant celebration for each culture represented within the school community.

- there is a flag of national origin for each student represented within the school community.

- there is a sign welcoming visitors to the school community representing each language spoken within the school community.

- cultural themes are presented at staff meetings, school-wide celebrations, on the cafeteria menu, etc., throughout the school year.

- an interpreter is identified for each language spoken within the school community.

Notes:

- each non-English speaking child is assigned a bilingual buddy.

- each multi-lingual teacher and staff person is listed as an in-school resource.

- cultural, gender, generational, or ethnic-based communication gaps are identified and staff development is scheduled accordingly.

- a school-wide image audit is routinely performed to ensure the diversity of images presented throughout the school community is reflective of the student population and communities served.

- a culturally-specific bulletin board is established for each culture represented within the school community displaying language, customs, foods, geographical map, political structure, major religions, etc., that is aligned with the social studies curriculum.

3. **Practical Learning Outcomes:** Each area of the core and elective curricula will have a culminating event that represents a practical learning outcome. Such events should be driven by school-wide needs:

A. Art: An Art Show where student art, silk-screened t-shirts, student-developed greeting cards, and fashions are displayed and sold.

B. Math: Students compete in local mathematics-related competitions or in a in-school math quiz bowl.

C. Science: Students compete in state and local Science Fairs or in an in-school Science Fair. Students engage in hiking, research, and other exploratory activities.

D. Literature: Student essays, poetry, and short stories are published in an annual anthology.

E. Writing: Students engage in a writing campaign soliciting donations, equipment, furniture, etc., based on school needs.

F. Speaking: Students engage in speech and debate competitions and develop presentations to solicit business partners.

G. School Newspaper: Students engage in the writing, layout, typography, photography, graphic arts design, illustration, publishing, printing, collating, and distribution of a school newspaper.

H. Social Studies: Students plan, present, exhibit, design, and discuss culturally-relevant issues, particularly as a part of culturally-specific thematic units.

I. Music: Students write and perform musical compositions culminating in the production of a school CD.

J. Radio/Television: Students create and present an in-school radio and television program.

K. Sports: Students create instructional videos of sports skills, techniques, research, nutrition, muscle building, muscle maintenance and repair, the anatomy, etc.

L. Special Interest Theme Walls: Students, parents, and teachers create and maintain special interest theme walls that may include such areas as: historical information, photographs, facts and most frequently asked questions, current magazine articles and newspaper stories, reference materials, student perspectives, dreams, aspirations, etc.

Notes:

M.Guest Speaker Library: Reference materials pertinent to all of the school's guest speakers including published works, video tapes of school presentations, vita, etc.

N. Entrepreneurship: Student-led group responsible for the school store and interfacing with all of the other related groups for exploring entrepreneurial opportunities.

4. **Effective Teams:** Develop a Strategy-Focused Team responsible for each teacher or student-driven activity. Each team will be responsible for following a format of data gathering and creating a report for the annual School Improvement Operational Manual.

5. **Research-based Programs:** Each area represented in the core and elective curricula will be responsible for identifying relevant research that supports the instructional or operational approach of the program that is to be included in the School Improvement Operational Manual.

6. **Integration of Core Values:** A cross collaboration of subject areas is required to design an interdisciplinary unit for each of the school's core values. For example:

A. Literature: Each classroom is responsible for reading, discussing, and writing essays about how the core value of "Courage" was demonstrated by the great eagle in the story of *The Eagles who Thought They were Chickens [Mychal Wynn]*.

B. Art: Groups of students are responsible for designing and displaying an eagle's nest in one corner of each classroom or within a prominent location at the entrance to the school. The nest is to be built from the dreams and aspirations reflected within the school community.

Students develop banners, t-shirts, flags, note cards, etc., which embody each of the school's core values.

C. Photography: Pictures of each student, teacher, administrator, and staff person are taken and enclosed in the eagle's nest.

D. Writing: Students engage in a school-wide writing contest based on the theme, "How can we demonstrate Courage within our school community?"

Students write letters to their heroes and heroines who exemplify the school's core values.

E. Community partnerships: Parents, community and business partners are asked to donate their favorite books relating to each of the core values.

F. Dramatic performance: Students and/or teachers present a dramatic performance relating to each core value.

G. Media Center: Books and book covers are displayed that relate to the school's core values. A reading, reference, and research section is developed specifically for each of the school's core values.

H. Student Newspaper: Students write articles relating to each of the core values.

Notes:

I. Music: Students write songs, identify contemporary and classical compositions that reflect the core values.

J. Special Interests: Each student club, extracurricular activity, and special interest group is required to develop a pledge or statement regarding how the school's core values will be reflected in their respective activities.

K. Expanded Learning Opportunities: Films, literature, and guest speakers are identified which reflect core values.

L. Core Curriculum: Historical figures who exemplify the school's core values are identified and discussed.

M. Student Dreams and Aspirations: Students are engaged in identifying, discussing, and presenting people who are living their dreams and who exemplify the school's core values.

Papers, essays, and collages can be presented and displayed.

N. Entrepreneurship: Students identify, create, and resale promotional products that relate to the school's core values (i.e., cups, bumper stickers, t-shirts, imprinted items, note cards, posters, baseball caps, etc.).

O. Customs and Rituals: Classroom and school-wide customs and rituals are developed to promote, reinforce, and recognize the school's core values.

7. **Integration of State Standards:** Each department is responsible for creating a time line of instructional units that are aligned with the state standards by subject area and grade level. Each department is also responsible for identifying supplemental resource materials that are aligned with the standards and that appropriately supplement classroom instruction.

8. **Publish Our Efforts:** A Strategy-Focused Team is established to compile a book outlining school improvement efforts in the form of a School Improvement Yearbook. Data, photographs, lesson plans, teacher and stakeholder perspectives, student performances, test preparation, best practices, research, and all school improvement-related efforts will be gathered together for publication.

9. **School of Excellence:** A Strategy-Focused Team will be established to research and train each teacher in the State and Federal Schools of Excellence Guidelines and Practices. The team will further complete and submit the required application.

    This team will further provide the nucleus of a school-wide grant writing team in support of school-wide funding needs.

Stakeholder Needs

While there are undoubtedly many areas of stakeholder needs that ultimately must be addressed by operational strategies, those that follow are typical of those areas which have a direct correlation to our efforts to increase student achievement and to close the achievement gap.

The demographic analysis of a typical student population often reveals that there is a significant achievement gap between the following identifiable groups of students:

- African-American students at all grade levels

- Non-English speaking Hispanic students

- Children living in poverty

- Migrant and working class families

The typical demographic analysis of a teaching and support staff may reveal that:

- the school lacks bilingual teachers or translators;

- there are few male teachers, with the balance of the men in the building being security officers and custodians;

- a disproportionately high number of the office referrals are made by teachers with less than five years of teaching experience, with the majority of office referrals being made by one teacher;

- a disproportionately high number of office referrals are made by middle class female teachers who refer poor male students to the office;

- a Staff Interest Survey reveals that teachers and support staff have experiences, passions or interests in the following areas: hiking, classical music, scuba diving, radio and television, the rain forests, body building, cooking, shopping, fine dining, writing, poetry, automotive mechanics, cabinetry, interior design, knitting, and jewelry; and

- a Multiple Intelligences Survey reveals that a dominant intelligence in each of the eight intellectual domains is represented within our teacher, administrative, and support staff (i.e., Verbal/Linguistic, Logical/Mathematical, etc.).

School-wide resource analysis:

- School has Title I funding, but few other resources.

- School does not have any business partners.

- Media center lacks up-to-date materials.

- School lacks technology.

- Playground equipment and school facilities are outdated.

- Assemblies are held in the cafeteria. The sound system and acoustics are ineffective.

These are typical of the types of issues that stand in the way of a school's pursuit of excellence. However, once the mission has been stated and the vision is clear, we must focus our energies on developing goals and operational strategies for each of the areas identified:

1. **Children in Poverty:** Teachers and support staff are responsible for reading the book, *A Framework for Understanding Poverty* by Ruby Payne, and for formulating an instructional action plan that deals with the unique needs of children in poverty and teaches students the hidden values of the middle class. Such strategies might include:

Notes:

- engaging all students in reading books profiling the lives of individuals who grew up in poverty such as, *Follow Your Dreams: Lessons that I Learned in School.*

- engaging students in classroom discussions about how growing up in poverty might impact a person's long-term dreams and aspirations.

- engaging students in pre-activities whereby they develop a series of questions for guest speakers who share their personal experiences of growing up in poverty.

- engaging students in instructional activities such as an essay competition, illustration competition, recognition for demonstrating the school's core values, etc.

- hosting an assembly whereby authors of books that are related to growing up in poverty can elaborate on the points from their books and interact with students through a question and answer session.

- hosting a book-signing reception for students who meet a predetermined selection criteria, together with stakeholders who are supporting the school's efforts toward achieving its vision (i.e., book reports, essays, community service, etc.).

- soliciting business donations for a drawing of door prizes based on expected student behavior during the assembly.

- providing a Town Hall meeting with authors and guest speakers.

- scheduling a series of assemblies following the same format with guest speakers who have experienced living in poverty.

- providing resource services for the unique needs of children living in poverty. Such services might include providing a washer/dryer, ironing board, clothing donations, toiletries, personal grooming and hygiene supplies, nutritional snacks, and a listing of social services organizations.

- engaging students in a letter writing campaign to local and national businesses to solicit donations for school and personal supplies.

- providing a list of school and personal supplies for students to select from as rewards for participation in classroom and school-wide activities.

- setting up business, community, and social services information tables at all school events.

- arranging for a regular schedule of vaccinations and inoculations.

- setting up a permanent Children and Family Resource Room.

- developing business partnerships with pediatricians, social services, psychiatrists, food banks, job banks, teen parent agencies, and other appropriate social and community programs and agencies.

- developing an introductory workshop entitled "Effectively Teaching Children in Poverty" for new teachers.

Notes:

2. **Negative Peer Pressures:** Establish a Strategy-Focused Team responsible for developing an implementation strategy for the instructional and community activities outlined in Dr. Peggy Dolan's book, *School Violence...Calming the Storm: A Guide for Developing a Fight-Free School.* Review the discipline data and identify those students who require specialized intervention strategies.

3. **Discipline Problems:** Establish a Strategy-Focused Team responsible for reviewing resource materials and developing intervention strategies for targeted groups of students based on student demographic data. Establish a second Strategy-Focused Team responsible for developing customs and rituals for celebrating students who demonstrate leadership skills and model the school's core values.

   Children at Risk: Establish a Strategy-Focused Team for implementing a Gentlemen's and Ladies club *[Inspired to Learn by Stephen G. Peters]* for gender-specific groups.

   African-American Males: Establish a Strategy-Focused Team for modeling the types of classroom and intervention strategies outlined in the book, *Empowering African-American Males to Succeed: A Ten Step Approach for Parents and Teachers.*

   Leadership Skill Development: Establish a Strategy-Focused Team for implementing the *Eagle Team Leadership Curriculum [Wynn],* for a cross-socio, cross-gender, cross-ethnic, and cross-academic group of students who have been identified as having untapped leadership potential.

4. **Parenting Skills:** Develop a Strategy-Focused Team responsible for analyzing instructional strategies, support materials, and student support services needed to assist in achieving the school's academic goals and each department's respective mission.

Strategies might include:

- providing each parent with a copy of the book, *Ten Steps to Helping Your Child Succeed in School [Wynn],* and a recommended reading list.

- creating a book club for reviewing the strategies and completing the activities outlined in the book.

- scheduling a series of parenting seminars to teach parents how to do the suggested at-home activities which will support the school's student achievement efforts.

- identifying and effectively fulfilling parent needs at school functions, i.e., child care, food, door prizes, guest speakers whom parents value, student performances/recognition, making parents feel special, etc.

- providing opportunities for parents to apply their unique talents, skills, and interests toward school-wide efforts, e.g., decorating, braiding hair, cooking, maintaining bulletin boards, doing nails, washing/ironing clothes, health and fitness, automotive mechanics, painting, cabinetry, brick masonry, gardening, computer technology, reading stories, or answering phones. Parents could also apply their professional talents

Notes:

in such areas as illustration, medicine, writing, publishing, law, landscaping, or construction toward school needs.

- developing a Parent Buddy Program between experienced and teen parents.

- developing business partnerships with parents' employers.

5. **At-Home Support:** Create a Strategy-Focused Team responsible for reviewing the student schedule and devising a plan for maximizing the instructional focus on the areas relating to the state learning goals.

Each department will further identify or develop:

- weekly tips for at-home reinforcement of the instructional focus.

- strategies with the before and after school programs for ways to reinforce the instructional focus.

- a program of rewards and incentives to encourage reading during breakfast, lunch, and in before and after school programs.

- a relationship between each child and individuals who can assist with homework (i.e., parents, extended family, siblings, mentors, business partners or other students).

- grading rubrics that minimize the importance of homework toward student grades.

- a parent room that has examples of how to set up study areas, resources and supplies, and to minimize distractions (e.g., television/radio).

- at-home visits to help parents set up work areas;

- a system for teaching parents how to set up before and after school home routines;

- a Parent Survey to understand parent needs for homework assistance and after school support;

- after and before school homework and study clubs across all core and elective subject areas;

- a relationship with a local church, YMCA, and community organizations that can also provide after school homework and study clubs; and

- classroom study buddies as a means of connecting high and low achieving students.

6. **Below Grade Level:** Create a Grade Level Team responsible for identifying ability levels and assessing preexisting knowledge during the first weeks of school.

    Each teacher will be responsible for:

    - identifying group facilitators and segregating students into homogeneous working groups;

    - creating one-on-one study opportunities between high and low achieving students;

    - creating a learning and study profile for each student to be maintained in a Student Study Profile binder;

    - conducting a strengths, weaknesses, multiple intelligences, personality types, and learning styles inventory for each student;

    - addressing study weaknesses through

instructional activities and workshops in such areas as note-taking skills, time management, organizational skills, learning styles, personality types, multiple intelligences, goal setting, study habits, prioritizing homework, test preparation, etc;

- following student data gathering and conducting a parenting seminar on how to utilize the data for structuring effective home support systems; and

- providing intensive reading programs to ensure that all children achieve grade-level reading ability within one school year.

7. **Nutritional and Personal Needs:** Create a Strategy-Focused Team to identify business partners who can assist in providing nutritional snacks consistent with the developmental needs of children. Provide appropriate nutritional snacks throughout the school community: i.e., classrooms, before and after school programs, in study halls, at P.E., etc.

   Also provide access to a washer/dryer, iron, personal grooming and hygiene supplies, clothes, etc., with volunteers to help ensure that each child is clean, appropriately dressed, and ready to learn.

8. **Long-Term Plans:** Create Subject Area Teams responsible for developing a time line and flow chart of the impact of their subjects on students' long-term plans.

   For example, algebra is considered a "Gateway" class in the area of mathematics. Students who succeed in algebra frequently continue into

Notes:

geometry, trigonometry, calculus, and higher-level courses in science and often in technology. Many other subject areas are frequently required for consideration into certain undergraduate programs.

The collaboration of the subject area teams should lead to such efforts as:

A. Creating a subject matrix on how certain classes provide the building blocks to other classes.

B. Providing examples of how honors and advanced placement classes impact grade point average.

C. Providing examples of the subjects that are commonly associated with certain career paths.

D. Creating illustrations of how subjects are used in popular student careers, e.g., math is used to calculate percentages, rates of return, and payment of income taxes in professional sports.

E. Conducting parenting seminars on how to help children select classes that provide the best opportunity for applying to college and how elementary grades and test scores impact middle school, and middle school impacts high school, and high school impacts college, etc.

Relevant Research

A key component to fulfilling the school's mission and achieving our vision is to identify the best available research that is pertinent to the issues unique to our school community. Within each of the seven major components illustrated above, we will attempt to identify:

1. **Published Research:** A Strategy-Focused Team will be established to continually identify pertinent research and research-based programs that are in practice.

2. **Pertinent Consultants:** A Strategy-Focused Team will be established to identify consultants with the expertise in each area of need within our school community.

3. **Focused Experimentation:** Where there is no available research or consultants to utilize, we will gather, analyze, and utilize in-school data to focus our efforts in implementing new programs and strategies based on our belief that they will be in the best interest of our students and help us to achieve our vision.

School/Community Connection

The following strategies outline operational components related to the major vision component of the School/Community Connection. As a result of busing, specialty schools, magnet schools, and numerous other changes in school districts that have moved us away from community schools, teachers and administrators, somewhere along the road, lost sight of the important fact that the surrounding community plays in the success of a school and it's impact upon school-wide climate and culture. The school is one of the most important institutions within a community. Our vision explicitly states that stakeholder collaboration is important to student success.

Goals and operational strategies for each of the areas identified might be stated as:

1. **Alumni:** The school's alumni is identified as one of the most valuable school resources.

    A Strategy-Focused Team must be established to coordinate such efforts as:

    -   creating an alumni Hall of Fame with photographs and biographical sketches and current companies and employers of the school's alumni;

    -   creating an alumni association and associate booster clubs for supporting school-wide activities;

    -   creating a series of alumni recognition activities;

    -   scheduling a series of study trips to alumni businesses and places of employment;

    -   creating an alumni database of skills, talents, and influences; and

    -   creating a series of customs and rituals that involve the alumni and their families in school events.

2. **Community Resources:** Create a Strategy-Focused Team responsible for creating and maintaining a database of community resources, i.e., heath facilities, social services, law enforcement, community services, churches, other schools, political representatives, businesses, business associations, foundations, fraternities/sororities, etc.

Notes:

A. Maintain an updated listing of community contacts, executive directors, and current elected officials.

B. Schedule study trips and instructional activities regarding elected officials and their respective areas of responsibility as they relate to the school and surrounding community.

C. Develop a resource database of television, radio, and print media contacts.

D. Create a directory of community resources for children and their families.

E. Host an annual Community Resource Fair as a part of the school opening celebration.

F. Establish a Strategy-Focused Team responsible for coordinating community nights throughout the school year at such venues as roller rinks, bowling alleys, restaurants, movie theaters, photo developing labs, community agencies, churches, etc.

G. Create a Community News Team comprised of student journalists responsible for reporting on community news and events in the student newspaper.

H. Invite community representatives to participate on Strategy-Focused Teams and School Improvement Planning Committees.

3. **Business Partners:** Establish a Strategy-Focused Team for developing and coordinating business partnerships:

A. Cultivate student leaders who can meet with and discuss the school's needs with potential business partners.

B. Create banners, recognizing all business partners, to hang prominently throughout the school community.

C. Create Business Partner Recognition Programs.

D. List business partners in the school's newsletter and student newspaper.

E. Identify specific areas where business partners can support the curriculum.

F. Invite business partners to all school-wide events.

G. Encourage teacher, student, and family patronage of business partners.

H. Provide business partners with an opportunity to create displays within the school community which connect their services to the school's curriculum, i.e., a school grocery, post office, automotive parts store, photo developing lab, etc.

I. Create special recognition plaques, awards, etc., to prominently recognize business partners.

J. Identify all of the available partners in education programs where businesses donate a portion of the their sales back to local schools.

Notes:

K. Identify business partners for all of the critical needs services of the school, i.e., framing, trophies, catering, bookstores, banners, t-shirts, school supplies, etc.

L. Develop relationships with the local Chamber of Commerce and business and professional organizations.

4. **Churches and Community Agencies:** Establish a Strategy-Focused Team to develop a relationship with the churches and community agencies serving the school community:

A. Identify the pastors, directors, and significant contact persons.

B. Create a database of the programs that they coordinate.

C. Create a community bulletin board for announcements of community events.

D. Host an annual Church and Community Recognition Day.

E. Have school staff attend the programs and services at local churches and announce that they are representing the school.

F. Invite church and community representatives to participate on Strategy-Focused Teams and in the school improvement planning process.

5. **Service Activities:** Have each department identify a community service project that is aligned with the curriculum. Such projects might include:

• serving meals to the homeless during Thanksgiving;

- having a book buddy at a Retirement Home;

- hosting a community clean-up day;

- hosting a fundraising fun run or walk-a-thon;

- participating in annual community or civic events, i.e., parades, voter registration, literacy programs, etc.;

- developing local and international school partners;

- working with Habitat for Humanity; and

- participating in clothing and food drives.

6. **Elected Officials:** Create a Strategy-Focused Team to create and maintain a database of all local, state, and federal representatives who make decisions that impact the school community:

   A. Schedule study trips to the offices of elected officials.

   B. Integrate letter writing into the curriculum regarding issues of concern to the school community.

   C. Identify the process for requesting proclamations and school recognition.

   D. Submit student work to the local, state, and federal offices (e.g., papers, artwork, etc.).

7. **Facilities:** Create a Strategy-Focused Team to identify the pertinent local facilities available to the school, e.g., parks, boating clubs, YMCA, churches, art schools, trade schools, colleges, universities, school district buildings, corporations, etc. for staff development, planning meetings, student programs, etc.

These examples clearly illustrate why closing the achievement gap requires that we establish Strategic-Focused Teams as a mechanism for moving the school's Vision from mere rhetoric to effective operational strategies. It is the only way to ensure holistic systemic and sustainable strategies that will lead to measurable increases in student achievement. Engaging in the process of identifying the problems shifts our focus from what we are to seeing what we can become. Once the Vision is written, such strategies ensure that the vision becomes more than just words, and that the school's Vision is communicated, embraced, and utilized to guide all school improvement efforts.

The Greatest Untapped Resource

As complicated and time-consuming as the process appears, the keys to success are the under-utilized human resources readily available within each school community, i.e., the stakeholders (parents, teachers, students, business partners, support staff, administrators, etc.). Once the major and minor components of the Mission/Vision are identified, there merely is the function of aligning what needs to be done with the respective passions of the various stakeholders within the school community. These passions are most frequently aligned with the multiplicity of intelligences, talents, and interests of those within your school community; the artists, planners, organizers, writers, poets, storytellers, painters, graphic artists, journalists, photographers, cabinet makers, politicians, salespeople, public relations specialists, press release writers, grant writers, public speakers, comedians, teachers, tutors, mentors, dancers, singers, actors/actresses, choreographers, musicians, song writers, athletes, personal trainers, nutritionists, hikers, joggers, walkers, quilters, knitters, coaches, entrepreneurs, fashion designers, interior designers, chefs, and brick masons. All are awaiting a vision of the village that you are attempting to create.

With so much talent to draw upon, I believe that any school community can transform itself into a place where teachers teach with passion and students learn with purpose.

Strategic-Focused Teams are responsible for:

- conceptualizing and implementing component parts of holistically-conceived strategies (e.g., visuals, communication, logistics, cultivating relationships, etc.);

- working with small groups of people to engage in the effective identification of pertinent data, analyzing such data, conceptualizing solutions based on such data, and carrying out implementation strategies based on those solutions;

- identifying the needed resources and expertise to successfully carry out implementation strategies;

- cultivating broad-based support and involvement from the school's stakeholders;

- performing a continuing re-assessment of problems and solutions; and

- being driven by the passionate pursuit of excellence within the problem-solving areas assigned to the group.

Each component of our stated Vision must provide the driving force toward developing a qualitative and quantitative strategy that incorporates the following three dynamics:

1. *Strategy.* Make strategy the school-wide agenda. Strategy must be communicated in a way that can be understood and acted on.

2. *Focus.* Create incredible focus. Every resource and activity within the school community must be aligned to carry out the strategy.

Notes:

3.   *Organization.* Mobilize all stakeholders to act in fundamentally different ways. Develop the logic and architecture to establish school-wide linkages to departments, services, and individuals.

Developing the strategy to achieve your vision, as in the entire school transformation process, should be a researched-based endeavor. You should be able to answer the following questions:

1.   What research will we base our organizational structure on for the execution of our strategy?

2.   While our headstart, elementary, middle school, junior high schools, and high school programs are based upon child developmental research, what research will we utilize as the foundation for organizing the adults responsible for executing the strategies needed to fulfill the mission of educating students?

The strategic implementation research outlined by the authors of *The Strategy Focused Organization* could be adapted to any school community. The research of successful organizations does not identify one common approach, but five common themes or guiding principles:

1.   Translate the Strategy to Operational Terms.

2.   Align the Organization to the Strategy.

3.   Make Strategy Everyone's Every day Job.

4.   Make Strategy a Continuous Process.

5.   Mobilize Change through Executive Leadership.

In my experience, there are five fundamental principles for guiding your efforts toward developing the holistic strategies needed to lead to systemic and sustainable increases in student achievement:

1. Engage in a candid and open discussion of all of the issues hindering student achievement. Whether real or imagined, all stakeholders must have an opportunity to articulate their concerns and their perceptions.

2. Group the problems into general categories (e.g., school safety, student achievement, school community relationships, resource needs, etc.).

   Note: These two steps have been taken, thus far, in the process of developing the school's vision.

3. Prioritize the problems.

4. Assess both problems and solutions through a Multiple Intelligences framework.

5. Develop Strategy-Focused Teams to further conceptualize and implement the needed solutions.

Principles four and five require a fundamental shift to school-wide problem solving. Traditional problem solving is to delegate a group of problems to a committee. For example, discipline policies and all related discipline issues are usually assigned to the Administrative Team or an Ad Hoc Discipline Committee; curriculum issues are usually relegated to Subject Area or Grade Level Teams; increasing parental involvement is usually left entirely in the hands of the school's principal (beyond the PTA/PTSA cookie sales or membership drives). Each of these groups typically work in isolation. Subsequently, their solutions are typically event-driven (i.e., cookie sale, guest speaker, policy change, etc.), rarely holistic, and are most frequently driven by one person (the school's principal, PTA president, department chair, etc.).

Beginning with the End in Mind

The often painstaking process of constructing the school's vision cannot be avoided. Clarity of focus is critical to the work ahead. The process itself, i.e., creating M.I. teams, engaging in a problem-solving analysis, and conceptualizing and implementing operational strategies, will be repeated over and over in each of the components to follow.

The only way to ensure that the school's vision is clearly defined and that it becomes commonly shared is to make it the driving force behind all school-wide efforts toward increasing student achievement (the fulfillment of our mission). This occurs by establishing goals, defining the measurement criteria, and determining the time frame during which assessment will occur.

At the point that we establish the school's Vision, we should familiarize ourselves with the questions that will guide our assessment efforts:

1. Did we begin the school year with a clearly-stated Mission?

2. Did we develop a clearly-defined Vision that represents the driving force behind all school-wide planning efforts and utilization of resources?

3. Did we develop a Strategy-Focused Team that is responsible for each component of our vision?

4. Did each Strategy-Focused Team establish a measurable goal with a time line for their areas of responsibility?

5. Did we establish the assessment criteria for each goal?

If it's in the vision, measure it.

The only way to ensure that we are proceeding toward achieving our mission is to measure our progress toward achieving the component parts of our vision.

Notes:

References

Armstrong, Thomas. *Awakening Your Child's Natural Genius: Enhancing Curiosity, Creativity, and Learning Ability*. New York: Putnam Books, 1991.

Deal, Terrence E. Peterscon, Kent D. *Shaping School Culture: the Heart of Leadership*. San Francisco, CA: Jossey-Bass, 1999.

Dolan, Margaret R. *School Violence...Calming the Storm: A Guide to Creating a Fight-Free School Environment*. Marietta, GA: Rising Sun Publishing, 1998.

Fliegel, Seymour. *Miracle in East Harlem: The Fight for Choice in Public Education*. New York: Random House, 1993.

Gardner, Howard. *Frames of Mind: The Theory of Multiple Intelligences*. New York: Harper and Row, 1983.

Glasser, William. *The Quality School Teacher*. New York, HarperCollins, 1993.

Hilliard, Payton-Stewart, and Williams. *Infusion of African and African-American Content in the School Curriculum*. Morristown, PA: Aaron Press, 1990.

Holt, John. *How Children Learn*. New York: Addison-Wesley, 1983.

Johnson, David, Johnson, Robert, and Holubec, Edythe J. *Cooperation in the Classroom*. Edina, MN: Interaction Book Company, 1988.

Jones, Laurie Beth. *The Path: Creating Your Mission Statement for Work and for Life*. New York: Hyperiod, 1996.

Notes:

Kaplan, Robert S., Norton, David P. *The Strategy-Focused Organization: How Balanced Scorecard Companies Thrive in the New Business Environment.* Cambridge, MA: Harvard Business School, 2001.

Kohn, Alfie. *Punished by Rewards: The Trouble with Gold Stars, Incentive Plans, A's, Praise, and Other Bribes.* New York: Houghton Mifflin, 1993

Lazear, David. *Seven Ways of Knowing: Teaching for Multiple Intelligences.* Palatine, IL: IRI/Skylight Publishing, 1991.

Maslow, Abraham H. *Maslow on Management.* New York: John Wiley, 1998.

Merriam, S.B. *Case Study Research in Education: A Qualitative Approach.* San Francisco, CA: Jossey-Bass, 1988.

Monroe, Lorraine. *Nothing's Impossible: Leadership Lessons from Inside and Outside the Classroom.* New York: Random House, 1997.

Multiple Intelligences: Teaching for Success. The New City School, 1994.

Oakley, Ed., Krug, Dough. *Enlightened Leadership: Getting to the Heart of Change.* New York: Simon & Schuster, 1994.

Ott, J.S. *The Organizational Culture Perspective.* Pacific Grove, CA: Brooks/Cole, 1989.

Parker, Palmer. *To Know as We Are Known: Education as a Spiritual Journey.* San Francisco, CA: Harper, 1993.

Payne, Ruby K. *A Framework for Understanding Poverty.* Highlands, TX: RFT Publishing, 1998.

Peters, Stephen G. *Inspired to Learn: Why We Must Give Children Hope.* Marietta, GA: Rising Sun Publishing, 2001.

Purkey, William and Novak, John. *Inviting School Success: A Self-Concept Approach to Teaching and Learning.* Belmont, CA: Wadsworth Publishing, 1978.

Ross, Ann, Olsen, Karen. *The Way We Were...The Way We Can Be, A Vision for the Middle School Through Integrated Thematic Instruction.* Kent, WA: Susan Kovalik & Associates, 1995.

Senge, P., McCabe, N.C., at. al. *Schools That Learn: A Fifth Discipline Fieldbook for Educators, Parents, and Everyone Who Cares About Education.* New York: Doubleday-Currency, 2000.

Schenck, E.A., Bechstrom, S. *Chapter I School-wide Project Study.* Portsmouth, NH: RMC Research Corporation, 1993.

Schlechty, Phillip C. *Inventing Better Schools: An Action Plan for Educational Reform.* San Francisco, CA: Jossey-Bass, 1997.

Texas Education Agency. *Effective Schools Research and Dropout Reduction.* Austin, TX: Author, 1989.

U.S. Department of Education. *An Idea Book: Implementing School-wide Projects.* Washington, D.C.: Author, (1994).

Wong, Harry and Rosemary. *How to Be An Effective Teacher: The First Days of School.* Mountain, CA: Wong Publications, 1998.

Wynn, Mychal and Blassie, Dee. *Building Dreams: K-8 Teacher's Guide.* Marietta, GA: Rising Sun Publishing, 1995.

Notes:

Notes:

Wynn, Mychal. *Building Dreams: Helping Students Discover Their Potential, Teacher, Parent, Mentor Workbook.* Marietta, GA: Rising Sun Publishing, 1994.

Wynn, Mychal. *Empowering African-American Males to Succeed: A Ten-Step Approach for Parents and Teachers.* Marietta, GA: Rising Sun Publishing, 1985.

Wynn, Mychal. *Follow Your Dreams: Lessons That I Learned in School.* Marietta, GA: Rising Sun Publishing, 2001.

Wynn, Mychal. *Ten Steps to Helping Your Child Succeed in School: Volume I.* Marietta, GA: Rising Sun Publishing, 2000.

Wynn, Mychal. *The Eagle Team: A Leadership Curriculum.* Marietta, GA: Rising Sun Publishing, 2001.

Wynn, Mychal. *The Eagles who Thought They were Chickens.* Marietta, GA: Rising Sun Publishing, 1995.

Supplemental Reading List

Achilles, C. *Success Starts Small: Life in a Small Class.* Final Report. Greensboro, N.C.:University of North Carolina, 1994.

Adelman, Clifford. *Answers in the Tool Box: Academic Intensity, Attendance Patterns, and Bachelor's Degree Attainment.* Washington, D.C.: U.S. Department of Education, Office of Educational Research and Improvement, 1999.

Barnett, W. Steven. *"Long-term effects of early childhood programs on cognitive and school outcomes,"* The Future of Children 5, no. 3 (1995): 25-50.

Begle, E. and W. Geeslin. *"Teacher effectiveness in mathematics instruction,"* National Longitudinal Study of Mathematical Abilities Report No. 28. Washington, D.C.: Mathematical Association of America and National Council of Teachers of Mathematics, 1972.

Bohrnstedt, George and Brian Stecher. *The 1998-99 Evaluation of Class Size Reduction in California.* Presentation to the North Carolina Research Council in Raleigh, N.C., 27 March 2001.

Bowles, S. and H. Levin. *"The determinants of scholastic achievement — An appraisal of some recent evidence."* Journal of Human Resources 3 (1968).

Boyd-Zaharias, Jayne and Helen Pate-Bain. *The Continuing Impact of Elementary Small Classes.* Paper presented at the annual meeting of the American Educational Research Association. New Orleans, LA: American Educational Research Association, 2000.

Notes:

Boyd-Zaharias, Jayne and Helen Pate-Bain. *"Early and New Findings from Tennessee's Project STAR,"* The CEIC Review 9, no. 2 (2000).

Brophy, J. *"Research Linking Teacher Behavior to Student Achievement: Potential Implications for Instruction of Chapter 1 Students."* Educational Psychologist 23 (1988).

Coleman, James, et al. *Equality of educational opportunity.* Washington, D.C.: U.S. Government Printing Office, 1966.

Cook, Philip and Jens Ludwig. *"The Burden of 'Acting White': Do Black Adolescents Disparage Academic Achievement?"* In The Black-White Test Score Gap, edited by Christopher Jencks and Meredith Phillips. Washington, D.C.: Brookings, 1998.

CSR Research Consortium. *Class Size Reduction in California: The 1998-99 Evaluation Findings Executive Summary.* <http://www.classize.org/> June 2000.

Darity, William, Domini Castellino, and Karolyn Tyson. *Increasing Opportunity to Learn via Access to Rigorous Courses and Programs: One Strategy for Closing the Achievement Gap for At-Risk and Ethnic Minority Students.* Report prepared for the North Carolina Department of Public Instruction and submitted to the North Carolina State Board of Education. Raleigh, NC: NCDPI, 2001.

Darling-Hammond, Linda. *"Teaching and Knowledge: Policy Issues Posed by Alternative Certification for Teachers,"* Peabody Journal of Education 67, no. 3 (1992).

Delpit, Lisa. *Other People's Children: Cultural Conflict in the Classroom.* New York, NY: The New Press, 1995.

Delpit, Lisa. *"The Silenced Dialogue: Power and Pedagogy in Educating Other People's Children," Other People's Children: Cultural Conflict in the Classroom.* New York, NY: The New Press, 1995.

Doherty, Kathryn. *Early Implementation of the Comprehensive School Reform Demonstration (CSRD) Program.* Washington, DC: U.S. Department of Education, Planning and Evaluation Service, 2000.

Druva, C. and R. Anderson. *"Science teacher characteristics by teacher behavior and by student outcome: A meta-analysis of research."* Journal of Research in Science Teaching 20, no. 5 (1983).

Elkind, David. *The Hurried Child: Growing Up Too Fast Too Soon.* Reading, MA: Addison-Wesley, 1981.

Ernst, Keith and Greg Malhoit. *The Achievement Gap 2001: A Progress Report.* <http://www.ncjustice.org/> Raleigh, NC: North Carolina Justice and Community Development Center, 2001.

Farkas, George. *Tutoring and Other Interventions.* Paper from the Center for Education and Social Policy, University of Texas at Dallas. Dallas, TX: University of Texas at Dallas, 1998a.

Farkas, George. *"Reading One-to-One: An Intensive Program Serving a Great Many Students While Still Achieving."* In Social Programs That Work. New York, NY: Russell Sage Foundation, 1998b.

Notes:

Notes:

Fashola, Olatokunbo and Robert Slavin. *"Schoolwide Reform Models: What Works?"* Phi Delta Kappan 79, no. 5 (1998).

Ferguson, P. and S. Womack. *"The impact of subject matter and education coursework on teaching performance."* Journal of Teacher Education 44, no. 1 (1993).

Ferguson, Ronald. *"Paying for public education: New evidence on how and why money matters."* Harvard Journal on Legislation, 28, no. 2 (1991).

Ferguson, Ronald. *"Can Schools Narrow the Black-White Test Score Gap?" In The Black-White Test Score Gap.* Washington, DC: Brookings, 1998.

Ferguson, Ronald. *"Teachers' Perceptions and Expectations and the Black-White Test Score Gap." In The Black-White Test Score Gap.* Washington, D.C.: Brookings, 1998.

Ferguson, Ronald. *"The Burden of 'Acting White': Do Black Adolescents Disparage Academic Achievement?" The Black-White Test Score Gap.* Washington, D.C.: Brookings, 1998.

Ferguson, Ronald and Helen Ladd. *"How and why money matters: An analysis of Alabama schools."* Holding Schools Accountable. Washington, DC: Brookings, 1996.

Finn, J., ed. *Class Size and Students at Risk: What is Known? What is Next?* A Commissioned Paper. Washington, DC: National Institute on the Education of At-Risk Students, U.S. Department of Education, 1998.

Finn, J., et al. *The Enduring Effects of Small Classes.* Paper presented at the annual meeting of the American Educational Research Association. New Orleans, LA: American Educational Research Association, 2000.

Finn, J. and C. Achilles. *"Answers and Questions About Class Size: A Statewide Experiment."* American Educational Research Journal 27 (1990).

Notes:

Notes: **Appendix**

Multiple Intelligences Theory

Bracing as it is to behold one's own array of intelligences, it is even more energizing if one can bring them to bear effectively at school, at home, at the work place, and in those regions of creative imagination which are so important to each of us.

— Howard Gardner

Dr. Howard Gardner developed the Theory of Multiple Intelligences, commonly referred to today as "M.I. Theory," while serving as a researcher at Harvard University in 1979. He and his colleagues were contracted by the Bernard Van Leer Foundation to investigate human potential. The Theory of Multiple Intelligences was published in Gardener's book, *Frames of Mind.* Gardner identified seven general areas of intelligence in his initial research findings, but stated that there may be more. He has since published an eighth area and identifies intelligence as not only doing well on a test or memorizing the fifty state capitals, but as solving a problem or creating a product that is valued in a culture.

'Solving a problem' encompasses computing two-digit multiplication, but it also includes forging a team, one capable of working collaboratively to accomplish a difficult task, from a group of individuals. 'Creating a product' includes turning clay into a bust, but it also means developing a new dance. And 'valued in a culture' means just what it implies: that others find merit in the work.

The educational applications of Multiple Intelligences Theory are far-reaching and have led to everything from expanded classroom lessons to the development of whole schools termed "Multiple Intelligences Schools."

While Multiple Intelligences Theory is widely recognized as the ways in which we acquire knowledge (learning styles) and ways in which we apply what we know, it also is reflective of how we think, or more succinctly stated, "how

Notes:

we know." Each of us has experienced the sensation of "knowing." Whether it is empathy for the pain of a child, solving complex problems, humming a tune, choreographing a complex dance routine, performing a martial arts kata or painting a landscape, we just know.

In Maslow's Hierarchy of needs, he sights the highest level of human development as the level of self-actualization. The level of being or the level of knowing. This is the synergistic level that we seek to achieve in solving the many complex problems within a school community that hinder our efforts to lift students to their highest levels of achievement. Effective Multiple Intelligences grouping (teaming) can help us to achieve this self-actualizing level.

How We Learn:

As an example, some people may rely greatly on Visual/Spatial Intelligence to learn. Such individuals would learn best through slides, overheads, graphic illustration, and other visual representations of what is being presented.

How We Apply What We Know:

Those same people may be highly Verbal/Linguistic in how they apply what they know. They may be very good at writing or speaking rather than being able to apply what they know through artist renderings or illustrations.

How We Think:

In yet another sense, the same individuals might be particularly proficient in problem solving, the conceptualization of complex processes, and in the sequencing of steps.

Thusly, they learn best through images (Visual/Spatial). They apply or communicate what they've learned best through writing or speaking (Verbal/Linguistic), and they create or "think" most effortlessly when solving problems or sequencing steps (Logical/Mathematical).

It is this final step, "How We Think," that we want to identify and utilize in our efforts to establish "Thinking or Problem-Solving Teams." These M.I. teams will be responsible for solving problems, implementing solutions, and carrying out the elements of our strategic plans upon which most rely on for the intelligence reflected in their group. Each of these intellectual domains will represent the pieces. When we pull together strategies and solutions from each of the teams, we will have the holistic approach needed, and thus, the synergy for achieving our vision.

The complexities of M.I. Theory is that no two people utilize the same combination of intelligences in exactly the same way. Also, no two people are equally well developed in each of the intelligences. While some people solve complex scientific or mathematical problems very well, others have a better understanding of people, and still others demonstrate a higher intellectual understanding of art or music.

In a typical school community you will find:

- individuals who never have problems with children or with their parents (Interpersonal);

- individuals who have well-managed, efficiently run classrooms (Logical/Mathematical);

- individuals who have beautifully inspiring, well conceived, and well-presented bulletin boards (Visual/Spatial);

- individuals who effortlessly integrate raps, songs, and music into their instruction (Musical/Rhythmic);

- individuals who explore the outdoors, plants, and animal life with passion (Naturalist);

- individuals who play basketball or golf, dance or workout or become passionately engaged in

Notes:

building complex models (Bodily/Kinesthetic); and

- individuals who recite poetry, present motivational talks, or write curriculum (Verbal/Linguistic).

My experience is that most of the talents and intellectual abilities needed to develop the strategies and solutions to the challenges confronting each school are largely existing within the school community itself. The challenge is to narrowly focus the unique intellectual capacity of teachers, parents, students, and support staff to conceptualize individual strategies that can be woven together into a holistic action plan. This sounds a lot more complicated than it actually is.

Developing effective Strategy-Focused Teams requires informally assessing the highly-developed areas of intelligence represented by each stakeholder within our school community, particularly, "How we think." Consider this to be a "talent search." Who organizes and plans things well? Who choreographs dance routines well? Who designs the best bulletin boards? Who works best with parents and students? Who is an inspiring orator? Who is best at building or constructing things? Who writes music or sings? Who appears to have great intuition about cultivating the spirit of collaboration and cooperation?

Developing Strategy-Focused Teams that are M.I.-specific requires a significant paradigm shift for those having participated on the age-old school improvement planning committees. Traditionally, those committees were created via volunteers or appointments rather than intellectual capacity. No offense. We are also challenged with moving from a traditional foundation of linear thinking, i.e., one dimensional solutions to the problems within our school community, to the holistic piecing together of the strategies conceptualized by the respective M.I. Teams.

For example, linear-thinking results in the typical strategies conceptualized in a school community's approach to discipline issues: "Punish the children!" An holistic approach would involve instructional components, signage, community communications, assemblies, procedural changes, intervention/prevention strategies, etc. Then, perhaps, punish the children!

How to Get Started

There are two approaches to Multiple Intelligences grouping: "Like Grouping" and "Cross Grouping." While each has its merits, "Like Grouping" is more effective and should be done first. The problem-solving discussions within such groups move quickly and effectively and the groups, as a rule, tend to be highly effective.

Benefits of "Like Grouping" are:

- faster problem-solving;

- group members appear to *hear* each other better;

- fewer disagreements and less need to explain;

- problem-solving efforts are often driven by personal passion;

- intellectual capacity and contributions of all group members are validated and appreciated;

- group accepts ownership of planning and implementation;

- natural cultural and gender diverse grouping occurs;

- cross-generational, cross-gender, and cross-cultural relationships are developed;

- a heightened sense of ownership of operational

and implementation strategies; and

- personal empowerment or group members.

Note:

Cross grouping should never precede Like Grouping. While Like Grouping validates individual intelligence if cross grouping precedes this intellectual validation long-held stereotypes and beliefs can contribute to the group being counterproductive. For example, in our schools we have historically valued Verbal/Linguistic and Logical/Mathematical intelligence above all else. Art and Music teachers have long-since lived under the stigma, "They're not 'real' teachers."

The example commonly seen in school communities extends beyond the lack of teacher validation of their intellectual diversity, but to students. Students highly developed in the arts are considered "talented," but not intelligent, as Ronald Stone notes in his book, *Creative Visualization*:

Western dependence on reason has meant that we frown on such things as the imagination. Schooling develops reasoning powers and implicitly, if not explicitly, treats the imagination as unimportant. It is not surprising, therefore, that children very soon give up being imaginative. As this process continues the growing person finds it more and more difficult to form mental images, simply because this particular faculty goes unused.

Students who are highly proficient in dance and sports (Bodily/Kinesthetic) are referred to as having "natural talent" and abilities, and again, are often considered less intelligent than those demonstrating talents and abilities in language arts, math, and science (typically the core curriculum).

David Lazear, in his book, *Seven Ways of Knowing: Teaching for and with Multiple Intelligences*, notes the intellectual foundation of Bodily/Kinesthetic intelligence:

Current brain research has revealed that bodily/kinesthetic capacities comprise a complex, intricate, highly integrated network of brain/body operations. The motor cortex of the brain executes specific muscular movements, with the right side of the brain controlling the left side of the body and the left side of the brain controlling the right side of the body. The cerebral cortex acts as a perceptual feedback mechanism, which both feeds information to the spinal cord and receives input from the rest of the body through the spinal cord. Once information has been sent and/or received and interpreted, the motor cortex brings about the appropriate body responses to match the information received by the cerebral cortex.

Once a culture has been established in which group members value and validate the multiplicity of intelligences, and thusly, the intellectual contribution of all team members, there can be benefits to "Cross Grouping."

- Individual group members are recognized as experts within their uniquely highly-developed intellectual domain and are deferred to leading the discussions pertinent to their domain.

- The group discussion is directed toward holistic strategic plans.

- Ideas are quickly discussed and solutions are holistically conceptualized leading to a framework for the smaller focus group discussions.

- Individual group members can carry the large group discussions back to a smaller more focused group for carrying out action plans.

Review the outline of each of the Multiple Intelligences domains on the following pages. Read all eight domains before attempting to establish your personal priority. Re-read each of the eight domains and indicate the priority for the three categories:

1.   How I best learn.

2.   How I best apply what I've learned.

3.   How I best solve problems.

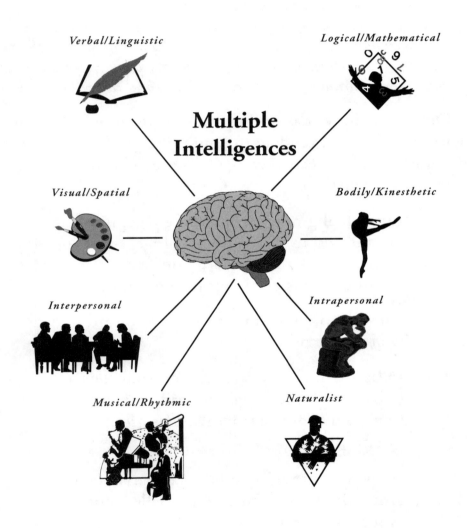

Verbal/Linguistic Intelligence (Language)

Word Smart. This intellectual domain is responsible for the production of language and all the complex possibilities that follow through both the written and the spoken word. People who demonstrate this intelligence tend to appreciate the subtleties of grammar and meaning. They may spell easily and enjoy word games. They understand puns, jokes, and riddles and have developed their auditory skills. They tend to memorize words and phrases easily and demonstrate an interest in the sound and rhythm of language.

This includes such categories as:

- *Poetry*

- *Humor*

- *Storytelling*

- *Abstract reasoning*

- *Writing*

People highly developed in this intelligence usually demonstrate abilities or interests in:

- *the capacity to use language, demonstrated in the form of oral and written communication;*

- *proficiency at acquiring information from reading, writing, talking, and debating; and*

- *a passion for things like poetry, humor, storytelling, debating, and creative writing.*

Notes:

Logical/Mathematical Intelligence (Processes)

Process Smart. This intellectual domain is associated with what we call "scientific thinking." Deductive/inductive thinking/reasoning, numbers and recognition of abstract patterns. People who demonstrate this intelligence tend to be logical in their thought processes, calculate well, and tend to be precise and methodical. They demonstrate the ability to move from the concrete to the abstract and enjoy computer games and puzzles. They tend to think conceptually and explore patterns and relationships. They organize their thoughts well and do well in applying a systematic approach during problem solving.

Typical of this intelligence is:

- *a highly-developed ability to figure things out and identify patterns; and*

- *a highly-developed ability to analyze and solve complex problems, particularly in subjects like math and science.*

People highly developed in this intelligence usually demonstrate:

- *great problem-solving capacity;*

- *proficiency with numbers and complex equations;*

- *proficiency at applying the scientific method to everyday problems, even relationships; and*

- *proficiency at sequencing steps and understanding complex patterns.*

Interpersonal Intelligence (People and Relationships)

People Smart. This intellectual domain is responsible for the ability to demonstrate empathy for and understanding of others. It also involves the ability to effectively communicate, verbally and non-verbally, with other people, and is often demonstrated through the ability to assume leadership roles.

Typical of this intelligences is:

- *the capacity to make distinctions in the feelings, intentions, and motivations of others;*

- *the ability to "read" people and interact effectively based on those cues;*

- *the capacity to make friends easily and function well on group projects and within group settings;*

- *the ability to share opinions and empathize with the opinions and feelings of others;*

- *a desire to work on group projects and within group activities;*

- *the ability to effectively mediate conflicts and cooperate with others;*

- *the ability to understand and recognize stereotypes and prejudices;*

- *the interest in volunteering to work with others; and*

- *the ability to offer constructive and appropriate feedback.*

Notes:

Intrapersonal Intelligence (Introspective, Spirit/Pride)

Self Smart. This intellectual domain reflects knowledge of the internal aspects of self and a heightened sense of intuition and spirituality. This intelligence allows us to be conscious of our self-identify and wholeness. According to Gardner, this intelligence is the most private and requires all other intelligence forms to express itself, such as language, music, art, dance, symbols, and interpersonal communication, often providing a sixth sense into the "spirit" of others. People highly developed in this intelligence tend to have a good sense of their strengths and weaknesses. Their metacognition, their thinking about their thinking, is especially refined.

Typical of this intelligence is:

- *being in touch with one's feelings and demonstrating an inner sense of self;*

- *demonstrating highly develop intuition regarding institutional or individual spirit, i.e., morale;*

- *having a strong focus on dreams and aspirations of future possibilities; and*

- *being proficient at concentrating, focusing, and inner reflection.*

People highly developed in this intelligence usually demonstrate abilities or interests in:

- *pursuing personal interests;*

- *understanding their own strengths and weaknesses;*

- *being or working alone;*

- *empathizing with the feelings and emotions of others;*

- *developing a strong sense of self, and are oftentimes do not defined themselves by group parameters; and*

- *demonstrate a highly-developed ability for introspection and self reflection.*

Visual/Spatial Intelligence (Images)

Picture Smart. This intellectual domain is responsible for the ability to create internal mental pictures. It is also utilized in our ability to find our way around a given location, including being able to get from one place to another. This intellectual domain is mostly located in the right hemisphere of the brain in what is known as the "parietal lobes." People who demonstrate this intelligence enjoy maps and charts, like to draw, build, design, and create things, think in three-dimensional terms, love videos and photos, enjoy color and design, enjoy pattern and geometry in math, and may like to doodle.

This includes such areas as:

- *Graphic and visual arts*

- *Design and illustration*

- *The ability to coordinate colors and patterns*

- *Photography*

- *Navigation*

- *Map making*

- *Architecture*

People highly developed in this intelligence usually demonstrate abilities or interests in:

- *fashion or interior design;*

- *animation, illustration or fine art;*

Notes:

- *multi-dimensional thought patterns;*

- *organizing information visually;*

- *good sense of direction;*

- *doodling, painting, sculpting, drawing and other arts and crafts activities;*

- *mazes, puzzles, hidden picture activities, awareness; and*

- *visually sequencing events and forming mental images.*

Bodily/Kinesthetic Intelligence (Movement)

Body Smart. This intellectual domain demonstrates the ability to use the body to express emotion as in dance, body language, and sports or the ability to use one's hands to create or change things. People who demonstrate this intelligence tend to be coordinated and agile. They tend to demonstrate good hand-eye coordination, balance, timing and equilibrium. Their gross or fine motor skills may also be well developed. They tend to be hands-on learners and demonstrate the ability to learn by doing.

People highly developed in this intelligence usually demonstrate through such areas as:

- *Sports*

- *Martial Arts*

- *Dance*

- *Gymnastics*

- *Rock climbing*

- *Water/Snow skiing and surfing*

- *Roller skating and bicycle riding*

- *Weight lifting*

- *Boxing*

- *Carpentry*

- *Building things*

- *Sculpture*

- *Surgery*

Musical/Rhythmic Intelligence (Music)

Music Smart. This intellectual domain includes such capacities as the recognition and use of rhythmic and tonal patterns, sensitivity to sounds such as the human voice, and musical instruments. People who demonstrate this intelligence tend to remember melodies well, enjoy listening to music, be able to keep a beat, make up their own songs, notice background and environmental sounds, and differentiate pattern in sounds.

This intelligence is demonstrated in such ways as:

- *creating and directing musical compositions;*

- *singing and playing musical instruments; and*

- *showing proficiency at remembering melodies, tunes, songs, or instrumental patterns.*

Naturalist Intelligence (Environment)

Environment smart. This intelligence demonstrates the ability to recognize plants, animals, and other parts of the natural environment, like cloud patterns or rocks formations. Demonstrates a heightened understanding of animal behaviors and the natural environment, such as the African jungle, Amazon Rain Forest, or urban jungle of New York City.

Typical of this intelligence is:

- *the ability to understand and interact well with animals;*

- *the ability to interact well in the natural environment; and*

- *a highly-developed ability in landscaping, gardening, hiking, and outdoor activities.*

People highly developed in this intelligence usually demonstrate abilities or interests in:

- *Outdoor work and activities*

- *Working with animals*

- *Working with landscape design, gardening, or farming*

- *Nature walks, bird watching, butterfly watching, changes in weather patterns, cloud formations, and a study of nature*

Each of us, provided that we do not suffer from any birth defect or brain abnormality, have all eight intellectual domains. However, no two people utilize the same combination of intelligences in exactly the same way to acquire or apply knowledge. Please re-read each of eight intelligences and number them in order of 1 through 8, from your most dominant to your least dominant. For example, are you better with people (Interpersonal) or better with understanding processes (Logical/ Mathematical)? Are you better at understanding music (Musical/Rhythmic) or the written or spoken word (Verbal/Linguistic)?

– Other books from Rising Sun Publishing –

A College Plan: For Those with College-Bound Dreams, [Wynn] (ISBN 1-880463-63-6 • $29.95)

An easy-to-follow planning guide for middle through high school students. Helps students to understand how grades, standardized tests, behavior, activities, classes, community service, essays, and the billions of available scholarship moneys can all be factored into a plan (beginning in the sixth grade !) that can pave the way into the college(s) of their choice. Also provides a step-by-step plan for parents, guardians, or mentors to get students into college without going broke.

Building Dreams: K-8 Teacher's Guide, [Wynn/Blassie] (ISBN 1-880463-45-9 • $29.95)

An indispensable resource tool for elementary and middle school teachers. Lessons and activities help teachers to develop more effective parent communication and a more positive classroom climate and culture.

Building Dreams: Helping Students Discover Their Potential: Teacher, Parent, Mentor Workbook [Wynn]
(ISBN 1-880463-42-3 • $9.95)

Guides teachers, parents, and mentors through exercises for facilitating discussion and direction for a student or group of students. Mentors learn how to move beyond the rhetoric of lecturing to meaningful and relevant dialogue; dialogue that will facilitate bonding and that will help students focus on long-term outcomes.

Don't Quit [Wynn] (ISBN 1-880463-26-1 • $9.95)

Mychal Wynn's critically-acclaimed book of poetry contains 26 poems of inspiration and affirmation. Each verse is complemented by an inspiring quotation.

Empowering African-American Males to Succeed: A Ten-Step Approach for Parents and Teachers [Wynn]
Book (ISBN 1-880463-01-6 • $15.95)
Teacher/Parent Workbook (ISBN 1-880463-02-4 • $9.95)

African-American males are the most "at-risk" students in America's schools. They are the most likely to be placed into special education, drop out of school, be suspended, be the victims or perpetrators of violent crimes, or be incarcerated. This book outlines a clear, cohesive set of strategies to turn the tide of underachievement to personal empowerment.

Enough is Enough: The Explosion in Los Angeles [Wynn] (ISBN 1-880463-34-2 • $9.95)

Provides an introspective analysis of the problems strangling those who live in America's urban battle zones and moves the reader toward solutions to help urban America help itself before it's tool late.

Follow Your Dreams: Lessons That I Learned in School [Wynn] (ISBN 1-880463-51-2 • $7.95)

All students are confronted with choices during their school-aged years, from kindergarten through college. Which group do I identify with? How seriously do I take my schoolwork? How important is it to establish goals? What are my dreams and aspirations? How can my time in school help me to achieve them?

Mychal Wynn shares his story about the lessons that he learned while grappling with such questions and how he became a high academic achiever along the road to discovering his dreams and aspirations.

Inspired to Learn: Why We Must Give Children Hope [Peters] (ISBN 1-880463-08-3 • $12.95)

Stephen Peters, former middle school principal, not only outlines his vision for the children in our schools, he goes on to share how he and his staff turned their vision into operational strategies.

School Violence...Calming The Storm: A guide to creating a fight-free school environment [Dolan] (ISBN 1-880463-50-4 • $29.95)

Outlines all of the components and provides everything that a classroom teacher or principal needs to create a fight-free school environment: *instructional lessons; charts; parent communication; letters to the community; classroom, cafeteria, school bus, and school-wide activities; a lesson on the human brain and what causes anger; sample newsletters; fight-free pledge cards; certificates, and more.*

Ten Steps to Helping Your Child Succeed in School: Volume I *[Wynn]* (ISBN 1-880463-50-4 • $9.95)

Outlines easy-to-follow steps for parents and teachers to better understand children so that we can better direct them. The steps help parents and teachers to easily identify a child's personality types, learning styles, Multiple Intelligences, best and worst learning situations, dreams and aspirations.

Test of Faith: A Personal Testimony of God's Grace, Mercy, and Omnipotent Power *[Wynn]* (ISBN 1-880463-09-1 • $9.95)

"This book has become more than a recalling of my hospital experiences, it has become a testimony of the power of the human spirit; a testimony of the healing power of the Holy Spirit; and ultimately a personal testimony of my relationship with God, my belief in His anointing, and my trust in His power, grace, and mercy."

The Eagle Team: Leadership Curriculum *[Wynn]*
Student Guide (ISBN 1-880463-16-4 • $19.95)
Facilitator's Guide (ISBN 1-880463-39-3 • $29.95)

An effective intervention and leadership program designed to help unlock the passion within students by leading them through a series of units that will help them to discover their dreams and aspirations as they develop the leadership and academic skills to be recognized as leaders within their respective school communities.

The Eagles who Thought They were Chickens: A Tale of Discovery *[Wynn]*
Book (ISBN 1-880463-12-1 • $4.95)
Student Activity Book (ISBN 1-880463-19-9 • $5.95)
Teacher's Guide (ISBN 1-880463-18-0 • $9.95)

Chronicles the journey of a great eagle, historically perched at the right hand of the great king in her native Africa, who is captured and taken aboard a slave ship, the eggs that are eventually hatched, and their struggles in the chicken yard where they are scorned and ridiculed for their differences. The story offers parallels to behaviors in classrooms and on school playgrounds where children are teased by schoolyard "chickens" and bullied by schoolyard "roosters."

To order materials or for further information regarding our products, staff development, or school improvement planning workshops please visit our web site or contact:

Rising Sun Publishing
P.O. Box 70906
Marietta, GA 30007-0906
770.518.0369/FAX 770.587.0862
Toll free 1.800.524.2813
E-mail: info@rspublishing.com
www.rspublishing.com

INDEX